THE FIRST TIME MANAGER

Robert Harris

ISBN-13: 978-1976133725

Contents

    What this Book is For   1

1. **Your New Job and Why You Are There**   3
   Things are different now 3; Culture and Structure 5; Management: fact and fiction 11; Your new environment 13; Doing the job 16; Morality 17; Dealing with change 19; The boss 20; What do you want? 22

2. **The First-Time Manager and Other People**   24
   Success with your people 24; Communication and motivation 27; What the research tells managers about people 30; Management styles and fashions 35; What else makes your people work? 36; Communication 39; Power, authority and responsibility 47; Leadership 48; Health 55; Management style 56; Your boss 57; Your boss's boss 59

3. **Can Your Organization Survive?**   61
   Why should you care? 61; The structure of organizations 62; Organizations, society and the law 63; The grip of the past 65; Survival of the fittest 66; The environment 67; Environmental change and responses to it 69; Takeovers and mergers 71; Organizational analysis 74

4. **The Principles of Management**   77
   The manager's role 77; Goals and targets 78; The overall aim 80; Management by objectives 82; Management techniques: their place in your job 84; Judgement, experi-ence and training 85; Dealing with complexity 86; Statistics 89; Pareto's Principle, or the 80:20 rule 104; Written records 106

Contents

5. Marketing 108

Marketing: what it involves 108; Listening to the market 109; The place of marketing 110; Marketing people 111; Marketing and communication 112; The marketing task 114; Advertising 118; Distribution channels 121; Selling and the sales force 123; Physical distribution 124; Product design 125; Pricing, positioning and the marketing mix 125; Sales promotion 126; Trade relations 127; Public rela-tions 127; Marketing: a summary 128

6. Managing Production of Goods and Services 129

Systems 129; The management of people 131; Production planning 132; Production management principles 134; Managing the production process 138; Group technology 140; Work study 141; Stock control 142; Purchasing and procurement 145; Quality control and quality assurance 146; Value analysis 149; Variety reduction 150; Premises location 151; Premises design and layout 152; Make or buy? 154; Research and development (R&D), and new products 155; Maintenance 156; The law 157

7. Finance and Accounting 159

What accountants are for 159; The accountant and the fi-nancial world 166; The accountant's dilemma 167; Basic accounting concepts: cash flow forecasting 169; The profit and loss account 171; The balance sheet 172; Gearing 176; Sources of funds 176; Costing 177; Break-even analysis 180; Budgeting 181; Project evalua-tion 182

8. Human Resources 185

Why HR departments exist 185; The HR department and discipline 186; The HR department's proper contribution 187; What the HR department does 187; Employees and the law 194; How you can help your team to develop 196

9. Five Key Skills **201**
Solving a problem 201; Managing your time 206; Chairing a meeting 207; Giving a presentation 210; Running a staff session 219

Further Reading *225*

Index *226*

What this Book is For

The job of a manager is demanding. It requires:

- a complete change of behaviour, from 'doing' to getting other people to 'do';
- an instinctive understanding of what makes people tick, amplified by knowledge of aspects of individual and group psychology;
- command of a small range of specialized, practical techniques;
- an idea of how organizations work and what the different departments are for.

This book aims to provide the first-time manager with a grasp of what he or she needs to know in order to function at least reasonably well, and possibly a great deal better than that. It does not offer the depth of a major management qualification such as a MBA; but then, it costs several thousand pounds less and does not take several years to complete. It is, however, meant to provide in an evening's read the main headings of what it took me many years' experience and a lot of study to learn.

When I wrote the first edition, in 1988, I had in mind my delight at being promoted to my first management job, and the subsequent horror of finding that I was drowning in work. I had no idea that managers have to manage what they themselves do, as well as looking after their team. Because I had no idea what I could afford not to do, I did everything thrust at me. Soon I was working from 7 am to 10 pm, as well as most weekends. I was saved from pushing myself into illness by a wise lady who saw what was going on, took me aside and sorted me out. Alas, she is no longer with us, but Mrs Baines, I shall for ever be in your debt.

My aim is to be the equivalent of my readers' wise lady, to be your Mrs Baines. I am not a woman, but I do know two things from personal experience: how easy it is to get close to failure in your first management job, and thus how vitally important it is for the first-time manager to master the essentials of management as soon as possible.

If at the beginning of my career I had had the knowledge I have now, I would have done some things differently, and been happier and more successful. I hope to equip my readers with those things I wish I had known, things I believe would have given me, and possibly you, a flying start.

The first edition of this book in 1988 and the second in 1994 were different books from this, the third edition. I have kept it up to date in the way organizations are developing and the new things they require their managers to do. In fact, around a fifth of this edition is completely new material, much of it offering practical skills in managing teams.

I hope this book helps you and I wish you every success in life, as well as in your career – the two are rarely the same, and in my belief, important though one is, it is greatly outweighed by the other.

Michael Morris

one

Your New Job and Why You Are There

Things are different now

Accepting a job in management means you have to operate in a new way immediately. Other jobs you may have done leading up to this one, or in student vacations, or even as a child delivering papers, will have done little to prepare you for the challenge now confronting you. The key difference is this:

Managers are paid not for what they do, but for the results they get.

Usually those results are produced, not by the manager, but by other people.

This means that the first-time manager who used to be 'one of the gang' at all times, at work and in the pub, cannot continue to be. While external appearances and behaviour may remain much the same, inwardly the manager changes. No longer does he or she share and join in with the gripes about 'them upstairs', for metaphorically at least, the manager is now one of 'them'. This does not argue for a class-based division between manager and workers, but for recogni-tion of the stark fact that the role and responsibilities of one group member have changed radically. (Anyone who does not believe that a change of role and responsibilities must cause radical changes in behaviour should look at people who have recently become parents.) The manager is now no longer a co-equal member of the group, pulling an oar with the rest, but now the coach and stroke, master-minding and coordinating their efforts to help them deliver success.

Management is all about getting practical results out of situations that can be difficult to cope with. Within certain limits, nobody minds how you go about it, just as long as the results flow. The limits, or rules, governing what is permissible and acceptable vary from one organization to the next, and even between departments within a single organization. To complicate things even further, those rules are sometimes not written down; but they are nevertheless very strong, and they can change over time.

Let's take the example of the police. It is said that a blind eye was sometimes turned to the fabrication of evidence, or the extraction of confessions by unfair means, provided 'everyone knew' that the suspect was guilty. Or the army: in spite of the Geneva Convention requiring prisoners to be treated in a humane way it has been said that, on occasion, prisoners were killed to avoid delaying an advance. Yet today such behaviour is sought out and punished, as the trials of errant police officers and soldiers show. These are extreme examples, chosen carefully to make a point accessible to all: managers in organizations need to be alert to how the tide of opinion is moving, or they could find themselves in very serious trouble.

In those two examples, behaviour on the ground used selectively to ignore the written rules but has now caught up with them. Else-where, actual behaviour has run ahead of the official position. To take an example from the field of education, some administrators are encouraging potential students to take courses which they are bound to fail because, they believe, the requirement for 'inclusiveness' takes precedence over educational success. Nowhere in their rules does it say so, but that is what is being done. Another education example: one institution has, quite rightly, an equal opportunities policy for staff. It seems to be interpreted nowadays to mean that men are to be recruited only as a last resort. Anyone seeing the word 'equal' might think it means what it says, but it actually means that discrimination against an unpopular group is permitted.

Faced by such a scene, apparently scripted collaboratively by Lewis Carroll's Red Queen (who said that words meant what she wanted them to mean) and the pigs from George Orwell's *Animal Farm* (who started with the slogan: 'four legs good, two legs bad', but ended by walking upright themselves), the first-time manager may be forgiven for feeling queasy. He or she may wonder what forces are at work to create such crazy situations; may even wonder if the people concerned are themselves unhinged. The answer, which may be depressing or reassuring, depending on taste, is that they are normal people operating in a political environment. There is no more to it than that.

Of course, the word 'political' carries freight. In the organizational context it suggests to some a distasteful level of sycophancy or selfish manoeuvring, perhaps involving intentional untruth. For some purposes, like the Red Queen, I am happy to see it in that light, but the sense used here is closer to Bismarck's notion of politics as 'the art of the possible'. Many things are possible; the art is to ensure that those that are in your best interests are those that prevail.

Introducing the idea of 'your best interests' does reverberate uncomfortably with that of 'selfish manoeuvring' towards personal gain, but it can encompass a far wider spectrum of implied goals. Often in organizations the most passionate debates are not between factions arguing about who ought to be on top, but on matters of principle. Here, the contest is between those believing that the orga-nization ought to go in a particular direction, and others who are con-vinced that would be wrong, disastrous even, and advocate an alternative. One might wonder whose interests are being served here: no doubt self-interest is not absent, but it is the interests of the organization that are the apparent topic of debate.

To sum up so far:

- Managers are paid not for effort or activity, but for getting re-sults, usually via the work of other people.
- Since other people are involved, not only in the manager's team but at strata above, below and level with the manager, many of the processes are political.
- Politics both influence and are influenced by the way the of-ficial rules are framed and interpreted.
- The official rules may not mean what they say, and the unofficial rules may be ahead of or behind the written ones.
- It is essential for the manager to grasp as soon as possible what the politics are of the context within which he or she works.
- For a first-time manager to fail to understand this and not to proceed with great caution could be damaging.

Culture and structure

This chapter began with a warning against some of the uncertainties that swirl around the first-time manager, in the hope that in the early days he or she will take guard. It now goes on to examine how those conditions come about, seeking to broaden understanding of what is known as the 'culture' of an organization.

The idea of an organization's culture is not easy to define suc-cinctly. One of the best approximations is: 'the way they do things around here'. The ways that various organizations go about doing business are many and varied, shaped by a wide range of influences. One is the nature of the task to be undertaken. A moment's reflection reveals that the way in which a well-run clinical psychology depart-ment works must be very different from that of, say, a rapid-transit parcel delivery firm. The one can run only at the pace of its patients, since mental health is not subject to quick fixes: it demands lengthy relationships between its professionals and their clients, run to a flex-ible timetable that is not susceptible to either rigid programming or re-engineering. Its atmosphere aims to be serene, tranquil and com-forting. Often, new clients have to wait their turn until capacity becomes available to treat them. The delivery firm, on the other hand, is frantic. Deadlines pop up all the time, and rescheduling and last-minute changes to plan take place constantly. Communication between the dispatcher and drivers is critically important. Every-thing is geared to getting the parcels delivered within the guaranteed period. The relationship between driver and recipient is fleeting, inconsequential and entirely businesslike: neither wishes to prolong their encounter beyond the minimum necessary.

In each of those establishments a different culture will prevail. This would be evident even to someone at the lowest level of the organiza-tional hierarchy: for example, a cleaner. Staff behaviour regarded as normal will differ greatly. In the one, a kind, gentle attentiveness will characterize dealings with clients and colleagues; in the other, at least briskness and, on occasion, something approaching hysteria are seen. Thus new employees could blot their copybook quite compre-hensively by behaving in what is seen as the wrong way.

Another factor governing culture is the structure of the organiza-tion. The organizational structure that was more or less universal until the last quarter of the 20th century was hierarchical and unitary: that is, all functions the firm had to perform were undertaken in-house. In its extreme form such an organization would try to become 'vertically integrated': in other words it would seek to own all the main activities necessary to its existence. Under that model a manufacturer of electric cable would want to own the copper mines that provided ore and the smelters that refined it, as well as the equipment which drew and spun the copper filaments. It might even go on to own the makers of electric motors and transformers that used large quantities of its product. There were occasional rebel firms that used say subcontractors for some of their activities, but on the whole it was thought desirable to integrate all the functions in order to control them properly.

Many, perhaps most, organizations still retain that shape or something very like it, but now a significant number have gone to the other extreme. They have thought deeply about what really adds value for their customers and retained it, seeking to outsource everything else. Thus IBM might have decided that its customers pay it to know a great deal about information processing, but not to own lorries; that side of things can safely be left to Federal Express. Working through the functions of an organization one by one, checking to see what contribution to its service to customers is made by each in turn, often leads to a massive whittling down of the firm's headcount. It need not sell any less, nor make less money, but it need employ far fewer people.

The firm whose processes are illustrated in Figure 1.1 garners inputs from suppliers, which it processes by means of functions that are entirely internal. It then sells the resulting outputs on to customers, again using its own, internal resources. It collects money from customers and pays suppliers.

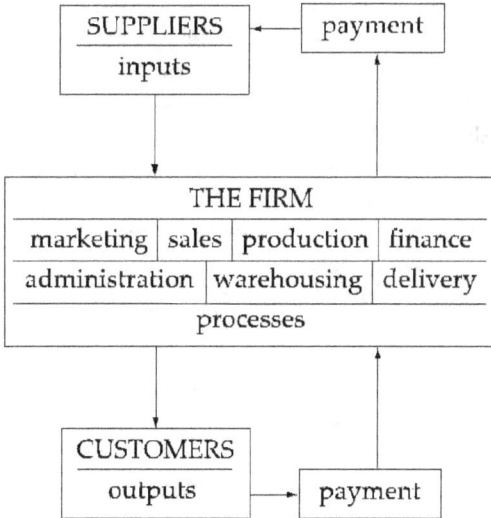

Figure 1.1 *The traditional organization*

The first-time manager

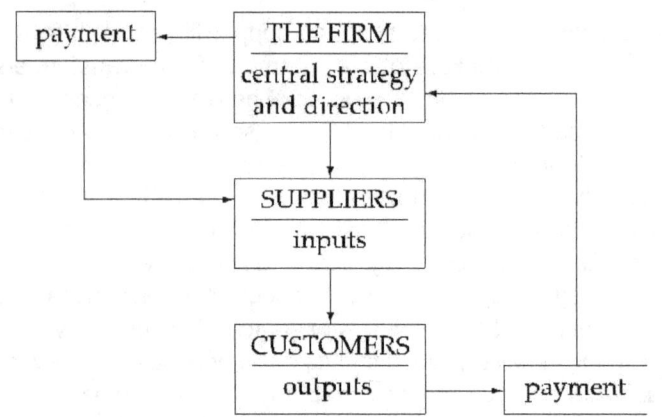

Figure 1.2 *The devolved organization*

The newer organizational form, where many functions are devolved to outsiders, looks and behaves very differently. Yet anyone looking at it from outside might find it hard to recognize any difference.

In Figure 1.2 only core activities are retained in-house. Everything else is devolved to others. The decision about what must be kept and what safely devolved is of crucial importance. It can be answered only after the most searching and rigorous examination. The danger is that the glib conclusion that an apparently routine function can be subcontracted could seriously undermine effectiveness. The example of an aircraft engineering contractor makes the point. Suppose that a key element in making emergency repairs quickly is the firm's ability to pick and dispatch a spare part within 10 minutes of an urgent order from a field engineer. Slippage from 10 minutes in-house to an entirely reasonable 40 minutes from an outside con-tractor that loses concentration momentarily could result in thou-sands of pounds of extra cost to customers in delays, loss of a take-off slot, loss of onward flight connections and so forth. In that case, clearly the storage and delivery functions are so crucial that they must be kept internal.

The fundamental tasks of management in both examples are the same: to get product to customers, collect payment and make profits. From then on they diverge. In the first example they have to keep the whole organization working together, working to improve perfor-mance where it is substandard. They can move good people from function to function in order to give them experience, which will in time broaden them to the point where they are ready to take on senior management responsibilities which bridge individual functions. The sheer size of the operation and numbers employed introduce com-plexities. They can be likened to farmers, seeking gradual improve-ments year after year which, over a long period of time, add up to major progress. Their attitude to the people they employ may be similar.

In the second case, they are more like hitch-hikers, looking always for a better ride that will get them to where they want to be. Relation-ships with suppliers are contingent on good performance: a few bad months, and contracts may be severed. There may be little sense of helping suppliers to develop their service (although it has to be said that such relationships do sometimes exist). The emphasis is on two divergent concerns: driving the suppliers harder and seeking the better deal, and constantly ensuring that the core offering to custom-ers is kept fresh and relevant as customers' needs change and the environment evolves. The demands that are placed on suppliers may colour the way in which staff are viewed and treated.

Overlaying all of this is the question of the type of business the organization is in. If it is hugely competitive and the firm is under constant pressure to perform, with results seen from day to day or month to month, people are likely to be under the same pressure. In such a setting there can be little toleration of underperformance. There might also be great rewards for those who succeed, but in such an environment past success rarely insulates people from the effects of a string of dismal results, and out they go. Equally, if the environ-ment is more settled and the results of today's actions do not become evident for a year or two, the organization is likely to be less demand-ing of day-to-day performance. Pressure there may still be, but its nature will be different.

So far this may seem reasonably clear, if a bit complicated. Unfor-tunately it gets more complex when you recognize that, even within a single unitary organization, different departments will have differ-ent cultures. A further factor that makes for cultural variation is the sector within which an organization operates. Broadly, three sectors can be discerned: private, not-for-profit (NFP, which we used to think of as the 'public' sector) and charitable. Most of the comments made so far relate to the private sector. Traditionally, the NFP sector was less pressured, rewarding its staff relatively poorly in return for security. In some areas that is still the case, but there has been a creep-ing in of temporary contracts and a devolution of functions which has blurred the distinction. As for the charity sector, people may expect it to be gentle in its approach and woolly in its thinking. This is often far from the truth. Some charities aim to operate with the effi-ciency and effectiveness of serious commercial operators, with a con-sequent effect on their internal cultures.

At a deeper level, the physical workplace itself can affect people's feelings about working there and the way they go about things. The routines of just getting along day by day cause people to develop habits of work and interaction. Coupled with the organization's view of what it is for, and the rules it erects to fulfil that destiny, all of this results in a set of unstated assumptions about how things are to be done and people treated. Established members of the group have a stake in the culture that thus emerges, and can feel strongly about its worth. Newcomers may observe all kinds of problems that it creates, but court trouble if they challenge it overtly or explicitly. Usually the only people who get away with such radical behaviour are in a posi-tion of considerable strength, yet they do not always survive even then. An example is of someone brought in to sort out an organiza-tion in deep trouble, where the staff are fearful. They know that the only means of survival involves great change, and will support an effective leader who steers them through it. In such extreme circum-stances the culture can be changed or even destroyed (which is some-times desirable). Individuals unsupported by such powerful forces have little chance of doing the same. Their only hope is to appear to fit in and work away quietly at making small improvements here and there. Nevertheless, many first-time managers have been appointed to sort out a mess in a small department. They may encounter a destructive or obstructive internal culture and must help to bring into being a new culture. To do this calls for great skills in leadership.

The importance of all this to the first-time manager lies in the fol-lowing summary:

- Being seen to fit into organizational culture is one of only a few major factors that will determine a manager's happiness and effectiveness in a job.
- Behaviours between people and departments that seems to the newcomer plainly stupid are often explained by the culture.
- Few people can tell the outsider or newcomer what the

> culture is, especially if they are long-serving. It is what they assume to be normal and so they do not notice it.
> - One of the most important tasks the first-time manager can set him or herself is to understand the concept of culture, and be able to recognize its different manifestations in different organizations and parts of organizations.

Management: fact and fiction

To many people the world of management is an exciting one full of beautiful people, money and power. To Hollywood directors and the more romantic TV producers that may really seem to be true. Others think it to be boring, petty and concerned with power plays con-ducted entirely in jargon and gobbledygook. The people who actu-ally inhabit that world know it to be very different.

To its practitioners, management is concerned with getting practical results out of difficult situations. In return for success they are awarded certain privileges. In every case, the good manager is more alive to responsibilities than to perks. When two or more gather together, the talk is usually about problems they face at work and how they might tackle them.

One way in which management differs from many other types of work is that managers are not paid for the hours they put in. Instead, they are paid to get results. Frequently the targets set are far too high and cannot reasonably be attained. Many a manager will attest that the word 'challenge', used so much in recruitment advertising, is no empty cliché. To keep their jobs and to realize their ambitions, they face and overcome really testing challenges every day of their working lives.

Those who are good at it are paid well. Ask them about the rewards of their job, and the money, if it is mentioned at all, will figure low on the list. Most of the time the main source of satisfaction is in a job well done, in the glow of knowing they have pulled off what most people would have thought impossible. Perhaps it is easy for the well-paid to be cavalier about money, some might say. But most managers are not rich and would be in real trouble financially if they lost their jobs. Despite that, they stubbornly insist on getting their biggest kicks from making things happen, not from being paid well. Even so, most will bargain strenuously for higher pay when the opportunity arises: they do have their practical side, too.

On the whole they are a hard-working group who take their work seriously. They have difficult balances to strike and maintain in a number of areas of conflict. Without their efforts, in the absence of people prepared to take on responsibilities, organizations simply could not exist. Without organizations nothing would ever be done that required concerted action by a large number of people. Our exis-tence would be played out under the primitive conditions of the pre-industrial world, with standards of living to match. Not that managers are solely responsible for all the benefits of industrial-ization – or its drawbacks – but theirs is an essential role in economic development. Without a flourishing economy, health and welfare services cannot be afforded, nor can national defence. Most people would think it desirable that those things should be available, however much they might quarrel about the forms they might take.

As a first-time manager it is quite right that you should take pride in your new appointment. It is also vitally important that you grasp immediately that the rewards – pleasant working conditions, higher pay, longer holidays, and perhaps other benefits – carry with them an expectation that you will strive to deserve them. Management is about getting things done, and in that way it resembles most other jobs. The unique aspect of management is that it does not do the work itself, but relies on other people to do it. Indeed, it is about getting other people to achieve the results. The manager may not have dirty hands, but that does not spell idleness. The nature of managerial work is different. It requires stopping doing what was done in the previous, non-management, job and taking on a new range of skills and activities, and adopting a completely new outlook. That sounds like, and is, the most significant challenge facing the first-time manager in the early days and weeks of a new job.

A further popular illusion should be disposed of. Some people think that 'management' is just a bundle of techniques. All the aspir-ing manager needs to do is study from books and – hey presto! – all is known that needs to be known. Techniques there are, and rightly so because they serve practical uses. They are no more to the manager than the tools a mechanic carries. Each one is designed for a specific task, and none is much use in the hands of the uncomprehending.

Management is a demanding calling, with no place for hangers-on. It makes demands not only on technical skill but on character too.

Managers must have a degree of courage, and they have to demon-strate integrity, as we shall see. It presents an infinite variety of chal-lenges, some of them daunting and all of them fascinating, but the rewards for success are great and varied.

Your new environment

Taking up an appointment as a first-time manager means grasping the basic message about the nature of the field. Furthermore, there are new bearings to be found in a new organizational environment. Above all, exactly why the appointment was made and what is expected needs to be understood.

It is not easy to do all of this under the interested scrutiny of col-leagues senior and junior, of peers and of rivals. What makes it really difficult is that everyone shows this interest in the first-time manager when he or she is nearly totally ignorant about the job and its place in the organization. Under such circumstances it is not easy to cut a dash. Indeed, it would be foolish to try. One certain way to make your spon-sors really worry about their decision to give you this job is to shoot from the hip. A readiness to state firm opinions on the basis of little information and less experience is evidence of fairly advanced stupid-ity. There is a 3000-year-old saying to the effect that it is better to keep quiet and be thought a fool than to speak and put the question beyond doubt.

There are many people who want the first-time manager to succeed. First, and most obviously, there are those who recruited you and do not want to be proved wrong; your success will be their success. Then there are your subordinates. They will take pride in working for a good boss in a section which is generally recognized as successful. Few people get much of a kick from association with failure, chaos and defeat, though such ghouls do exist.

There are also your colleagues from other sections, the smooth running of which depends on your section's performance. They do not want to be on the receiving end of poor output from your depart-ment. Finally, there are the people of goodwill whom you meet at all levels of organizations. They like to see someone doing well, and were among the first to congratulate you on your new post. Despite all the stories of corporate politicking that you hear, these people are around in greater numbers than some folk think.

There will also be a majority who do not care very much one way or the other. Those who have heard of you regard your appointment as just another fact of life. From time to time you will have dealings with these people, and as your career progresses they will grow to represent a constituency of friends or enemies, depending on how you behave towards them. Courteous and open behaviour at all times is becoming, and you will rarely know when a piece of behav-iour will be noticed to be set in your favour or against you. This factor operates on two principal levels. There is the humble security guard or cleaner whom you always greet, and who gets into conversation with the chief executive about who comes in early and works late, and mentions your name; then there is the griping session about you behind your back, when somebody whom you scarcely know speaks up on your behalf.

In organizations all sorts of grapevines exist which are hungry for news to transmit. They reach right through an organization: what do you want them to say about you? The best answer is probably 'Nothing, but if it has to be something, then let it reflect well on me.' Even if you do not attract too many strong supporters you can avoid needlessly making too many enemies. Do not overlook the fact that there will be a tiny number of warped personalities who will work to undermine you. They could be contemporaries or above or below you. Those at the same or a lower level are possibly worried that you will thwart their ambitions. There could be other explanations from a very wide range of possibilities. Those at more senior levels may have some private vendetta against your boss and try to get at him or her through you. Again, nobody should jump to what seems like an obvious conclusion. Human beings are complex and can have all kinds of contradictory feelings about their fellows.

Bear in mind that the enemy does not always approach with a scowl and a raised club. A certain degree of reserve and saying no more than is necessary should get you safely past the individual who seems just a bit too friendly. You may encounter unusual incidents which could be interpreted as attempts at sabotage. The only way to deal with them is to use common sense and reason. Do not get drawn into arguments. If that approach does not work, withdraw with dignity and ask your boss for advice. Later, when you have learned more about the internal tensions and the motivations of colleagues, you will be better able to deal with such matters unaided. Always behave with courtesy and do not become heated, however strong the temptation. Never respond in kind to someone who has lost self-control: all that ever does is hand the other side real grounds for criticizing you.

So much for the defensive side, of trying to avoid making embarrassing mistakes early on. There is a strong positive side to it, too. At first, people will not judge you by how much or how little you know, but by two other factors: how you behave personally towards them and others, and how you go about tackling things. A real drive to understand what the organization does, and how it does it, earns a lot of Brownie points. Going about your job with energy, fairness and personal pleasantness takes you even further. People love to answer questions about their work, and their answers form a great part of your education. They will know you are ignorant and will be happy to help. They are flattered by your interest. So teach yourself and form relationships with colleagues at the same time, a game where everyone wins.

Up to now, virtually no mention has been made of the techniques of management. That is intentional, for the primary task in the first-time manager's early days is to be seen by the other, earlier inhabitants of this bit of jungle, so as to allow them to decide whether or not you are a threat, harmless or a potential ally. Everyone knows how this works nowadays. A glance across a room may yield enough information to allow us to decide that we dislike somebody. Then we are introduced, and a few minutes' conversation shows that we have made an absorbing new acquaintance. We have witnessed the falling of the defences erected by primitive instincts for survival. These defences cannot be battered down: indeed, attempts to do so can result in reinforcing them. Only the owner of those defences can lower them, and then only at the rate that instinct will allow.

These ideas may seem strange to some first-time managers. Surely, there's a job to be getting on with? And shouldn't everyone be judged on the basis of performance, and that alone?

Certainly, there is a job to be done, and urgently. But you would like to do it effectively and for some considerable time. It would be a pity to make much of that time more difficult than it need be. One way to do so is to ignore basic facts of human nature. An investment of a few hours in making people feel that you are a sympathetic and pleasant new colleague should pay off handsomely. Also, it may be true that the formal system says that everyone is judged on the same impersonal basis. In that case, your performance should be all the more recognized, as your care with people will make you more effec-tive in your job. Look at it the other way. In every organization there is someone whose performance is always poor, yet who leads a charmed life because they are liked. It should be nobody's ambition to emulate that, but everyone can learn about how to insulate oneself from the consequences of results. Good relations with those around you can influence the way your performance is perceived, and hence judged. Indeed, the quality of your relationship with the people in your team will largely determine the degree of your success.

Doing the job

When it comes to the technical side of the job, there ought to be fewer imponderables. If your boss has any wits at all it will be made quite clear what is expected of you and when, and also the minimum performance acceptable. The extent of your authority and the resources for which you are responsible will be named too. If, for some reason, this information is not available, you must request, demand and, if necessary, insist that you are given the answers. If they are not in writing then confirm them in writing to your boss, keeping a copy, of course. Your boss will also arrange for your induction into the department's systems, and be available to answer your questions. He or she wants you to succeed – never forget that.

There may be a temptation to flee from the very idea of targets. They do have great advantages to the manager, in that they state quite unequivocally what he is expected to achieve; there can be no disagreement or misunderstanding. The poor wretch with no measurable target may, for a time, think that all is well, but eventually someone descends from on high to demand why things are going so badly. All he or she can do in response is to squeak: 'Compared to what?'

One manager who had no targets for his unit asked what they were, but got no answer. He thought that this meant he should invent his own, which he did, and quite sensible he thought they were. One day his boss visited him to say that he was sacked. When, not unnaturally, he asked why, he was told: 'Things just haven't worked out.' That was as close to an explanation as he ever got.

So, if at this early stage the first-time manager encounters muddle and haze around the topic of targets and how achievement is measured, it would be well to keep the CV polished. Any interviews offered should be attended, and the recruitment agencies dealt with should be told he or she is still available. It would be wise not to tell the agency which found the present job, as they may stand to lose commission, and in any case may feel duty bound to tell the employer, their client. Organizations with muddled targeting and measurement systems and methods are doomed.

Morality

In dealing with colleagues at all levels, and especially with subordinates, the manager must act with integrity. There will be temptations to economize with the truth, in order to have a quiet life. There are occasions when tact, compassion and common sense demand less than a full statement of one's beliefs, but self-preservation is rarely a sound reason. It is important, for trust is like life itself: you can lose it once and once only. The first time the manager is caught out trying to get away with something other than the truth is the last time that manager will ever be trusted. Trust is the basis of all your dealings with people. Once it has broken down, people suspect an unworthy motive behind everything you do and say, and will take nothing at face value. At that point the manager ceases to function properly.

There is more to integrity than just avoiding the telling of direct lies. It touches on every aspect of the manager's work. Not only does it forbid deliberate misrepresentation, it also means taking responsi-bility for events in the department. If one of the manager's people makes a mistake, the manager takes the rap in public. If one member of staff fails, it is the responsibility of the manager, and not the direct fault of that person. The manager shields and defends staff as much as possible, even if it would be easier and safer to let them take the blame. If people make mistakes, it is the fault of training and motivation, not their stupidity and carelessness.

Of course, nobody should attempt to defend the indefensible: people do have to take responsibility for their own actions, and accept punishment where due. But even the most flagrant abuse of the rules does not absolve the manager from duty towards the miscreant. In such cases the organization's disapproval will be registered publicly, and there may be nothing that can or should be done to save the individual from dismissal. However, the manager can speak in mitigation, can take a little time to speak to relatives (if the employee agrees), and can make sure that the person's good points are not overlooked by potential employers. The offender will accept punishment as inevitable and will also be frightened of the consequences of a blot on his or her record. The manager can help bring about the realization that this is not the end of the world, and that there is someone available for advice before the trouble starts again. In circumstances like these the manager will need to be careful to say nothing which could be used to support an action by the ex-employee at an industrial tribunal.

That is an extreme example. There are many more ways in which a manager can treat people with decency and understanding while not infringing their privacy. Integrity warns a manager of the danger of interfering, rather than being available to help when needed. On occasion the manager will have to make the first move. A teenager weeping has to be approached rather than be left to ask for help, and can be offered the privacy of the manager's office while regaining composure. Both the person concerned and any witnesses will value such concern for human dignity.

Some first-time managers may feel that this is just a rehearsal of an obvious point about behaving with decency. For such people the reminder may be superfluous, at least in present circumstances. When the department is run off its feet and the telephone never stops ringing, it can be difficult for anyone to remember their people's right to respect. When the pressure is on, it is too easy to slip into treating your staff as an obstacle, rather than the means, to achieving your aims. From that position it is a short journey to regarding them as expendable cogs in the machine. If a manager ever reaches that point, staff will detect it.

It is not easy to decide what and how much your staff should be told. 'Economy with the truth' was mentioned earlier; the difficulty lies between, on the one hand, knowing that your staff have a right to know about the bad as well as the good news on issues which affect them, and, on the other, that there are matters which are properly your concern alone. There is also confidential information which you may not disclose or even hint at. The manager who does let too much slip, in the hope of achieving a sort of camaraderie with staff, runs great risks. If your people see that you cannot be trusted with sensi-tive information they will be more reserved about the very things you need most to hear about.

The staff deserve to be told about how things are going: if things are bad, only a fool would pretend otherwise. The manager will talk about the situation frankly, within the limits of confidentiality, and stress what is being done to remedy things, demonstrating that it is a rational response with a high chance of success. In this way the manager discharges the twin responsibilities to the staff and the organization at large. As a result, the staff know that they may have to work harder and in different ways, in order to help the organization or the department to turn the corner. They know why they have been asked, how important it is, and that it ought to succeed. In any organization in trouble worry coexists with willingness to help out. The manager encourages and uses the latter, and in doing so banishes the former. 'Things are going from bad to worse' is replaced by 'We are getting it sorted out'. There is a world of difference between the mental states which underlie each of those statements, and in the activities towards which each of them will direct energies. Worry is counter-productive; sorting out a problem is worthwhile and fulfilling.

And never, ever, have favourites.

Dealing with change

It is not unknown for a first-time manager to be suddenly pitchforked into a department with really major problems which he or she is expected to sort out. The staff know it; they know that changes must take place; they know what most of the desirable changes are, and they yearn to see them made. Many first-time man-agers disappoint them, for all the right motives. The manager may feel that they need a little stability among all the uncertainty, and holds back on necessary change. That attitude displays a becoming sensitivity but a wrong interpretation of the problem. The best way to act is usually this:

- look carefully at the problem;
- get the staff's ideas on what ought to happen, making sure that all have their say;
- decide;
- check the decision with colleagues who will be affected and with the boss;
- implement the decision.

Your people expect you to manage, and to provide the conditions under which they can work properly and productively. Don't let them down or, if you must, explain why, show them that you have tried, and they will forgive you.

The first-time manager may have to modify behaviour in other ways as well. Someone who has been 'one of the gang' will have to withdraw gently to a more aloof position. If inclined to act in a way which, coming from a manager, could offend or upset people, he or she ought to think about making changes. An obvious example is bad language. It may be acceptable among former colleagues, but it is definitely inappropriate in a manager. This has nothing to do with conformity to a boring stereotype, and everything to do with respect for others.

The boss

Given that your boss wants you to succeed, the only major area of possible dispute between you is any difference between your ideas of what success comprises. There might also be a subsidiary source of friction from the way in which you tackle the job, it is true.

One thing that the first-time manager realizes early on is the truth in the perennial boss's moan: no subordinate can do his or her own job as well as the manager could do it. There can be exceptions, for example, where a generalist is responsible for technical specialists. Some bosses stop at that point and never think further. Those with intelligence and a grasp of reality understand that, not only is that inevitable, but it may well be right and proper. The boss is usually older and more experienced, and ought therefore to be able to do most subordinate managers' jobs easily. That is one reason why the boss is not employed at a lower level, where his or her ability would be under-used. Moreover, the superior has an advantage that the subordinate can never have: as the recipient of much of the junior's output, the boss knows exactly what is wanted and what is superflu-ous. Much as the boss will train subordinates in producing what is required and not wasting time on extras, they will never achieve the same degree of understanding.

If your boss shows signs of dissatisfaction with your work, the only course of action that makes sense is to show willing, and get an explanation of what is wrong and what is really wanted from you.

There is a general rule (apart from the general rule that all general rules are suspect) that governs the first-time manager's dealing with the boss, and with higher beings still. It is that most inexperienced managers give far too much detail in their reports to their seniors and in response to their questions. 'How are things?' is probably just a conversation-opener, or a request to be told if anything is off-target, and if it is, what is being done about it. Too many first-time managers will respond as if they have been asked the ancient Chinese civil service entry-examination question: 'State everything you know', and have taken it too literally. Just as the examiner was looking for the ability to isolate and address what is important and neglect the trivial, so the boss is looking for the ability to rise above everyday detail and provide an answer in terms that match his or her needs, not yours.

Above all, be loyal to your boss, rejecting criticism, whatever your private view. If his or her behaviour is so odious that you really cannot bear to defend it, at least do not join in. However tempting it may be, do not allow yourself to let off steam to colleagues. In the unfortunate event that it is clear to all that the boss is an irredeemable fool and a knave, do not try to deny the obvious but confine yourself to praising his or her good points (yes, we all have them).

The same sort of loyalty is mandatory towards higher management and the organization as a whole. However difficult it may be to defend a particular decision or instruction, it is the manager's responsibility and duty to present it positively and constructively to staff.

A famous American industrialist used to tell his managers not to give him any surprises. It is a good maxim for any first-time manager to observe in relation to the boss. If trouble looms, give early warning. If stories are circulating, let him or her know. If the boss is away and someone senior looks in and asks questions, answer truth-fully, but tell your boss all about it as soon as you can. If there is any-thing about the senior person at all, he or she will repay support like that, and your reputation for discretion and soundness will rise.

A final point on bosses is not to curry favour. The question of how much of a relationship people seek outside the workplace varies with the individual's tastes and the organization's culture. In some US-based firms it is expected; many European companies shrink from the idea. Research done in the United States suggests that pro-motion is strongly linked to after-hours socializing. That may or may not be exclusive to the United States. Even then, do not presume on the relationship and expect favours. These are all further aspects of granting him or her due respect as a human being first, and as your supervising colleague second.

What do you want?

The spotlight now moves back from the boss to the first-time manager. You will have expectations of this job. It may be too soon after the appointment for you to envisage anything beyond learning the job and trying to survive in it. Or you may have been at it for some time and feel that you are getting on top. When that stage comes it is worth standing back and asking yourself some very fundamental questions about what it is all for. Every job can be seen as an educa-tional opportunity. As such, it is a stepping-stone towards self-devel-opment. There will be aspects of it that fascinate you and those you dislike: one way of defining a good job is where the one does not out-weigh the other. Fairly soon you ought to be able to decide whether this function is one in which you want to stay, and if not, whether you want to be in this field at all. A further dimension is that of whether the present organization is right for you.

The whole point of this exercise is to make sure that what you do today and tomorrow is moving you in the direction you want to go. Chance can and will produce some lovely surprises, but it is a little uncertain as a basis for deciding what you want to do with the rest of your life. Conversely, people who make out that they have a career plan stretching from school to retirement, with defined moves every few years, are most kindly thought of as poseurs. We change, we learn more about ourselves, our environment changes and things happen to us that make more than medium-term plans useless. Indeed, Professor Charles Handy foresees us spending the greater part of our working lives operating a 'portfolio' of jobs which itself will evolve over the years.

The manager can never start too soon to think about what aspects of jobs suit, and which do not. Over a period of time this process leads to a deepening understanding of what we really want to do, so that, before half your working life has passed, you know what you want to do with the other half. The knowledge may lead to a complete break with an earlier career, or it may mean exploring an interesting tribu-tary to the main stream. Either way, it can make the difference between a working life of fulfilment and one in which one-third of your most productive years are spent in misery and strain.

Key points and tips

- Understand the idea of 'organizational culture'.
- Being made a manager requires you to develop new perspec-tives.
- A manager's primary responsibility is for the output of other people.
- Managers need clear targets that they understand and believe they can achieve.
- Straight dealing is essential.
- If you want to change things, involve the people affected.
- It is helpful to have clear objectives for what you want out of life, and to know how your work will support them.
- If your field of work turns out to be wrong for you, dare to make the change. This is not a rehearsal.

two

The First-Time Manager and Other People

Success with your people

Until now, your main responsibility has been for your own performance. Now that you are a manager you have suddenly acquired another responsibility. Not only do you have to perform well yourself, but you have to coax good performances out of the people who report to you. Indeed, your boss's view of how good you are at your job will be based largely on one factor: how well your people have performed.

This extension of responsibilities is always dramatic and, unfortunately, often traumatic as well. Handled badly, it can lead to a lot of misery for subordinates and a severe setback in the manager's career.

Just as any failure by the first-time manager to handle people effec-tively reflects adversely on views held by others, so that failure reflects on his or her boss.

Since you are not really keen to fail, but would prefer to succeed, what should you do? First, you should make sure that you never forget that your people's success is your success. There is only one way in which a manager can succeed, and that is through them. When a first-time manager comes to grief, it is usually because nobody explained that elementary truth. Having been promoted partly because of good performance, he or she can easily assume that an extra amount of the old skill is called for. Not so. Those first-time managers who have failed have usually worked incredibly hard. They failed because they spent precious time and effort on the wrong target: improving their old skills or the wrong new ones rather than developing the right new ones.

Inevitably, when you look at your team you will find people who are good at what they do and others who are not. Those in the latter category clearly need urgent attention. First, you need to know why their work is below standard. The explanation usually falls under one of these headings:

- they lack the tools;
- they lack technical skill;
- they do not understand what is expected;
- they have been told to do the wrong thing;
- they are not getting the cooperation they need;
- they lack the desire to do well;
- their intellect is too low for the job.

To deal first with the most intractable; the last item, where someone just seems to lack the mental equipment needed. It is, of course, per-fectly possible that this is the case, but it is rarely so. The first trap to avoid is that of thinking that someone's inability to express them-selves clearly is proof of stupidity. Skill with language is not given to all, and sometimes not to the brightest. Einstein did not speak at all until he was five, though he made up for it later. Just because some-body cannot talk fluently about a task does not mean a lack of under-standing of it. It can be equally dangerous to assume that the fluent talker has actually grasped what he or she speaks about. Moreover, the fluent talker may not be a doer.

Another factor to bear in mind is that there is a great deal of illiter-acy around. People who have trouble with reading and writing develop all sorts of wily strategies for concealing their difficulty. Thus the person may not be stupid, just unable to cope with the level of literacy and numeracy involved. That sort of problem might be susceptible to training, but it will need to be done with tact and dis-cretion, and preferably neither at the workplace nor given by a colleague.

It may be that the job is just not fair on the person. It might call for decisions about a number of unstructured situations which really ought to be dealt with at a higher level. Alternatively, it may be possi-ble to create simple rules which are easy to follow, and remove the need to take decisions. An example is where customers' complaints are dealt with. Examination of their range and type shows that most of them fit into a number of clearly defined categories. If a list of cate-gories is produced and guidance given on how to spot and deal with each, the scope for decision is virtually eliminated. The really difficult ones can, and ought to, be referred upwards. Thus the person's task is simplified, perhaps to the point at which they can handle it. Equally valid would be the opposite approach. The front-line staff could be empowered to deal with every query in the way they see fit. To reduce the risk to the organization, and the stress on the individ-ual, a great deal of training and support might be needed.

By such means managers help people to become more competent, less worried and hence happier. They also find that their section becomes acknowledged as a good place to work, with all the benefits that flow from high morale. The point of such helpful behaviour will not be lost on the colleagues of the person who was in trouble but is now on top of the job. Previously they will, by turns, have been exas-perated by and sympathetic to the poor performer. At times they will have prayed for a replacement, at others, they will have wanted to help; indeed, they will almost certainly have tried. The appearance on the scene of a new manager warned them that trouble might be in store. The way you treat the weakest among them conveys strong mes-sages about the sort of person you are and how you mean to behave. They were worrying about whether you were the devil incarnate or an understanding fellow-human with a job to do. The behaviour described will go a long way to earn respect, trust and cooperation.

Some approaches to the most difficult of the possible reasons for a person's poor performance having been considered, the other items from the list on page 25 can now be considered. If technical skills are lacking, the answer is probably to review the task to see if they really are needed, and if they are, to provide suitable training. Easily said, but sometimes difficult to accomplish. The help of a human resource and training specialist can be very useful in such situations.

Before any expert is brought in, a little do-it-yourself analysis should be undertaken. A look at the task itself and a discussion with the employee may throw up the most unexpected findings. It may turn out to be completely pointless, a result which is certainly not unknown. Often, when changes are made in organizations, odd jobs are overlooked which the change has made superfluous. Or the job may gradually have assumed an importance to the organization which crept up on people because the movement was so slow. In that case you and your boss may decide that it ought to be upgraded, since the level at which it is being done now is just not adequate in view of its importance. In that case, training will come into it but not as an early response.

When redesign of a job is involved, do not be afraid to ask for views and ideas from specialists, colleagues, the boss and the job-holder, too. Far from losing points for appearing ignorant and indecisive, you will gain them for showing the wisdom to learn from others and to accumu-late information before taking action. Once the change has been made the job-holder should be able to hit the ground running too.

Communication and motivation

The next issues on the list of underperformance factors were to do with unclear or inaccurate instructions. One of the greatest contribu-tions that a management consultant makes, when reviewing how a department does its work, is by concentrating on what the depart-ment must do. This means eliminating everything that does not have to be done. Usually this investigation unearths activities which were once very necessary, but have become obsolete. Others can be found to have somehow grown in the absence of any conscious decision to create them. Often they were proper responses to temporary prob-lems; but when the problem died down the solution did not. It is easy to laugh and maintain that it could not possibly happen in your organization. It does, for it occurs in every organization on earth. The clever ones are those who recognize this inevitability and keep them-selves under constant review to check these wasteful practices before they really get a hold. There is no good reason to leave the skeletons in your cupboard for some beady-eyed consultant or internal auditor to discover and make a name at your expense.

The remaining human item on the list of reasons for under-performance concerned a lack of motivation. So how do you get people to want to do well?

Because so much hangs on the answer, that is one of the most-researched areas of organizational life. Armies of sociologists and psychologists devote their lives' work to its study. The consen-sus of informed opinion boils down to three guiding, and somewhat conflicting, rules:

Long term, nobody can be made to do things: they themselves must want to do them.
The art of motivating them is rather like selling them something. It involves finding out what they want in life, and showing them how helping the organization will help them to get what they are after. Ultimately, they buy it willingly, or they reject it.

People are different.
Some need the stick, some the carrot; some work best with loose guidance, others feel unhappy away from their tramlines; some start fast, others have to warm up first. Any two people are capable of drawing diametrically opposite conclusions from identical in-formation.

People are the same.
They want to do well, they like recognition for their efforts, they re-spond to encouragement, they like to know where they stand.

Later we shall touch on the research which supports some of these assertions. For the time being it is enough to say that most people will recognize them as broadly true in their experience, and do not need earnest and serious studies to persuade them.

A moment's reflection shows that people go to work from a variety of motives. Most of us need a certain minimum of money and are pre-pared to put up with a degree of misery to earn it. Some will accept a great deal of misery in return for large quantities of extra cash over and above their basic needs. Yet there are poorly paid people who love their jobs so much that they almost have to be thrown out of the building at night. Behaviour as diverse as this can be explained in all sorts of ways, but the single fact on which all psychologists agree is that: *behaviour is caused, it does not 'just happen'.*

The causes may lie deep within the person, or may be more super-ficial. They may be the result of upbringing or of inheritance. What-ever it is, the cause is there somewhere at some level. Just because you cannot identify the cause you must not think that it does not exist. Clearly, there is little that you can do to change the psychologi-cal make-up of your people, and it would be an impertinence to try. What you can do is to try to help them become motivated.

At the heart of motivation lie the three ideas of the person, the task and the context.

The person
Finding out what combination of satisfactions will keep this unique person working to the limit of ability, and supplying them.

The task
Finding out what tools, systems and resources are important to getting this job done well, and supplying them as far as possible.

The context
A cultural setting in which the person feels comfortable.

Once those three requirements are satisfied, the argument runs, the person will be perfectly motivated. Of course, a lot can go wrong to stop the ideal from being reached. For instance:

- wrong diagnosis of the person's needs;
- the possible supply of satisfactions exceeds the person's appetite;
- the full complement of possible satisfactions is not being delivered;
- the job has been poorly designed;
- inadequate resources are supplied;
- the person lacks technical ability;
- the culture is not right for them;
- something changes.

Then again, two people doing the same job side by side could easily rate very differently the importance of having this job, or any job at all. One might like going to work, the other hate it. One might see it as a job for life, the other as a stepping-stone. One might not care about the money, the other be very concerned about it. Even the most per-ceptive manager could not understand all that there is to know about each member of staff. The good manager does grasp that they, their motivations and their behaviour all vary, and will strive to under-stand as much about them as possible.

Trying to understand the individual is difficult enough; it becomes even harder when there are laid over it the demands made by the job itself. Taken together, these problems conspire to stack the odds against any manager succeeding. This illustrates what a remarkable challenge it is to become an effective manager. Few who take up that challenge are extraordinary human beings. Those who do so, and succeed in that calling, can make an exceptional contribution to the lives of the people under them and the success of the organization which they serve. Widely diverse types though successful managers are, the single thing they have in common is the ability to get people going and to help them work effectively, whether alone or in teams.

What the research tells managers about people

At this point the first-time manager might wish that there was some simple set of rules governing human behaviour. Help is nigh.

Seven major researchers have given managers insights into what governs the behaviour of people at work. They are Abraham Maslow, Frederick Herzberg, Douglas McGregor, Elton Mayo, Henry Mintzberg, Daniel Goleman and Erich Berne. Here is a brief summary of the light that each shed on the field.

Abraham Maslow

Maslow described how people seek to satisfy first their most basic, animal-like needs which are essential to physical survival. Once those are satisfied they cease to be of interest, and attention moves progressively to higher-level needs. Thus someone given £20 when hungry and wet would choose to spend it on shelter, dry clothing and food, but not, for instance, on a book. Once the low-level needs were satisfied by dry clothing, shelter and food the higher-level needs would seek satisfaction, and he or she might look around for a book to read, or turn on the radio for music, or visit friends for company.

The lesson which this carries for the manager is that people need reasonable pay and conditions, but when those lower-level requirements are met, they start to look for other satisfactions, such as civil-ized treatment, liking their colleagues, finding their work interesting and believing it to be useful. The manager who does not realize this may try to solve all problems with people by raising pay, for example. All he does is to supply more of a response to a low-level need than is necessary, and neglects the higher levels altogether. Nobody is likely to decline the extra pay, but their dissatisfactions will remain.

Frederick Herzberg

The thrust of Herzberg's work was in much the same direction as that of Maslow, but it did contribute important additional dimensions. His view was that, in the modern world, motivating factors fall into two camps. Some are positive: their presence has a real and sustained effect on performance. An example might be the appreciation which a manager shows for an exceptional level of performance. Others do not motivate positively, but are none the less crucial. These are the factors whose presence is taken for granted, but whose absence does demotivate. Examples of such factors are sufficient income, adequate equipment or civilized treatment (and many more). These Herzberg labelled 'hygiene factors'.

The message in this for the manager is that today there are certain standards which are expected to be observed as a matter of course. There will be no medals for doing so, but a failure to provide ensures that staff will be discontented. Quite separate from these are the real motivators. They include recognition, opportunity, appreciation and the chance to put one's personal stamp on one's work.

Douglas McGregor

McGregor's best-known work was to develop two stereotypes of managers. One, who operates on McGregor's 'Theory X', believes that people need to be driven and will backslide if given the slightest chance. The view is that people are wholly selfish and untrustwor-thy. The other managerial type operates on 'Theory Y', believing that people really want to do well, and that it is the manager's job to help, encourage and inspire them.

Many people recognize that there is truth in both of these generalizations, and settle for a mode of operation somewhere between the two, adjusted as the occasion demands for different situations and different people. Clearly, when the building is on fire there is no place for a consultative meeting which seeks views on what ought to be done: the manager slips into Theory X mode and orders everyone out.

Elton Mayo

Mayo is best known for the 'Hawthorne experiments', run at the Hawthorne plant of General Electric in the United States. This work provided insights into the subtleties of motivations at work. Brutally paraphrased, it showed that staff took little notice of the company's efforts to motivate them, or of its demotivating behaviour. The great-est influence was the degree of effort which they saw going on around them. The conclusion was that people do not want to stand out as either good or poor performers. Thus, whatever management does or fails to do, people will set their own pace and stick to it.

One interesting finding of the Hawthorne exercise was that output rose considerably in those areas of the plant in which the researchers moved, but fell back when they passed on. The feeling was that this was due to the boost to morale caused by becoming the subject of interest.

Henry Mintzberg

Professor Mintzberg is a prolific writer and profound thinker on management. The part of his work considered here is his analysis of what managers themselves actually do. His research led him to the belief that managers perform 10 roles, which can be grouped under the main headings of interpersonal, informational and decisional. This can come as a shock to many, who think that managers are there only to take decisions.

The full list of the roles he observed is as follows.

Interpersonal roles

Figurehead	Is identified with the group by the outside world
Leader	Provides leadership within his or her group
Liaison	Works with others in the group's interest

Informational roles

Monitor	Watches what is going on
Disseminator	Spreads news and information, keeping the group current
Spokesperson	Represents the group externally

Decisional roles

Entrepreneur	Takes opportunities available to the group
Disturbance handler	Spots trouble and deals with it
Resource allocator	Plans and decides who gets what within the group
Negotiator	Gets the best deal available

Not surprisingly, an important outcome of Mintzberg's observations was that managers are so beset by such a wide range of demands that they have little time for reflection. By his calculation less than 30 min-utes a day is typical.

The use to the first-time manager of this analysis is to show the wide range of competences that will be called on if he or she is to be fully effective. Any areas in which the manager recognizes weak-nesses deserve attention and development. Any worthwhile boss to whom you take this issue will not criticize you but congratulate you for your professionalism. If you feel unable to discuss it with that individual, it is a severe criticism of him or her. Perhaps the HR department may help.

Daniel Goleman

Dr Goleman is a specialist in behavioural and brain sciences, perhaps best known for coining the term 'emotional intelligence', which he used as the title of his best-known book. He proposes that we have in essence two types of intelligence, rational and emotional. Goleman argues that emotional intelligence is of far greater value than rational intelligence to an individual, and by extension, society. He argues not against the rational variety – after all, the many technological boons of our society might not exist without it – but for greater recognition of the importance of the emotional version. He says that while people with higher IQs tend to end up in better-paid work, IQ contributes only 20 per cent of the factors that determine life success: his interest is in the other 80 per cent.

In that may lie the book's most important message for people inter-ested in their careers: that the people who get things done most effec-tively and get promoted are those exhibiting high levels of emotional intelligence. They may be the happiest, as well.

Goleman defines emotional intelligence as being able to motivate oneself and persist in the face of frustrations; to control impulse and delay gratification; to regulate one's moods and keep distress from swamping the ability to think; to empathize and to hope. The impli-cations for the manager are clear. Life is full of frustrations, in the face of which dismay must not be shown. Even the most distressing cir-cumstances must not get the manager down, at least as far as the world is concerned, and the ability to think is vital. Empathy with colleagues is essential: what is *really* going on in their minds?

Erich Berne

Under the heading of 'transactional analysis' (TA), Berne described the ways in which people interact, classifying behaviour as adult (A), parent (P) or child (C). He argued that the ideal way for people to interact was A–A, and ascribed most of the problems that arise to straying from that model.

Adult transactions are characterized by mutual respect, openness and empathy. Parental address is judgmental, imperious and critical. In child mode, emotion and selfishness predominate.

For example (mine, not Berne's), let's take an airline passenger on a busy flight where the staff are rushed off their feet, who asked for a drink of water 10 minutes ago. He or she might remind staff in the following ways: 'I know you are busy, but I should have told you I need that drink to take my tablets' (A); or 'You have had plenty of chances to get my drink. I still want it, you know' (P); or 'I really want my drink. I tried asking nicely but you're just not interested' (C). The danger is that the C statement invites the staff to make a P response ('Can't you see we're busy? Wait your turn'). The P statement invites a C response ('We are doing our best but it isn't easy, you know').

Any of those mismatches would guarantee a letter of complaint, but the real fun starts when interchanges are P–P or C–C. 'Where's the drink I asked for 10 minutes ago?' 'If it's so important, get it your-self' (P–P). Wow! Or 'I want my drink!' 'I want my rest-break that I didn't get!' (C–C).

If the passenger reminds staff in A mode, the chances are that the steward will respond immediately and feel glad to have been able to help him or her, a very different feeling from that sparked off by any of the other interchanges.

Berne says that it is best to use A mode always, whatever the temptations to respond differently to people who are upset and using another mode. In reply to either of the P or C examples above, a response explaining the delay in terms that the other can understand ought to calm him or her down and even shame him or her into behaving properly. 'I am sorry, we had not forgotten you, but unfortunately we are two staff short because of illness. We have had to clear up after a sick baby, and one passenger has had a small medical emergency. At present I am dealing with some luggage that has come out of a locker and is blocking the gangway, which is both dangerous and against the law, but I will get your drink as soon as I can, I promise.' After something like that, the passenger would probably apologize to the steward for troubling him or her.

The use of TA to the manager is obvious. Staff, colleagues and people from the outside world may not have been trained in TA, and may therefore address him or her in P or C mode. Recognizing it for what it is, rather than responding instinctively, the manager can use A mode to bring the conversation on to a plane where sensible busi-ness can be transacted by calm people.

If anyone finds this field of interest, all these people are worth reading in the original. They published extensively, and any academic library, or larger public library, will carry their work.

Management styles and fashions

A first-rate way of making a fool of oneself is to propose as new an approach tried and rejected by earlier generations. Thus, while the first-time manager needs to know something of the current thinking among specialists in the management of people, he or she can also profit from understanding the shifts in approach which have taken place over the years.

In broad terms, the twentieth century saw two approaches to the management of people. The Victorian era gave rise to the first-ever formalized theories of management, the so-called 'Classical School'. Roughly since the Second World War, the 'Human Relations School' has held sway. Their characteristics can be summarized by the fol-lowing lists of propositions.

Classical School
- The organization is like a machine, enabling the person at the top to pull a lever to make things happen at the bottom.
- There is a clear chain of command from top to bottom.
- People are told what to do and how to do it.
- Human feelings are irrelevant.

Human Relations School
- Behaviour is influenced by attitudes; attitudes are affected by how people are treated.
- Better treatment results in better performance.
- Threats are very poor motivators.
- People want to do well and appreciate efforts to enable them to do so.

Echoes will be detected in this of McGregor's two theories. It is self-evident that most people need to use both the X and the Y theo-ries, either in a moving combination all the time, or separately as dic-tated by events. In any case, quite apart from any conscious decisions about their behaviour, managers come pre-programmed with a set of beliefs and values which, to a large extent, determine the degree to which they are instinctively authoritarian or liberal. That is no reason for abandoning all attempts to consider one's behaviour, for nobody should assume that the way one's instincts dictate how one behaves is necessarily the way to get results.

Ways have been developed of identifying and reconciling these different strands in the make-up of the individual manager. The writers Blake and Mouton devised a grid for mapping a manager's preferred style. The extent to which he is dedicated to getting the job done ('task orientation') as against having friendly relations with col-leagues ('people orientation') is assessed. People rate a particular score depending on the answers they give to a large number of ques-tions. The mix can change – indeed, it must – with the situation. Thus a really hard-driving infantry officer, faced in combat by the need to take a particular enemy position, will score nine for task orientation and one for people orientation. At night he may change completely, to a rating of three-eight, perhaps, in observance of the old army motto that officers eat last.

More recently, the precepts of the HR school have to some extent been set aside. The drive for efficiency, which led in the 1990s to widespread de-layering and downsizing, was, for the most part, con-ducted with little obvious concern for its effects on the motivation of those who continued to be employed. Although labels such as 'post-industrial', 'neo-industrial' and 'post-modern' are in use, it may be too soon to identify and label a predominant school of thought. History, by definition, can only be seen in retrospect.

Meanwhile we may view with concern the re-emergence of a man-agement style that views people as consumables to be used up rather than assets to be nurtured. If there is any justice, and if history truly does not repeat itself, such brashness will be punished and eventu-ally scorned, as it was a generation earlier.

What else makes your people work?

So far some of the most important factors bearing on people's atti-tudes to work have been discussed. There are further influential matters to consider, under the main headings of *ability* and *prepared-ness* to contribute.

Ability to contribute is affected by:
- personality
- skill
- health
- training
- knowledge
- organizational setting.

Preparedness to contribute is influenced by:

- confidence
- motivation
- perceptions of the task, the boss, the organization, and probabil-ity of reward and punishment.

Personality

People can be unfitted for a particular job in many different ways. An obvious example of a personality misfit is of an introvert in a setting where dealing with people is important. Thus the personality of the person needs to be matched to the demands of the job. By the same token, an extrovert required to work alone with no human contact will probably fail to perform properly. The wise manager bears all this in mind when recruiting, reviewing, transferring and promoting.

Health

People in good physical and mental health, given the right sort of work setting, feel as if they can take on the world and win. When they are under the weather even minor things can get them down. Many first-time managers are fortunate in having no personal experience of how health worries can affect people. These worries can be real or imagined, and they can apply to the health of the worrier or to that of someone close. The range of people close to each member of your staff may be quite wide: partner, children, parents and in-laws, grandchildren, brothers and sisters – who could add up to a dozen or more – quite apart from friends. Thus at any one time there is quite likely to be at least one problem affecting each member of the team.

A worried person will not perform well, and may even upset other members of the team. The manager should not be too hard on such a colleague: if it has never happened to him or her, it certainly will one day.

Knowledge

People who know the most are not always the best performers. Indeed, in some settings, they can be paralysed by indecision arising from their knowledge of all the things that could go wrong. That is not to argue against knowledge, but to say that judgement is just as important. The person who knows a lot but lacks judgement cannot take sensible decisions. Equally, somebody whose judgement is sound, but who has little knowledge of a particular field, is in no position to take a decision. However, he or she can usually identify the information needed to bring about that position. In the real world, knowledge and thought usually lead to understanding, which is the parent of judgement. Thus knowledge and practice in a particular field do tend to raise a manager's performance.

A manager should encourage people to extend their knowledge and their understanding of their own field and of the setting within which the organization at large operates. Study introduces new information, new perspectives on things and new ways of dealing with issues. To anyone interested in advancing their career it is an excellent way of preparing for promotion.

Organizational setting

As far as most staff are concerned, most of the time, their manager fixes the setting within which they work. The manager is the organization for all practical purposes. There are matters which impinge on people over which the manager has little control – whether they can be allocated a parking space, pension arrangements and the canteen menus, for example. However, in many ways what people do and how they do it are largely fixed by the manager. He or she may not be able to change much in their working lives, but as long as his people recognize that someone is doing their best for them, they will work all the better. To be seen to be trying to get better equipment, support, furniture, wages and so on will cause people to warm to you. It is better to succeed than to fail, but failure can be forgiven if sincere efforts were visibly made. It is important that this is done in such a way as not to raise hopes unduly: that could only lead to demotivation when the inevitable failure comes. However, even under the most unpleasant conditions it is possible for the most junior manager to ameliorate the setting in which people work. Even in the most unpromising situation, the sense that you are brothers and sisters in adversity can help people to pull together.

Perceptions

This word may seem a trifle precious, but it is used because it has a precise and useful meaning. Psychologists use it to denote the impressions that people gain of events and things. Some people even argue that there is no objective reality, and that perceptions are the whole of existence. They would say that because your shoe was hidden under the chair, you cannot prove it was there. You saw it go under, and you fished it out afterwards, but while it was out of sight there is no proof that it existed. Only while you were perceiving it through sight or touch could it be proved to exist. Furthermore, what kind of proof of existence is your perception anyway? You may be imagining the shoe for some reason. That line of speculation may keep philosophers and psychologists in work, but it is of limited use to the practical manager. Its value lies in drawing attention to the idea that one person's way of seeing things is not the only way. 'Facts', 'truth' and 'reality', even in relation to the same event, mean widely different things to different people. Those differences arise for all kinds of reasons: social, cultural, personality, life experience and upbringing are some. All these influence how we see the world. Thus you, your supervisors, colleagues and subordinates are all car-rying around different mental models of what was said, agreed and done. Even if you were all to agree on exactly what did happen (which is unlikely), there will be disagreement over its value and importance, and over whether and how to react. In other words, you all formed different perceptions of the implications of the event.

This variety is not something to deplore, but to be recognized and taken into account in dealings with other people. Confronted by these ideas people often fall back in horror, demanding to know how, if all this is true, anyone ever manages to deal with any other person. Practical experience shows that to be an extreme reaction. Most of the time we manage to rub along reasonably well with one another. The manager is concerned with leaving as little as possible to chance, and therefore allows for the fact that his or her understanding may not coincide with that of someone else. That brings us to the next topic of this chapter, communication.

Communication

So widespread has the recognition of the importance of communica-tion become that this topic is almost a cliché. It would be folly if that caused people to think of it as something that little can be done about, a fact of life like the weather. It is an important matter, and a lot can be done to deal with its problems. The manager who cannot communi-cate effectively cannot manage, so it is a matter of vital interest to the first-time manager.

At work it is essential that we communicate effectively with one another. On the simplest level, you want your staff to do something, so you tell them: you communicate. They do it and report back: they communicate. As has been seen, the human apparatus for transmission and reception is rather good at overlaying messages with all sorts of unintended meanings. Receivers can hear things never said, transmitters can say things in a way they did not mean. Chaos looms.

Chaos can, at the very least, be postponed, and even banished alto-gether. The key is to recognize the pitfalls already described and to allow for them. This does not mean treating colleagues like ignora-muses, but simply recognizing the fact that you are all human beings and accepting everything which that implies. The same approach applies whether you are dealing with seniors, subordinates or peers, to ensure that each side is carrying away the message in the form in which it was meant to be put across.

At the heart of this issue is the question of whose job it is to make communications work: the transmitter or the receiver of the information or instruction. As a general rule, both carry that responsibility in equal measure, but since the manager has a responsibility to people and carries the can if things go wrong, it is in the manager's interest to make sure that they go right.

The obvious technique available to the manager is simple and easy to master. It comprises passing the message, and then getting the person you are dealing with to play back what it is you want them to do. Most people know the childhood whispering game, when a message is whispered from person to person around a ring. Misun-derstandings change the message as it goes, with the result that what started as 'send reinforcements, we are going to advance' becomes transformed into 'send three-and-fourpence, we are going to a dance'. (Readers unfamiliar with pre-decimalization currency will be fascinated to know that three shillings and fourpence is equivalent to about seventeen pence.)

That easy technique soon becomes second nature, but it should be applied subtly. People asked to repeat what they have been told will react waspishly. A subordinate can, instead, be asked how they will tackle the task. It will soon become clear if they are talking about a different job from the one you asked them to do. When you ask your boss to do something, you can ask what problems he or she foresees or where that information or permission might come from. Again, the reply gives away any misunderstanding.

When taking instructions from the boss it is important to check your understanding of them. A playlet:

First-time manager. Just to make sure I've got that right, you want me to get three units of 8080A into your office by ten tomorrow morning. Right?

Boss: Yes. *Or*: No, three dozen. *Or*: No, I leave at ten and I want to check them first; make it nine o'clock. *Or*: No, 8088. *And so on.*

The scope for misunderstandings is great, and when they occur the damage can be enormous. To reduce the risk of an occurrence, the groundwork starts before transmission begins. Listening is probably the most crucial element. The manager, transmitting information and instructions, must listen to staff. The staff, the receivers, must listen to their manager.

Listening

Listening requires concentration and sensitivity. It therefore rarely works well when the listener is:

- tired
- angry
- emotional
- worried
- preoccupied
- suspicious
- unwell
- dying to say something
- in any other way distracted.

To make the listening part of your communication work well, you therefore need to do rather a lot before even starting to think about transmitting. If by some fluke none of the more extreme distractions listed above does apply, your people will be busy and will therefore have a lot on their minds. You have to start by wrenching their thoughts away from their present focus before you begin. It may take a minute or two, or longer. However long it takes, the good commu-nicator does not start to transmit until he has gained the attention of the audience.

Once they are paying attention, that attention has to be held. This involves constantly refocusing it. Teachers who spot attention wandering bring it back with a jolt by asking a question, a useful technique at times. It must be borne in mind that on the side of yourself and of your audience there are further human problems to contend with.

Some more communication problems

- people hear compliments better than criticism;
- prejudices and values affect perceptions;
- reticence;
- thinking about what has been said blocks reception of what is be-ing said;
- there are feelings behind the words which the words alone can only hint at;
- not everyone listens actively, following the basic rules of good listening.

The rules of good listening are very powerful. Properly followed, they help you to understand and know your colleagues better, and to increase their respect for you. Every single piece of effective listening that you undertake improves your performance as a manager.

The basic rules of good listening

- banish distractions, physical and mental;
- relax, and turn off the mental jabbering of your thought processes;
- get the others to relax;
- work hard at listening; aim to grasp what is going on in speakers' minds: what did they mean by this, why did they not say that? Show that you are listening: maintain eye-contact and if you have to break off or make a note, explain why;
- give people space to complete or qualify what they are saying;
- notice body language: is it contradicting what is being said?
- as each point is made, play it back to check you have understood and to assess how others react.

Inevitably things will be said with which you disagree. This is not the time to argue back, still less to impose your point of view. There will be plenty of time for that later if it becomes necessary. Listening is different and separate from persuasion, but you cannot move on to the persuasive phase without it. Unless you listen effectively, you:

- do not understand fully the points being made;
- do not really know what your colleagues are after;
- have no idea why that point is being made now, in this way and by this person;
- cannot gauge the other's sincerity.

Persuasion

The whole point of communication is to get something desirable to happen or to avoid some undesirable outcome. In order to do this, people's understanding of events and their perceptions sometimes have to be changed.

Sometimes just passing information is all that is needed. The recip-ient receives it, interprets it and acts on it as you would wish. Alas, for much of the time it is less straightforward, and the point you wish to convey is not accepted.

The first thought should be to give due weight to the objection, for it might be right. Many a manager has been saved from folly by another person's viewpoint. Even so, there will occasionally be courses of action with which we privately disagree, but which we nevertheless have to implement. If a matter is in that category it is pointless to stimulate discussion. It has to be presented for what it is, a *fait accompli*. After that presentation it is the manager's duty to make sure that it is seen in the most favourable light, but loyalty should not go as far as to forfeit personal credibility in the defence of the plainly unacceptable. Staff must be told that it is necessary and why, and the manager must avoid a disloyal dissociation from the policy. When the reaction comes, as it will, the manager will recognize and accept the objections as valid. Then, and only then, will he or she try to fix attention on the future and how the changed situation is to be dealt with. Word-pictures can be drawn of how things will be under the new arrangements, getting people thinking not of what has been lost but of making things work – it is important to be and remain positive. The explicit statement that resistance is pointless should be avoided, for nothing is more likely to stir free-born people to rage, resistance and even sabotage.

What the manager wants to see is all that energy of protest being channelled into solving the problem, which in this case is making the adjustment to a possibly unpleasant new situation. It may mean more work or fewer resources, or a removal of func-tions, or new methods or a score of other perfectly understandable grounds for grievance. Whatever it is, a manager's people will respect straight talk that accepts their right to hold and express their views, and then gets them to work on adjusting to the new circum-stances. The manager will then be fulfilling one of the job's highest functions, that of helping to reconcile the staff's best interests to those of the firm.

That was an extreme example, and deliberately so. Mercifully, not all the situations in which persuasion plays a part are charged with so much explosive potential. How can persuasion be exercised in this context? It becomes easier the better you and your people know one another. The basic rules are:

- listen to the objections;
- acknowledge them;
- show the positive side of the proposals first;
- recognize openly their less desirable side;
- explain vividly and simply how the net result will be a gain for the organization, the department and the individuals;
- give people time to come round, while remaining positive.

If they still will not accept, the manager is faced with a choice between three courses of action: to withdraw, to revise the proposals or to impose them. Withdrawal may cast you as a soft touch or as a wise person, depending on how you do it. Revision, if it is possible, scores highest for wisdom. Imposition forfeits goodwill, but some-times it has to be done.

If you have honestly considered the objections and still believe that the proposal is, on balance, right; if you are certain that revision would fatally undermine the proposals' thrust and effectiveness; and if you believe that the cost in goodwill is outweighed by the improve-ments, your duty dictates that you impose the proposals. One of the things you are paid for is your judgement. If unexpected trouble does result you will be able to say with a clear conscience that you did what you thought to be right, that you had considered the conse-quences, and that the gains appeared to outweigh the disadvantages. In most organizations it is recognized that managers will make mis-takes, as part of the process of making things happen. The organizations to avoid are those which are so risk-averse that their managers never dare do anything, for fear of getting it wrong.

When a manager has to impose it must be accompanied by an acknowledgement that he is doing it and an explanation of why. Staff should be asked for their support in putting into practice the propos-als to which they object. That may call for some courage, but nobody admires a coward, and no one said management was going to be easy. Again, it shifts attention to the future and what you are all going to do, and away from the past and the battle you have just lost.

Written communication
Oral communication is both easier and more difficult than its written

counterpart. It is more difficult because of problems of vocabulary, concentration and mishearing. It is easier because it is simple to check the real meaning behind the words. Written communication does convey an authority which can be entirely spurious: the fact that it is in print at all makes it impressive. That can make it seem like the last word on the subject, to be obeyed however much it contradicts common sense. Then there is the problem of expressing yourself comprehensibly. Some people, who speak quite normally, freeze when they have to write. Their brain switches into a different gear, and they use terms like 'with reference to' instead of the word 'about', and close their letters with 'Assuring you of our best atten-tion at all times' which is the biggest waste of typing and reading time ever invented. The professional communicators who give the best example are journalists, particularly those on the mass-circula-tion papers. They use simple language and short sentences. They use the active voice rather than the passive (eg 'I want to review the budget because it is looking increasingly suspect', not 'the suspicion under which the budget is increasingly coming means that it ought to be reviewed'). The first tells everyone what is to be done, why and by whom. The second has to be read twice to work out what it means, and even then it omits mention of who is to do the review.

Along with the need for simple vocabulary and short sentences goes the need to break down indigestible lumps of information into manageable morsels. If it is unreasonable to expect people to manage the whole lump in one go, feed it to them a point at a time. Replacing long sentences with tabulated lists is particularly helpful.

One rule of communication is to tell people where you want to take them before you start out. Some organizations develop styles and conventions for documents. In case yours is not one of those, here is a suggested layout for a presentation to your boss, requesting permis-sion for something you want to do.

A presentation like this saves the boss's time. Often the rightness of the recommendations is obvious and they can be approved without reading the rest of the document. Where he or she has to read on, at least the conclusion you are leading up to can be seen, rather than being kept in suspense until the last page. If the document is more than a couple of pages in length, especially if it contains many lengthy sections, it helps the reader if you preface it with an 'execu-tive summary'. As the name suggests, this sums up the whole docu-ment in brief in up to 100 words, which is about the length of this paragraph.

1. *Recommendation*
   What I think we should do.
2. *Objectives*
   What it is designed to achieve.
3. *Method*
   How I plan to do it, when and where.
4. *Background*
   The situation that has made action necessary.
5. *Implications*
   Costs, both monetary and other benefits.
6. *Justification*
   Reason for doing this and doing it now, risks of doing it and risks of doing nothing.

The underlying idea seems sound: that any recommendation should be capable of explanation and justification in quite a brief document. Managers' time is too precious to be taken up in writing or reading documents that are over-long. However, experienced writers will attest to how much more difficult it is to write concisely rather than at great length.

So much for the boss; we shall now return to the people whom the manager is responsible for. Depending on all sorts of factors, like the nature of the task, physical location and the organization's culture, you may need to write more or less frequently to them. There are some pointers to observe.

Written instructions
- write clearly, simply and concisely;
- banish detail to appendices;
- draft and redraft until your meaning is clear;
- if possible, put the draft away for a day or two, then look at it as if you were a recipient;
- check with staff and departments that might be affected;
- reread it for accuracy and as a true reflection of what you mean;
- if it is really important, get your boss to check for confused mean-ings;
- put it through any necessary clearance procedures;
- publish.

Even then the job is not over. When your people have read and dis-cussed the document, go through it with them to check their percep-tions and answer any queries about operational problems.

Power, authority and responsibility

Power can be intoxicating; some psychologists maintain that the urge to gain it is the mainspring which drives us. You tell someone to do something and he does it. You ask for something and it appears. All this is heady stuff.

On your first day as a manager, you sit at your desk. People look expectantly at you, perhaps even anxiously. They all seem eager to please. You must not let this go to your head. If you do, it will show that your idea of your job is exactly upside-down.

One of the things you are paid for is responsibility. In order to help you to discharge your responsibilities you have been given authority, from which flows whatever power you have.

It is not really your power at all. Rather than belonging to you, it attaches to the job that you are temporarily occupying. In the fullness of time you ought to gain a further source of authority, resulting from the display of attractive personal qualities. Equally, a bully or a wimp will find that his authority is reduced by the unattractiveness of his behaviour.

Thus authority springs from three sources:

- your position;
- your qualities and behaviour;
- any special skill or expertise you have.

The first is automatically conferred by the organization to enable you to get things done. The second is harder to get, for it depends on peo-ple's judgement of your qualities and behaviour. They are not obliged to approve of them. That type of authority is easy to lose, too, for one good show is not enough – you have to continue to exhibit qualities and behaviour of which they approve.

One mistake which is sometimes made is to grant someone respon-sibility without the authority to discharge it. If you are ever in that position, lose no time in bringing it to your boss's notice. It is a basic principle in the design of organizations that authority and responsi-bility should be equal. Your boss should therefore be very glad that you drew attention to the problem. If there is little interest, write confirming the problem's existence and your lack of authority to deal with it, and repeat your request to put things right, keeping a file copy. That covers your back for, make no mistake, you will get the blame for your failure to cure the problem. Then start to look for a job straight away. It is a rotten organization and an inadequate boss who will let you take the rap for things you cannot control.

Leadership

Leadership is a vital part of the manager's job. It has already been dis-cussed in part under the heading of Communication (page 43), where mention was made of the idea of getting people to do things that they do not want to do.

That thought introduces the very essence of leadership. The organization pays the manager to get things done. Bullying and misusing authority might work short-term, but will usually create bigger problems than they solve. The victim may do as instructed, but seethes at the slight on his or her dignity. From then on the victim will be bent on revenge, and may well succeed. It is usually not worth taking the risk. There may be very rare occasions when the damage to the relationship is less important than that to the organization, but situations deserving this approach must be carefully selected.

The main elements of leadership are:

- creating an atmosphere of high expectations;
- establishing clear objectives and guidelines;
- setting an example of effort and achievement;
- helping people to reach their potential;
- helping people to work together, not merely in mutual toleration but as a team;
- acknowledging effort and achievement;
- protecting and defending your people;
- representing your department and people effectively;
- treating people with respect;
- and, if you possibly can, making it all fun.

Let us look at these points one by one:

High expectations
It is up to you to set the atmosphere in which your people work. Expect only a little of them and some might exceed the norm but the

majority will learn that there is little point in making an effort. The true leader gets them to adopt targets that they believe are beyond their reach, then helps them to achieve those goals. Their awe at their own performance will drive from their minds any wonder at their leader's miraculous powers. Of course, it is important not to set people up to fail, for that leads to misery and self-doubt.

Clear objectives and guidelines
People become confused and irritated if they are asked for one thing and then expected to deliver another. That annoyance quickly turns into criticism of the person who confused them in the first place. It is a particularly effective way of earning scorn rather than respect; and respect is at the heart of leadership.

Setting an example
The boss who asks his people to put in great effort, but himself spends working time on the golf course, soon finds that these exhor-tations are ignored. Likewise, coming in late, leaving early, taking long lunch-breaks, inexplicable absences during the day – none is setting the right example to people. It is even worse if they are penal-ized for lateness while the boss gets away with it.

So when you are going out it makes sense to let your people know where and why. They do not have to know all the details, but they do need to know both that your trip is in the furtherance of team goals and if they will be able to reach you in an emergency.

Helping people to reach their potential
Your people are all different. They are diverse in their backgrounds, ages, circumstances, education, training, experience, personalities, beliefs, intelligence, abilities, appearance and ambitions, as well as in other ways.

Probably the most significant item on that list is 'ambitions'. People can be bright but content with their lot, and such people have their place on every team. Others will care passionately about getting on. This presents you with a dilemma: if you help them you will lose them, but if you do not, they might stay around for only a little longer. What should you do?

For once the answer is simple. If you help them, you will get:

- good and improving results while they are with you;
- a reputation as a developer of people.

If you do not help, you will:

- lose them more quickly to someone who will give them a chance;
- be recognized as selfish.

Anyone inclined to promote his or her self-interest should remember that the ambitious subordinate of today may be the boss in a few years' time.

So much for those who are ambitious. There is another type whom you need to look out for, and who probably needs more help than the ambitious person. That is the person who cannot do the present job properly. The simplistic answer is to fire them but you could try to find out why, and see if you could work on it together. If the person is clearly grossly inadequate in the present role, and is completely inca-pable of improvement, move them on to something new. People do know that they are bad at their job and will be relieved to move on to something more manageable.

You have to be very sure in your judgement before taking such drastic action as to sack someone. There is, of course, the effect on the individual to consider. Then there are the practicalities: replace someone, and the chances are that you will get a replacement who is much the same in many ways, but has other problems it will take you time to uncover. For a start, there is a need to fit into the team; then learning the basics of the job. It takes at least six months to see if you have made the right choice – what do you do if you got it wrong?

On balance, at first it is best to give people the benefit of the doubt. Try to identify the cause of the problem, and only when you are as sure as you can be, deal with it. Identification can take a long time and cannot be hurried. First, the person has to learn to trust you. The first reaction on being asked a lot of questions by a new boss could be defensive, so make allowances. Before doing anything else, consult the organization's HR specialists. All sorts of trouble can be caused by dismissals deemed unfair or discriminatory, so there will be pro-cedures to observe.

You have to make it clear from the outset that you perceive underperformance. That presents you with the two obvious choices, to dismiss or take a chance – and you have chosen the latter. This dis-cussion is important so it takes place away from interruptions, at a carefully chosen time and in private, and you will give no hints to others about why you are paying extra attention to this person. Be sure to allow plenty of time for discussion and be ready to listen more than you talk. Don't do it on a Friday, when there is all weekend to worry before being able to ask for clarification of some point. Your aim is to help this colleague to pull out of the past pattern and into a new one of success. You believe that the capacity is there, but success will come only if he or she really wants it. Is he or she prepared to make the effort? If so, you will help, but most of the effort must come from the colleague. Agree a timetable and a definition of success. Agree the rules under which you will deal with each other, and ask for any questions.

If your attempt to solve the problem in this way fails, you will know that you exhausted every possible avenue. If it succeeds, your reward will be the knowledge that you have done your job by the organization and the individual. That person was in trouble and is now more effective and self-confident. Their loyalty to you will be great. Such things are rare, precious and not to be under-valued.

Acknowledging effort and achievement

People like to be thanked for what they have done. You would think that nobody needed telling that, but it is a sad fact that few managers remember this elementary piece of good manners. Some would say that doing their job is what people get paid for, and that they should not expect to be thanked as well.

That is a curmudgeonly view. It slips into the idea of people as mechanisms: pour money in and get effort out. It is well known that pay is certainly not the only thing that people get from their work. In any case, how can a manager possibly know when people have made a great effort? What may be easy to the manager is perhaps a great challenge to subordinates. It is folly to risk disappointing someone who has tried really hard by not acknowledging it. What incentive do they have to keep up the extra effort?

The most desirable thing to reward is achievement, of course. Nev-ertheless, people can come last and still contribute a lot to the depart-ment's accomplishments. They should not be ignored just because they did not take first prize.

The rewards themselves do not have to be large or expensive. Just a 'thank you' is usually quite enough. A brief explanation of how the department and the organization have benefited is even better. Best of all is public acknowledgement.

Protecting and defending your department and people

Every organization goes through difficult periods and, from time to time, every department comes under fire. Your people will be watch-ing your response.

If your reaction is to turn round and blame the people under you, it is unlikely to impress anybody: your boss, your staff or your other colleagues. Insist that your people are good – the best group in the organization in many ways – but that circumstances have not made life easy for them. Things would have been much worse if a team of that quality had not been on the job.

This goes as much for your dealings with individuals in your department as for the group as a whole. There is nothing to stop you from tearing strips off your people in private if you believe that will help them, but to the outside world you defend them. Even where their actions have been indefensible you have something to say to show they are not entirely bad. In those circumstances you do not try to defend so much as to mitigate. People whose bosses support them, especially in times of trouble, will go a long way to support their boss in return.

Representing your department and people

Just as you defend when attacked, if others are making it difficult for your people to do their jobs you get things sorted out. You do not do this in a way which will look to your people like surrender. Furthermore, if your people have any justified grievances, you at least try to get changes made. You may fail, but you are seen to be trying.

Getting and giving the credit to your people for their good work is also important. Where somebody does something especially good you make sure that it is known about elsewhere in the organization, and beyond if appropriate. Helping your department to build its reputation as a unit is important, and so is helping individual members of your staff to build their personal reputations. If a presentation has to be made to senior management on a matter which one of your people has worked a lot on, why make the whole of the presentation yourself? You could, instead, make it clear at the outset that you take responsibility for the presentation, but since Jane and John did all the background work on the project, you feel that they can explain it best: over to them.

Respect

You have a sacred right to your point of view, and so do other people to theirs. Much of what has been said so far can be classified as courtesy or good manners, an acknowledgement that the other person has rights, too. Good manners can be completely superficial; respect goes much deeper. Where your behaviour towards others springs from a fundamental respect for their rights, you are unlikely to misuse your relationships.

Insincerity, on the other hand, is detectable. Some are quick to spot it, others give the benefit of the doubt for longer. Either way, when it is eventually detected, it destroys goodwill, loyalty and motivation faster than anything.

Making it all fun

People do best the things that they enjoy. Why should they not enjoy their work, getting pleasure from personal achievement and being part of a winning team, and taking satisfaction from practising and improving their skills? The organization's eight or ten hours a day do not have to be a mental version of toothache. It has little to do with the number of hours people work – indeed, some of the people who enjoy work most spend a lot of time at it. Stories abound of 'hot' departments which work until late at night which, on first acquain-tance, sound like the salt-mines. A closer look shows that people from other departments are fighting to get transferred to them; far from the present inmates seeking an escape route, they work hard to stay put.

Such an atmosphere usually starts with one person, the departmental manager. He or she does not have to look like a film star, or resemble a hero or heroine in any other way. What they do have is the ability to make their work fun; their enthusiasm catches and spreads, and before long the whole department is in a state of excitement. Everyone gets satisfaction and fulfilment from doing their own bit well, plus an extra kick from seeing the whole team succeed. The people who can create this atmosphere are rare, and some are excep-tional in other ways as well. But what they do to inspire their teams can be learned. This means that nobody need give up hope if they cannot do it naturally. They can learn the skills and put them into practice, and will surprise themselves at the results.

Team building

It is important to consider what is meant by the word 'team'. A true team is more than a collection of people who just happen to work together. It *is* a group, but one which is distinguished in an important way: its results are more than the sum of its members' individual contributions.

So the manager will want to ask: 'How can I get my people to work like that?'

It is hardly original to remark that people come with all sorts of dif-ferent personalities. Some are leaders, or at least have in their make-up slightly more than the average ration of bossiness and the urge to control others.

When teams are being put together, or when an existing team is being reviewed, the question of personalities must be considered. If you want firecracker performances, go for people with a dash of leadership qualities about them. They will be difficult to control and downright argumentative, but they will make things happen all right. On the other hand, there are many tasks where individual ini-tiative is inappropriate. Nobody wants an accounts clerk to exercise creativity in the way that the accounts are made up: sticking to the rules and the routine is essential.

The worst situation to create is one in which a bright, energetic, ambitious and competent person is put under someone who is defen-sive, jealous, petty and incompetent. Therefore consider the ques-tions of personality type from all angles. Get the mix right in your team and it ought to work beautifully; if it is wrong, there will be trouble.

That is possible when assembling a team from scratch, but few new managers are in that position. What can be done about an existing group to enable it to function like a team? Many researchers have looked at this subject and derived a variety of answers. Many working managers find the advice of Dr Meredith Belbin of particu-lar help. He focused on what people actually do in effective teams, and found that such teams contained people who played eight team roles (which he later expanded to nine). This does not mean that all teams must comprise nine people, but that all nine team roles have to be performed. Some people can play more than one. He also devised a way of identifying the preferred style of any individual – which helps people to find out what they are good (and not good) at in the team. These roles are quite separate from the professional expertise which people bring to team work. His analysis deserves more than a summary here: it is worth reading his book.

In everyday parlance we speak of the manager 'motivating the team'. It is my belief that this is possible, but only when the manager holds a big stick, not when the main weapon is the carrot. Then the only source of motivation is from within the person – the need to achieve must come from inside the individual; nobody can impose it from outside. The manager's task is to *create the conditions* under which people can become motivated. Get the conditions right, and motivation will follow.

Health

Managers have available all sorts of tools to help them carry out their jobs. They take great care to select the right equipment and to main-tain it properly. They usually neglect woefully the most important piece of equipment of all, their own minds and bodies.

Keeping yourself fit to work is clearly a fundamental prerequisite of work of any kind. The threats to a manager's health are specific, and spring from the nature of the work. The causes of poor health include:

- a sedentary job;
- the pressure of events: always more to do than there is time for;
- worry about things that have gone, or could go, wrong.

Your people may also be exposed to similar or different risks, depending on the nature of your department's work. These risks pose real threats to physical and mental well-being.

Watch your people, and look at yourself in the same way. Are they tired and irritable? Unstable? Losing concentration? Drowsy in the afternoon? Putting on or losing weight? Taking frequent sick-leave? Constantly catching colds? Unable to sleep at night? All these can be symptoms of stress or stress-related malfunctions, or of the ways in which people sometimes try to deal with them, by using drink or drugs. Time off for alleged sickness is noticeably higher among people performing routine tasks. They can suffer stress from con-stant pressure to do this work more quickly, and boredom from its repetitiveness.

Difficulties at work need not spring from work-related problems. Trouble in a person's private life can affect work performance. This is not easy for the manager to deal with, but it is a managerial responsi-bility to do so. While unable to help directly with such a problem, the manager may be able to reorganize holiday schedules or working hours to help someone cope. It may seem little enough to the manager but it can be a godsend to a person under pressure.

People can also be worried by imagining that their work performance is not up to scratch. They are often right, and when they are they know before the boss finds out. By far the best way of dealing with this is through the staff appraisal procedure (if there is none, ask to have one installed and if that is refused, go and work for a firm that has one). This is a system which requires managers to report in writing on the performance and progress of each subordinate. In a proper system, the manager discusses and explains his evaluation with the subordinate; if there is agreement – and there usually is – a course of action and a timetable are agreed for improvement together with targets for the future.

In a system where that is done once or twice a year everybody knows where he or she stands. People know which are recognized as their strong points, and they know what they have to brush up on. It eliminates large areas that people could worry about fruitlessly if left to themselves. It also concentrates their efforts at self-improvement on the right targets, as well as showing that support is at hand. It is therefore both humane and efficient.

Management style

Management style is a term used to denote the way a manager goes about performing the leadership role.

Managers are individuals, with their own unique personalities, backgrounds and beliefs. Therefore there can be no one style of behaviour which all should observe, a kind of mould into which they should force themselves. If they were foolish enough to try, either their insincerity would show or the strain of prolonged, successful pretence would take its toll.

There is no contradiction between this statement and earlier asser-tions that certain types of behaviour are desirable. While certain approaches to the job are of proven effectiveness, the way that differ-ent people put them into effect can vary widely. For example, someone who smiles rarely need not be miserable, just undemonstra-tive. When such a person bestows praise for a job well done it may sound gruff when compared to the way in which a more outgoing person would do it. That is not the important issue at all. What really matters is remembering to do it. How it is done is, and must be, a reflection of that unique personality.

Thus leadership style is not something synthetic which is donned as you walk through the reception area. It is the real you, tempered and improved by your knowledge of how to get the best out of people, and acting within the context of the known organizational culture.

Your boss

Some people think that the only thing that they ever need to do is to please their boss. Such a generalization can be misleading and dan-gerous. Misunderstood, it could lead to crawling. The sort of boss you are better off without may be impressed by such behaviour, but anyone worth working for will not be taken in.

There is however a wider sense in which your job is to please your boss. It depends on his being impressed by good performance of tasks which are in the organization's best interest. The boss's management style ought quite quickly to tell you what sort of person he or she is: weak or strong, loyal or treacherous, competent or not. Whatever it is, you need to find out very quickly indeed. If he or she is a stickler for detail you will have to make sure that your figures are correct to the required number of decimal places; if the preference is for a broad-brush approach, you can round up or down the odd hundred or thousand without doing harm. Until you know how the world looks from out of your boss's eyes, your strengths may go unrecognized and your weaknesses may be floodlit. Thus, in the early days of your appointment you will be learning not only the job itself but also your boss's attitudes and values. You will be learning about what is expected but doesn't appear in your job description, and also getting to know the person upon whom your immediate career prospects depend.

Whatever the perceptions of your boss may be elsewhere in the organization, there will be criticism of him behind his or her back. A pleasant person may be criticized as weak, or a hypocrite; an effective go-getter as ruthless; or an older person as tired. Remember the earlier discussion of loyalty, and say only those things that give support and which you would be prepared to say face to face. Apart from the moral aspect, there is always someone who will remember your words and quote them, carelessly or maliciously, in the wrong place. If you don't say it, you can't be quoted.

As time goes by you will learn more about your boss. If he or she is not good at areas in which you have strengths, demonstrate those strengths and wait to be asked for help. Help offered is rarely refused, but direct offers of help can be misunderstood. Where your boss has strengths, learn from them. A good manager is a keen trainer, and a session with one will teach more of direct relevance to your job in an hour than most business schools can manage in a week.

Do your boss's career ambitions coincide with your own? If so, and you work well together by complementing one another's strengths, you could make a team that will go far. As you get to know each other you can explore and discuss the plans and aspirations that you both have. In the best partnerships, which can occur at unequal levels in an organization, the people concerned know each other well, and openly acknowledge their strengths and weaknesses, likes and dislikes.

Your boss will have worries too, arising from pressures that, to you, seem awesome. (Soon enough you will be raring to have a go at them yourself.) How the boss deals with them and how he or she appears to you are tests of just the same sort as how you appear to your staff. Indeed, you can apply all the manager-development ideas in this book to your boss. One that scores well on 70 per cent is a very good boss indeed.

The most difficult boss to deal with is the one who fears you. Perhaps unable to do the job, he or she observes your competence, and jumps to the conclusion that you represent a threat. Such worries may be completely groundless, based on little more than a tendency to see plots everywhere. On the other hand, contemporaries may have been leapfrogged by juniors. Whatever the reason, there is only one course of action open to you. It is to do your job conscientiously, taking care that you present yourself to your boss as a loyal sup-porter. Any dealings you may have which could appear ambiguous should be recorded in writing. Even your own private, dated note of a conversation could clarify misunderstandings later. If your boss is set implacably against you, at least you will have some basis for defence and explanation of the actions which are criticized. If mis-trust springs from nothing more substantial than caution, open and loyal behaviour should quickly overcome the problem.

There may be temptations to educate your boss. They will be particularly strong if you are formally trained in management and he or she is not. If you really are convinced about the need for and desir-ability of introducing new ideas, explain them in everyday language. Technical terms should not be used: they will look like an attempt to appear clever, and nobody loves a smart alec. Ideally, it will not look as if you got it out of a book, but as if you made it up for yourself: it is just an idea that you thought might make things easier. If you fail to convince, do not persist. Unlikely though it may seem, the boss just might know best and, if not, no amount of preaching will bring about a conversion. You will just have to let matters take their course, and try again later if the opportunity presents itself.

Do not shrink from contact with your boss's contemporaries in the organization. At first they will judge you by your boss. If he or she is not rated highly you need to establish your own reputation, independent of the department's; if the opposite, your job will be so much easier. So whenever you have contact with them let them see how organized, on the ball, thoughtful and knowledgeable you are about the organization's operations. Needless to say, none of that should be done so as to create the impression that you are putting on a special display, for nothing would count more against you. One day you may find that they have taken over your department, or jobs may come up in other departments. Being known already will do you no harm at all.

Your boss's boss

Inevitably there will be times when you come into contact with this august being. He or she will be on the look-out for many things on visits to your department, one of them being talent. Such a presumably astute person will be singularly unimpressed by any showing-off on your part. Just deal with the questions politely and positively.

One thing that you do not have to do is to tell your boss's boss the whole truth about everything in the department. Try to keep to the positive things, and when asked about those negatives which are not your responsibility, try to refer the question elsewhere. If the nega-tive is a matter under your control, answer truthfully about the problem and tell him what you are doing about it. It is important that you both support your boss and do not look shifty. This person is no fool, and can spot evasiveness and disloyalty at 50 paces.

As far as you can, try to talk only about those matters on which you have complete knowledge. Do not discuss anything beyond your competence; and explain why you are confining yourself in this way. You will earn respect for it.

Key points and tips

- Think about the saying, 'There are no bad soldiers, only bad officers.'
- Communication is as much about receiving as transmitting.
- Motivation is key to performance, but cannot be imposed.
- Gain insight into behaviour by reading studies of people at work.
- Leadership involves persuasion. This takes time but, long-term, works better than imposition.
- To maximize clarity, read and reread important documents before sending them out.
- Before sending them out, put yourself in the shoes of each recipient. How might he or she respond? If all possible responses seem negative, keep thinking.
- Leadership involves helping.
- Never forget 'Please' and 'Thank you', and when deserved, 'Well done.'
- A team is more than a group of people.
- Look after your boss's interests.
- Assess and understand the culture of your organization.

three

Can Your Organization Survive?

Why should you care?

The longer you intend to stay with an organization, the more this question will matter to you. You will also care if you are trying to build an impressive-looking CV. It will do you no good to be associated with a collapsed organization or one which got into a lot of well-publicized trouble.

Whether or not your organization is likely to collapse is therefore an important question. The power to predict its failure may seem well beyond the first-time manager. However, the techniques used by experts in this field are available to anyone, and the main ones are described in this chapter. It is usually a lot easier to predict *whether* an organization will fail than *when*. Indeed, many an unfit organization chugs on for years despite all the warning signs. Nevertheless the first-time manager needs to recognize as soon as possible whether to pursue a career with the present organization or to create an escape plan.

The question of fitness to survive is not entirely defensive, about whether or not to leave a ship that seems to be sinking. It can be used equally well to evaluate a potential employer.

While the private-sector firm is the type of organization most likely to fail, bodies in the public sector do die as well. They can also have large areas of their activity closed down or hived off, leaving a much smaller core which offers fewer opportunities and less security for individual managers.

The structure of organizations

Ever since the emergence of the modern, complex organization in the first half of the twentieth century, there has been a single model of structure which firms, public-sector bodies and not-for-profit organizations have broadly followed. That structure followed functional lines, which is to say that they were broken down into divisions or departments that fulfilled essential functions such as finance, sales, production and others. Indeed, many still are organized in that way, especially (but not exclusively) in the public sector. However in the last decade a powerful movement has arisen to reorganize firms to ensure that the essential processes are performed with maximum effectiveness and efficiency. That rearrangement has radically affected the way in which organizations work.

This, its most radical advocates say, involves no less than destroy-ing the old, functional divisions between people which sometimes resulted in more effort going into internal political battling than in meeting customers' needs.

The trouble with sudden, radical change is that even when it is well intentioned, it assumes that everyone who plans and implements it is all-seeing. The result of such top-down changes has been close to disastrous for some of the companies that have followed that path. As a senior manager in a major financial services group said, 'We had no real idea who those odd-looking people were who sat in corners working at PCs all day, or of what they did. So when our reorganiza-tion swept away all the dead wood, they went too. Too late we real-ized that they were the people who made our antiquated IT system work, and it's costing a fortune in temp agency fees to cover for them. But the temps don't have anything like the depth of knowledge that our own people had, so we are in serious trouble. We just hope we can sort it out soon.'

Despite the direst warnings from advocates of this approach, known as BPR (business process re-engineering), that the change had to be rapid and radical, most organizations have moved at a more prudent pace. They are re-aligning themselves to ensure that the pro-cesses are what matters, not the internal empires. Whether or not that results in the fulfilment of the gloomiest predictions, time will tell. So far the evidence is mixed. Some organizations have improved their processes beyond recognition. For others – so it seems to their cus-tomers – the main change has been to route all calls from users to a call centre staffed by undertrained ignoramuses. Or maybe it is only *my* bank that is like that.

Organizations, society and the law

In the private sector a firm may feel itself tempted to take profit-seeking too far. It could reduce its costs by cutting corners on safety, or by not heating work areas adequately, for example. Society believes those expedients to be undesirable, and forces all firms to observe minimum standards of performance in these and many other fields. Thus the ideal of complete *laissez-faire* towards business has not been followed by any government in the UK for several gen-erations. Enterprise is to be encouraged, but has to be tempered by care and concern for customers, suppliers, employees and the natural environment.

The first-time manager encounters the law in a variety of fields:

Personnel	*Selling and Buying*
Recruitment	Trade descriptions
Pay	Advertising
Discipline	Packaging
Rights	
Manufacturing	*Operations*
Safety	Accounting
Pollution	Taxation
Noise	Company law
Location	Insurance
	Vehicles

That is far from a complete summary of the ways in which an organization is controlled. It relates, furthermore, to only one type of law.

It is necessary to recognize that there are two main branches to the law: civil and statute. Statute law arises from Acts of Parliament, enhanced and extended by ministerial regulations, breach of which can lead to prosecution by the state.

Civil law comes from a very different source. Its roots lie back in the days when an aggrieved citizen could petition his chief or his sovereign to right a wrong, perhaps to stop his neighbour's cows from wandering on to his land and grazing his pasture. Civil law is based largely on precedent, recognizing the wisdom of supporting past decisions and of trying to build a body of case law which grows more comprehensive and reliable with every decision.

Just as the rest of the village expected our ancestors to behave with due regard to their neighbours' interests, grazing their cattle only where they had the right to and so on, today a wider society demands that we all observe the same basic rules. Today organizations, too, are regulated, as well as individuals.

Most of the regulations which chafe industry have been brought upon it by its own misbehaviour. Factories have long been forbidden to pour untreated waste into rivers, a measure which was passed because many did just that, poisoning fish and causing offensive smells. The same goes for smoking factory chimneys, and everyone accepts the desirability of that sort of control.

If the organization pursues its own interest too hard and at the expense of others, therefore, it risks controls being imposed on its behaviour. Obviously it is proper for a manager to seek profit as far as possible within the legal constraints. It is less easy to say what should be done about areas which the law does not control, but which are clearly beyond the pale in the view of most people.

It is difficult, if not impossible, for the first-time manager to take responsibility for such a decision. Indeed, one who does so is unlikely to find superiors admiring his or her judgement, for the limits to authority should have been recognized. The proper task was to bring the matter to the attention of his superiors, to spell out clearly the opportunities and potential difficulties, then to follow instructions.

Governments frame the laws which Parliament enacts. Governments are run by politicians. Thus politics are at the heart of regulation.

Organizations need to keep in touch with politicians if they are to understand them and, by doing so, influence the course and nature of any regulatory process. Politicians need to keep in touch with organizations in order to represent the full range of legitimate interest in the constituency. Inevitably, party attitudes will obtrude at some point in these dealings. Attitudes within parties can crucially affect the subject of this chapter, the organization's ability to survive.

The grip of the past

There is potential for harm in the assumption which can creep up on individuals and entire nations, that it is entirely right to continue automatically to do what we used to do, and that it somehow becomes more right the longer we do it. It is so much simpler to follow precedent than to innovate, and anyway making changes always causes such a fuss. It is easier all round to keep things as they are.

People at the top of organizations face a remarkable challenge in trying to stay up to date. They are selected both by and for their expe-rience, all of which was necessarily obtained in the past. They are ex-pected to chart a way into a future in which the events of the past may be an unreliable guide.

The most obvious example is GEC-Marconi. For decades the firm had been the UK's flagship electrical and electronic engineering group, built up from small beginnings by Lord Weinstock. When he retired from direct management his successors in effect bet the whole firm on the 1990s dot.com boom. When the boom turned to bust the shares plummetted from £10 to 10p. Weinstock was said to have been uneasy at the strategy but was persuaded to accept it. With hindsight Weinstock's wisdom is clear, but hindsight was not available in the 1990s. What would you have done? The answer is not easy.

Every manager carries a mental model of the organization. The view of someone at the top will differ markedly from that of juniors, a fact which he or she could learn by eavesdropping in any canteen.

Their views differ for all sorts of reasons. They come from different generations, they have different experiences of life (nobody born after 1978 can remember the Iron Curtain and few a divided Germany, for instance), and the direction taken by their education and training was almost certainly different. Even down at the level of goods and services which today we take for granted, there are mark-edly different experiences and expectations. People do adapt, of course, but they cannot alter what was irrevocably fixed in their early lives.

Built into each of us is a tendency to hold on, to a greater or lesser extent, to the past. Most of us do not like change very much, and that is a major handicap to adaptation to a changing world. Its evolution-ary value is that we also do not rush to embrace the novel, which may turn out to be not only new but also dangerous. The risk to organizational life is that we hold on to the old ways for too long, delaying changes which may bring great benefits until we are forced to adopt them. Some managements are good at evolving, sensing changes in the environment and reacting appropriately to them. Others are certain that the present course is not only right, but will remain so for the foreseeable future. Too often they begin to consider the need for adaptation just as they step over the cliff. A purblind approach can and does cause organizations to fail.

An organization which is so governed will change eventually. Regrettably the change is usually more costly the longer it is delayed. Even more regrettably, the pain too frequently falls not on the architects of the problem, but on the employees and owners. When change does come to the rigid organization it is usually sudden and catastrophic. Major closures and sackings take place, sometimes leading to the economic devastation of whole communities.

Survival of the fittest

Running through the imagery used to describe the successful organization are vocabulary and concepts borrowed from Darwinian biology. In nature, the successful organism is one which adapts to the environment in which it finds itself, acquires the resources it needs for survival, and establishes itself in sufficient numbers to ensure survival through even major catastrophes. If an organism is too cautious in expanding its population when conditions are favourable, it will be pushed out by more aggressive competitors for the same resources. If it is too greedy, it could strip its environment of resources and die out, or make too many enemies among competitors. Thus the successful organism occupies niches which it can dominate, but if it is to continue in existence it must take account of changes going on both within the niche and around it. In order to do so it needs three abilities, to:

- sense information from its environment;
- interpret that information;
- create appropriate responses, either changing itself or altering the environment.

The parallels with the life of an organization are obvious. To know what changes are taking place it must have the means to get informa-tion. Those changes may be taking place in its supplies of essential inputs – capital, raw materials, equipment and premises, and people.

Merely knowing that things have changed is not enough; there must be assessment, evaluation and interpretation to make sense of the sit-uation. That must be followed by a decision whether or not to change, and, if so, in what way. Making the change may be costly, but it is usually preferable to the alternative of increasing feebleness and eventual extinction. It should be emphasized that here we are dealing with the species as a whole, not with individuals. They will inevita-bly die, but the species lives on. It is the same with organizations: individuals come and go, but the existence of the organization as a whole continues.

The rigid organization, deaf to the increasingly urgent messages from its environment, runs down gradually until it fails, or falls to a predator. Its decline is usually in a series of steps, each larger than the last.

The adaptable organization, on the other hand, recognizes the danger of rigidity. Even if it is not proof against all that the environment can throw at it, its positive pursuit of appropriate change will mean that it is in better shape to endure.

The environment

The setting within which an organization operates is complex. This applies with a vengeance to the large organization, but even the smallest is linked to and affected by events over which it has no control and little or no prior knowledge. A plumber in a Scottish village is affected by the politics of southern Africa (where the copper in pipes comes from), the threat of war in the Middle East (whose oil makes the plastics), and the state of trade with the USA (whose firms make many central heating controllers). Nearer to home, demand is affected by the government's fiscal policies (which condition whether customers feel well off and able to spend), the national economy (whether the banks and building societies have money to lend), not to mention the weather.

The environment of that one-person business is too complex to monitor directly. Thus, in order to stay in business the plumber does two things:

- concentrates on just the key issues;
- adopts surrogate measurements.

Instead of trying to keep up with all the matters which affect the firm, the plumber picks the ones which really matter and concentrates on them. They are only few in number, so there is still some time in which to pursue the trade of plumbing. The key factors identified are:

- enough work on hand, but nobody waiting too long;
- prices not too high in relation to competitors;
- prices high enough to cover costs and make the desired level of profit;
- operating within the supply of working capital;
- bank's forecast of the economic and financial scene in three and six months' time.

That list is not too difficult to contend with. A lot more time can be saved by fixing a few of what might otherwise be uncontrollable variables. The cost of materials would be an example. Variation is allowed for by putting an expiry date on quotations, and by providing for prices to be raised to cover unexpected increases in materials costs.

A further way of simplifying the monitoring task is by using surrogate, rather than direct, measurements. Instead of trying to keep up with the financial wizards of Edinburgh and London, the plumber lets the bank digest the signals and asks for its interpretation.

The robustness of an organization relates to its stance towards its environment. Its culture, the quality of its managers, the state of the economy, fashion, legal regulation, the strength of its finances, its technology, and where its raw materials come from are all factors.

To what extent can problems in these areas be predicted? It is pos-sible to write a list of threats which could present themselves. It could include such issues as skills shortages, which are relatively likely to occur, as well as earthquakes, pestilence and flood. All are possible, but which are sufficiently probable to warrant inclusion?

Surprising though it may be, most commercial casualties seem to stem from major, long-term trends. In other words, a glance in the rear-view mirror would have yielded as much information as was needed to predict the future. When the Distillers Group was taken over by Guinness, its share of markets had been declining for years. The question was never whether it would be taken over, but when and by whom.

There is a minority of problems which can be just as devastating in their effects, but less easy to foresee. These are the shocks which are simple to list but unlikely to occur. When they do happen, it is there-fore a considerable surprise.

There are many forecasts around, all of which ought to be listened to but only some of which should be heeded. Those which worry us most are the most sensational. All are plausible, but the problem is often not when they will happen, but if. Examples abound of dooms-day forecasts which have not come true – yet.

There is only one piece of advice which can be given on how to tell the hucksters' forecasts from the real thing. It is to read them all, but to do so critically. Those which display a logic and consistency that cannot be faulted, while being in tune with the known facts of the situation, must be the most persuasive, however odd they may seem. At the same time, the view of the majority must not be automatically discounted. There is a way in which forecasts can be made not to come true, either because the warning was heeded and disaster averted, or because the majority's stubborn insistence in marching to a different tune from that of the forecast overcomes the forecast's logic. The crash of the US stockmarket in the late 1990s, widely predicted by eminent authorities, might be such an example.

Environmental change and responses to it

In the 1990s a new school of management thought emerged, called Business Process Re-engineering (BPR), also known in some circles as Core Process Redesign or Process Innovation. It arose in response to two main factors: the continuous change on a huge scale with which organizations were faced, and the ascent of IT. Echoing an accounting idea that enjoyed a brief vogue, of 'zero-based budget-ing', it started by asking this question: 'Suppose we weren't in the business we're in, doing things in the way we do; suppose we were starting from scratch; how would we set things up, given the way that things can be done today?' Zero-based budgeting was thought to be a useful idea, in that it prompted management to think about the possible radical change inevitably dictated by changed situations. Only its most enthusiastic advocates thought its usefulness extended much further. BPR, on the other hand, was applied with a vengeance. It was highly ambitious, seeking sudden, major improvements in performance twinned with falling costs. To do this it sought to think the unthinkable, to tear up rule-books and discard assumptions. It was an energetic reaction to a perceived emergency.

A further, major change in the environment in which organizations operate was in the role of IT, which had expanded enormously. Now it was both enabling much of the change and driving some of it. IT drove change forward by changing the nature of information, and enabled change to take place by providing analytical and communications media of extraordinary sophistication and speed. Summaries of information, which previously had taken weeks of hard work to prepare and collate for consideration at board level, could now be done automatically in seconds. Large customers began to collaborate with suppliers in unprecedented ways, making great savings and gains in efficiency as a result. Consequently a great divide began to open up between those organizations who were using IT effectively and those who were not. The former category found that they no longer needed several of the layers of management between the front line and the board.

This down-sizing also met a pressing business need, to reduce costs. It was accelerated by a fashion for outsourcing, that is, closing internal departments and buying-in the same functions from specialist suppli-ers. That had been an aspect of organizational life from time immemo-rial – very few organizations had ever tried to run all their legal affairs in-house, for example. This time it was different, because of its scale and extent. In some firms, almost everything that could be spun off was, and many firms embraced this approach wholeheartedly.

Another key environmental change was in the competitive climate. Competition began to be felt from much further afield than hitherto. That competition, especially when it came from the Far East, was keenly priced. Now that they, too, had access to the same com-puter-driven systems for design and production, they began to pose a much more dangerous threat. This time they could not only under-bid, but could also approach or exceed Western standards of quality.

Meanwhile, customers themselves were also going through the same sorts of reorganizations. Part of the effect from the mindset that spawned the idea of outsourcing was to look to suppliers to do more of the work that had previously been done in-house after taking delivery. Thus buyers put suppliers under pressure to move away from mass production and towards what came to be called mass customization. Suppliers were themselves aware of the threat posed by business done increasingly on a global scale. They were searching for ways to become more valuable to their customers so as to win some loyalty, and so agreed.

This drive to widen the variety offered within the product range ran directly counter to all the received wisdom that had previously applied. Ever since Henry Ford invented the production line in the 1920s it had been believed that variety had to be minimized. He summed it up memorably in the famous aphorism, 'They can have any colour they like as long as it's black'. What had changed? Why was it now thought possible to customize practically anything for anyone? The answer lay in IT.

For the second half of the twentieth century, the motor company founded by Mr Ford, along with its competitors, had offered an increasing variety of options, including in the range of paint colours. Latterly they were changed every season and had bestowed on them ever more fanciful names. The complexity that this implied threat-ened chaos. Imagine trying to keep control of a production line in which one car out of several thousand to be made that week was Mr Smith's 1600cc version (he didn't want the standard 1300cc) in Spring Lilac metallic, one of the special 'custom' colours for which £100 extra was charged, with Graphite upholstery, not the usual pink. A paper-work system would collapse, but chaos was kept at bay by the slow advance of the computer into production control systems. As that advance developed into a rush in the late 1980s and early 1990s, fuelled by the huge increase in cheap computing power, the ability of the manufacturer to keep on top of enormously complex schedules grew. Now it had become possible for Mr Jones's personally-speci-fied VW Golf to be scheduled for production on a particular day at the factory in Wolfsburg. Moreover, the time it would leave the factory on a lorry bound for the cross-Channel ferry would also be planned and therefore its arrival at his home VW dealership in Wolverhampton could be predicted, give or take a couple of hours. (Much of that presupposes that Mr Jones wasn't himself taking part in the IT revolution by ordering from a dealer in the Netherlands, using the Internet, which he may well have done.)

Takeovers and mergers

All organizations can be classified into one of two categories:

- potential takeover predator;
- potential takeover victim.

It is possible for an organization to fall into both categories simulta-neously. A medium-sized organization can be on the hunt for victims but at the same time be a larger body's next meal.

In assessing the fitness of a particular organization to survive, it is particularly important to know whether it is more likely to be the drinker or the glass of water. Once upon a time the takeover targets were obvious. In the public sector they were very few, and in the private sector the bidders were easy to spot and their favourite targets simply identified. During the more turbulent times in which we live today, competition is so much more intense that there are more people on the look-out for acquisitions. At the same time, the environment has become so choppy that one organization can be temporarily rising while another is falling, presenting an opportu-nity for one to bid for the other. Overlaid on that are the facts that an expansionary phase of the economy offers the finance to fund take-overs, and a recessionary phase makes all kinds of bargains available.

Then again, there are firms which are intentionally set up in order to be taken over. Their founders decide to create something which they can sell out after 10 or 20 years, and retire rich while still quite young. The purchaser might buy it with any number of ideas in mind. Most threatening to the manager is the situation in which the firm is bought in order to close down an inconvenient competitor. Next most threatening is where the assets are to be stripped and only a shell left in operation. Usually it is in the stripper's interest to leave at least a viable operation in existence so that money can be earned from operating it, or so that there is a credible business to sell on to another owner. In most cases, however, the buyer sees the purchase as enabling an improved grip on the market.

In looking at such a firm it is important to identify why a competi-tor might buy it. Non-competitors do not matter in this context, as their reasons for buying will be to get into the market: they will want to build up the victim rather than dismantle it. Competitors who mean to keep the firm running will buy in order to:

- increase market share by adding activities which they do not currently undertake;
- reduce competition;
- get hold of technology;
- increase the productivity of their sales force;
- increase the productivity of their manufacturing assets.

Raising productivity means raising output per head, so they may well be looking for heads to chop off. Almost inevitably they will be in the victim firm. The part of that company which is to be closed will depend on the reason for the purchase. For example, if the victor wants to improve the productivity of its own factory it will close down the victim's and transfer production there. By such manoeuvres production could be rationalized, leaving selling untouched, or the sales function be transferred to the new parent, leaving production as before. Sometimes both can be stripped out completely. The production and selling people of the victim company are at risk in either case. The administration, warehouse and distribution people are likely to lose out substantially in any event, for theirs are areas in which considerable savings can be made.

Should a manager therefore seek out an employer who appears to be takeover-proof? First, this question should be kept in perspective: traumatic though takeovers can be, many organizations are never affected. If it is a matter of personal concern – and it would be foolish to ignore it altogether – a significant division of one of the major takeover predators could be the safest place to be. Takeover-proof it may be, but the style of management exhibited by these firms does not suit everyone. Equally important, the sorts of opportunity offered need to be carefully assessed. Typically, such a firm is run very efficiently indeed. This means that it may be an excellent training-ground, but such firms do have the reputation of forcing the pace. If that excites and challenges you, put them on your list. If you doubt your toughness and resilience, think again; or have a go, but be prepared to move on if it does not suit.

The results of takeovers are by no means all bad. One manager in the sales force of a British firm of international repute tells an interesting tale. Under the original management he was unhappy: targets were high and rising all the time. As one who had risen from the ranks, his promotion was blocked because the firm made a point of holding back a number of key junior management jobs for directly-recruited train-ees. Uncannily, a high proportion of them were related to board members. Not unnaturally, he was rather peeved by this.

That company was taken over recently by one of the specialists in takeovers, and many heads rolled at high level. The junior manager reports a far better atmosphere at his level. People are now judged by their results, and sales targets are much lower. Instead of chasing volume at any cost, the new owners encourage him to earn the maximum profit for the firm from the deals he does. Not only do the new owners talk better sense, they also listen.

That story illustrates the general approach of most takeover specialists. They quickly fire the top level of their new acquisition and find that there are excellent people immediately below who, for years, have been raring to run the company, and know all there is to be known about it.

Organizational analysis

Throughout this commentary runs the idea that some organizations are better adapted to their job than others. So far we have not looked in detail at this rather generalized notion.

One of the most useful tools for assessing and comparing organizations is the SWOT analysis. SWOT is the acronym for Strengths, Weaknesses, Opportunities and Threats. The idea is to examine the firm's capabilities: what is it good at (strengths), and what is it bad at (weaknesses)? Then it is related to its environment: what opportuni-ties are open to it and what threats are there to its well-being?

If this is done for one's own organization and its competitors, a much clearer picture emerges of where they stand in relation to one another. It can greatly improve understanding of what is going on in a market, what could happen, and who the leading players would be. At the very least it offers the first-time manager some useful ques-tions for the recruitment interview; at best it can point up major areas for attention.

The organization which seeks to do the things essential for survival will be doing this for itself. It will recognize that the only permanent features of life are impermanence and uncertainty. Far from resisting them, it positively welcomes them because it knows that they will throw its less aware competitors off balance, while removing old prob-lems and presenting new opportunities (and problems) to the alert.

Not every organization is in that happy state. In order to be able to spot opportunities and to exploit them, and to identify problems and deal with them, it will be in a constant state of evolution. Since all the changes which the organization makes to itself are responses to changes in its environment (or to its perception of it, which amounts to the same thing), the internal changes will follow the pattern described by those in the environment. Environmental changes are occurring all the time, on short, medium and long cycles. Short-run cycles are such things as advertising and promotional tactics, which can alter from month to month or from one season to another. Medium-run cycles concern matters on the time-scale of production technology, in which today's research breakthrough might translate into a new factory three years hence. The long-run changes are the really big ones, brought about by changing age-structures of the population, by changes to the distribution and amount of wealth, or by more fundamental technological innovation. Those examples are simply indicative, rather than complete lists in watertight compartments.

Readiness to adapt does not come about spontaneously, but needs to be caused by top management. The survivor organization:

- has the will to succeed in the first place;
- has a clear understanding that change is essential to progress;
- has the ability to identify the right direction to travel;
- provides the necessary resources;
- creates the context for progress;
- inspires its people;
- achieves its goals;
- once those goals are achieved, defines new goals;
- learns from its mistakes.

It also realizes that energy is not enough; motive power has to be applied intelligently. It is therefore a thoughtful as well as a hard-driving organization. It gives much consideration to the problem of information, the system for providing which can go awry in a number of ways.

Consider the process through which data must pass. (The distinction between data and information is important here. Data are individual items which, alone, give no real clues to a larger situation. Aggregated, they can give those clues, which is to say that they become information. An example is sales invoices: each one tells you something about an individual customer, but if you want to know how sales in total and by product and customer sector are doing, you have to perform some arithmetic and produce summarized totals. The invoices represent data, the summaries, information.)

First data are sensed; but the sensor may be faulty, or pointed away from the direction from which the true threat comes. Data are then processed into information; that processing necessarily reduces detail in order to allow the bigger picture to emerge. Part of what is lost could be an important pointer. Then the information is analysed and judgements are formed over its content and import, processes fraught with potential for misinterpretation. The next problem is that the solution designed may be incorrect; or even if a perfect plan emerges from all the problem-areas so far encountered, it may be executed badly.

Looked at in that light, it might seem like a miracle that anyone ever does anything even half right; or that it is no more than a happy accident when they do. Such fatalism may, on occasion, be realistic, but organizational life can hardly be conducted on the basis of crossed fingers and hope. Equally, nobody should ever fall prey to the idea that he or she is in charge of their own destiny. An awareness of all the things that could go wrong carries with it an important message: that constant attention to all aspects of operations is essen-tial to organizational survival.

The manager therefore does not try to watch everything all the time but instead apportions attention according to particular rules, which are discussed in the next chapter.

Key points and tips

- Organizations do fail: keep yours under constant review.
- Signs of failure are clear in hindsight, so try to develop some foresight.
- Organizations that survive are those that change neither too quickly nor too slowly for their environment.
- An organization's environment comprises a large number of influences.
- Understand your organization's environment and assess the likelihood of survival. Repeat this from time to time.
- If all the logic points to failure, it probably will fail. The only problem is to predict when.
- Become aware of the law as it affects organizations and their managers.

four

The Principles of Management

The manager's role

A manager has a real job to do, a fact which is not always appreciated by subordinates. It can look easy from the outside: a comfortable office, other people to do all the work, and a bit of glad-handing to do from time to time.

In fact, the manager's job is much more substantial than that. The organization has its aims, and it is the manager's job to achieve them by using the allocated resources. On occasion, the resources might not be adequate and more have to be sought. However, the fact remains that the manager's job is to organize and control resources – equipment, materials, skills and money – and inspire his people to achieve the desired end.

In some organizations the manager seems to be expected to work out unaided what to do. Someone in that position is the victim of bad management. It is unreasonable to demand that goals should be scored while the goalposts are hidden and the ball is invisible. In those circumstances it can be difficult even to tell which game is being played, football or hockey.

In any organization in which reason and common sense play a part, efforts will be made to help managers to understand exactly what is required of them. Opinions differ over which is the best way of doing so, but there is universal agreement that it is difficult to achieve. That is not because there is stupidity on either side of the dialogue, but because of the eternal problems of communication between people.

Some organizations tell their managers at all levels what they are to do, expecting those instructions to be carried out with little or no discussion. Even where a different regime is supposed to operate throughout an organization, there are managers who run their individual fiefdoms in that way. The trouble with this approach is that the better managers are not very good at implementing other people's ideas without question; being the people they are, they want to run things in their particular way. Conversely, the sort of manager who prefers to cede individual responsibility to seniors is not neces-sarily the kind of person who can play a full part in taking the organi-zation forward. Indeed, that person is not so much a manager as an administrator, running other people's schemes as instructed. It is a type found in every organization, but most frequently in the public sector. One has to wonder where the next generation of imaginative senior management is to come from, if the pool available to draw from is full of grey administrators.

Naturally, there are occasions on which all managers must and will accept the discipline of working to goals which are not entirely their own. On the other hand, if the whole organization is run completely on the principle that those at the top are omniscient, it will be severely and progressively impoverished. The lower-level people with a real contribution to make will leave in frustration. Those who remain will be quite incapable of succeeding the top management when it eventually retires or moves on. Thus one elementary principle of management is that nobody is ready for promotion until a suc-cessor has been developed.

Goals and targets

Clearly there has to be a degree of central direction in any organization. It would be intolerable if everyone were to pursue personal interests and subjective ideas of where it should go. In many of the best-run organizations, which term includes departments within otherwise undistinguished bodies, the centre defines a target and states constraints. They might comprise a doubling of profits within the next five years (the target), to be achieved on 50 per cent more working capital (the constraint). When they have recovered from the shock of such a demanding requirement, individual managers can get down to interpreting the goal as departmental targets.

The task is not then at an end. Ideas on how targets are to be achieved have to be developed into departmental plans. Let us say that the profits increase could be reached by a 70 per cent rise in sales (which would breach the working capital limitation) or by tripling prices (which would kill off too much market share). Thus each of these extreme routes is rejected, and a combination of extra volume, price increase, raw materials reduction, manufacturing efficiencies and financial policy changes is substituted. To get to that position there will be a great deal of negotiation and argument between departments, but once that point is reached each senior manager knows what to do to ensure that his or her department makes its con-tribution to the organization reaching the overall goal.

Then the departmental managers can send the message down to their subordinates, defining what has been agreed as the department's contribution, and to what time-scale. It is then passed down from layer to layer of management, at each stage being broken down into progressively greater detail. Within departments there may be considerable modification of the overall rules, so that, for example, the lorry fleet may be allowed to think in terms of a steep increase in its costs and working capital requirement, provided that it is offset from elsewhere in the distribution budget (say, by closing one of the regional warehouses).

By such means every manager in the organization can see what their personal contribution is to the grand plan. It is now each manager's job to work out in detail how to bring it about. Figure 4.1 shows that this cannot be done in isolation: while some areas of responsibil-ity are wholly under the control of a department, many concerns are common to more than one. Starting at the lowest level of the organi-zation, operating plans are formed. They feed up through the organi-zation like the sap moving up from the roots of a tree. At each higher point, the plans from the lower levels are pulled together, amended if necessary, and passed on upwards. The process of aggregation goes on until, at the top of the organization, everything fuses into a single entity, the overall plan.

Bargaining, negotiation, pleading, manipulation, cajoling and bul-lying all come into play in this process. The first-time manager may simply be unable to see how to effect the economies or volumes required. Not merely challenged, he or she can be frightened by the scale of the demand. It is the responsibility of the superior manager to help to raise the sights and concentrate not on how difficult it is, but on the way it could be pulled off. In just the same way, the junior manager will both need the help of subordinates to devise the plan and encourage them to see how demanding targets can be reached.

Excellent performance is achieved by thousands of small acts like this throughout an organization. Refusal to accept that yesterday's performance is good enough for today, pushing back the frontiers of

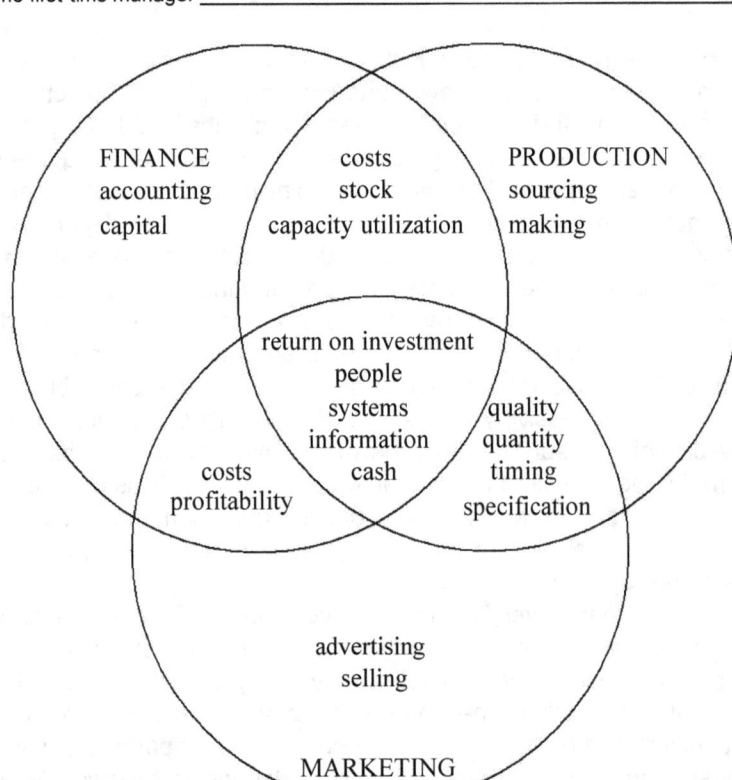

Figure 4.1 *How departmental interests overlap*

what people see as possible – that is how organizations become great and maintain their momentum.

The overall aim

In order that all the subordinate plans come into being, the lodestone of the organization's overall aim is needed. Its function is to unify and coordinate: by making the plans of everyone in the firm point in the same direction, it enables them all to pull together in the common cause.

This aim is often not easy to define. There was a short time in the last century when it became fashionable to define a firm's aims as 'making money'. Certainly that is preferable to making losses but, like pleasure, money-making usually results from the pursuit of some other goal.

Whatever the aim is, it must be within the organization's powers to accomplish. More is needed than just a brilliant idea, or the ability to make a product or provide a service. Finance will almost certainly be required, and the skill to manipulate the various resources available. Moreover, the aim has to be consistent with managers' and share-holders' values. Usually, the attempt to define an aim results in the generation of a range of options. The test that should be applied to each option is the extent to which it is:

- desirable
- feasible
- acceptable.

The SWOT analysis (page 74) will have identified options which could be pursued. The management now applies this test to rank the various options in order of preference. Since judgement is at least as important here as measurable factors, there is great scope for an indi-vidual manager to make a personal contribution to the debate.

Major assumptions will have been made about the plans' acceptability to staff. Now comes the test of those assumptions, the point at which they are put across to people. Arriving at the definition of the overall aim and the resulting plan was a complex enough process; but it often proves simpler than making sure that the message is:

- received accurately
- understood
- accepted
- and, finally, implemented.

Too many well-formed plans have foundered in this process. They have been subject to one or more of the following problems:

- received inaccurately
- misunderstood
- rejected
- not implemented

and, as a result, have failed miserably.

Small wonder, then, that managers gave an enthusiastic welcome to a technique which promised to banish these problems for ever. It would make sure that managers at all levels knew exactly what they had to do. It spawned work for consultants like no other technique before it. It is called 'Management by Objectives', or MBO for short. (This should not be confused with 'management buy-out', which shares the same acronym but refers to the managers of an organiza-tion buying it from its owners.)

Management by objectives

This technique takes as its basis the idea that running through the organization there should be a clear chain of command, which should be exercised as the primary tool of top management.

Few would challenge the idea of people liking to know where they fit into the scheme of things, what they are responsible for, and to whom. MBO says that it is the job of the person at the top to set an overall objective, and to require subordinates to show how they will contribute to its achievement. They, in turn, have their subordinates show what they will do to make sure that the objective is achieved, and so on down through the organization.

In that way, the overall aim of the organization is contributed to by every person in it. The top person ensures that:

- the issues affecting the achievement of the organization's main aim are addressed by everyone;
- the non-influential issues are ignored or deliberately neglected.

The mechanisms used to bring and keep the members of the organi-zation into line vary with the consultant offering the programme. Their common content is to require each job to be specified in detail, no bad thing in itself, and then to have each manager define and agree with their boss the key and lesser areas of responsibilities bearing on success in the job. Then performance standards are agreed between subordinates and superiors. The main governing factors are also defined. Actual results are compared with the target for each area, usually monthly. Finally, any adjustment needed to perfor-mance is agreed for the following month, and so on.

In principle, MBO offers the top manager the power of far tighter control over what is done and to what standard: no wonder it appealed. Why, then, isn't everyone using it?

Nobody quarrels with the idea that people are paid to help their employer to reach the organization's goals. To the extent that MBO helps to bring that about, it can only be welcomed. Unfortunately, there are two key problem areas: paperwork and self-protection.

As has been said, different consultants sell different versions of the MBO package, but most seem to involve fearsome quantities of paper. Every month the middle manager has to report to his or her boss in writing about performance against target. He or she also has to deal with similar reports from subordinates, perhaps between five and ten of them. Meetings have to be held to discuss the reports. Some organizations have found that the real benefits of greater inte-gration of the organization's aims with the individual's actions are outweighed by the extra administrative load imposed.

Self-protection comes into the equation when people resist being too ambitious, for fear that they will create a problem for themselves in the form of ever-increasing targets. It can seem sensible to be careful, or even pessimistic, in the target you accept and the perfor-mance you deliver. Thus, the greater control which the top exercises under MBO becomes feared as an instrument of imposing ever-mounting demands. People protect themselves from the threat that they perceive, and performance gets worse instead of better; or nobody saddles themselves with the target that could be achieved for fear of ratcheting-up expectations. A system designed to improve performance can therefore reduce it.

A further problem arises from the fact that MBO has to assume that a lot of the performance factors are fixed. The great interlocking pyramid of personal goals against which progress is measured is somewhat inflexible. Change the goals because the environment dic-tates it, and all the measurements have to start again against new goals. Couple that with the much leaner levels of staffing of manage-ment nowadays compared to those of some periods in the past, and there emerges a picture of too few people with too little time to erect paperwork mountains.

MBO has not been discredited as a management technique any more than the muzzle-loading rifle has become less able to kill at 20 paces. Its value is considerable, in that it showed not only the desir-ability, but above all, the practicality of integrating personal aims with those of the organization at large. Perhaps its most abiding legacy is the emphasis which it placed on the central role of objec-tives. The truths which it popularized were by no means universally recognized before it came on the scene.

Thus, it has left a lasting message for those organizations which could make no use of MBO because of the mechanistic view of the organization on which it is predicated. They may not be able to use an MBO package, but they need constantly to keep their objectives in view. An old people's home, a research laboratory and a design studio are examples of organizations which simply cannot be run sat-isfactorily as if they were machines. A large car assembly plant must be, and therefore could apply MBO with good results.

Management techniques: their place in your job

If you are paid to operate a particular technique, say a computerized PERT model (programme evaluation and review technique – a method of planning and controlling complex projects), used to control a large civil engineering scheme, that technique will play a big part in your working life. You are an exception among managers, since few of them find that any one technique, still less the whole range, is of use most of the time.

The whole point of the techniques, boiled down to its essence, is to help the manager to organize information so that the stage at which the point is grasped comes sooner, cheaper, more comprehensibly, or in any combination of these. At centre stage is not the technique, but the manager's understanding of the issue in question. Understand-ing is the end, the technique merely the means.

What goes for techniques also applies more or less to measurement. We measure where it aids understanding, and only where it is realisti-cally possible. The idea of what can be measured may surprise many who left school with a perfectly respectable GCSE in maths. Statistical techniques exist which are rarely touched on at school, even today, but which greatly help the manager's understanding. If you are lucky enough to work for an organization which has its own statisticians or operational researchers, see if you can get them interested in what your job entails. They might show you all sorts of short cuts and per-fectly proper tricks with figures which will reduce the time you spend slaving over a spreadsheet or calculator. At the same time, they should also be able to enhance the depth of your understanding of the quanti-fiable aspects of your job. One or two of the more elementary and uni-versally useful methods are touched on later in this chapter.

Judgement, experience and training

Despite the emphasis on measurement which overlays so many texts on management, in the end the manager is there not to do sums but to exercise judgement. It is exercised on information, whether it tells of quantity or quality. Measurement greatly aids understanding, but it is the start of the process of management rather than its entirety.

The manager's judgement is honed by experience, a curious entity. Some people who claim 40 years' experience have, in reality, had one year's experience 40 times over. They have neither reflected on events nor developed understanding. True experience is gained not just via existence, but by observation, reflection and experimenta-tion. In other words, a certain amount of effort is involved.

The part that experience plays can be seen when two managers, one experienced and one not, are confronted with an apparent emer-gency. The inexperienced one will probably dive immediately for the alarm button. The more experienced colleague will spend a little time pondering the evidence before acting. The same decision may emerge in the end, but without losing an undue amount of time in doing so. The real value of the more considered approach lies in what goes on between the hearing of the problem and acting.

What the experienced person is doing is, basically, fourfold:

- deciding to what extent the information can be trusted;
- deciding whether or not any further information is needed, and getting it;
- reviewing the possible courses of action, and selecting one;
- weighing any potential undesirable outcomes of action and inac-tion and making up his or her mind.

Experience helps at all stages. Through seeing more examples of ambiguous information than the colleague, and giving more thought to the way in which such information is generated and conducted, the more experienced person is also able to create a richer list of options for action and is well placed to assess the likely outcome of each, and is thus armed to take a more informed decision.

The obvious course of action is not necessarily the best. Indeed, masterly inactivity might be best of all, in certain circumstances. A US statesman once advised his president: 'Don't just do something, stand there.' His experience told him that frenzied activity would achieve little in that case, and that an impassive pose would be the most impressive attitude to adopt.

Put to good use, experience does give a manager a head start. Having dealt with problem X a dozen times in his career, there is hardly any need to think what to do when the thirteenth jumps over the parapet. The danger comes if preparedness spills over into complacency. Seeing what looks like a problem X, the knee-jerk reac-tion responds automatically to what subsequently proves to be a problem Y, skilfully disguised.

At this point the less experienced manager could despair. What hope is there of gaining ten years' experience in anything less than a decade? Fortunately, there is quite a lot. The answer lies in education.

Today's manager has available without doubt the richest choice in management education since time began. In any major city there are various institutions vying for custom on a wide variety of courses. Degrees and diplomas can be gained. Even out in the depths of the country learning is accessible. The choice of distance-learning programmes is ever widening and represents a greater range than the old-style correspondence courses could ever muster. The Open University, and the National Extension College, are just two of the organizations which offer management programmes which can be followed at home and at the manager's own pace. New opportunities present themselves via the Internet almost daily.

The whole point of formal study is to shorten the length of time it takes to learn. Much of what is taught, the student could have worked out eventually unaided; in that case, learning it on a course concertinas the time taken to acquire the knowledge. Other informa-tion which is gained on courses comes from far greater minds than the student's, and from disciplines never before encountered, so it can safely be assumed that, unassisted, learning could never have taken place. Study cannot and never will supersede experience entirely; it does complement it massively, and adds greater depth to the conclusions that the manager draws from day-to-day life.

Dealing with complexity

Many of the situations which a manager has to deal with are very complex. They often do not look like it on the surface, but digging for the underlying facts often reveals a complexity which was not at first suspected.

The principles of management

The human brain is a wonderful thing, but faced with a complex situation it can switch into panic mode. A better response is to stay rational and apply techniques for dealing with such situations.

Exactly what you do depends on the nature of the problem in ques-tion. In umbrella terms, you:

- classify;
- assess for size and impact;
- list probable outcomes;
- list available responses;
- assess likely consequences of each;
- select action.

Take an apparently simple problem: a sudden fall in the orders coming into a children's shoe factory. The full explanation may lie in decisions taken in millions of homes up and down the country, about what shoes to buy and when. They all filter through into thousands of shops selling the merchandise; they in turn experience pressures. One may have the bank insisting that buying is reduced in order to lower the overdraft. Another may have stocked up with a competi-tor's brand. A third may have become fed up with slow delivery of orders and switched to another supplier. Multiplied out by dozens of possibilities across thousands of shops and millions of families, it adds up to an incomprehensibly complex picture. The manager should not panic, though. The complexity comes about because so far everything seen has been data; what is needed is information, the aggregation of data into meaningful, summary form. The main potential reasons for the problem appear on this list of seven possibllltles:

- competitor activity;
- retailer liquidity;
- retailer stocks
    - in total
    - of this brand;
- consumer demand;
- the firm's reputation and past service;
- promotional effectiveness;
- sales force abilities.

Every manager in any market is capable of listing the main possible reasons for a situation in just the same way. He or she will seek infor-mation which will test the situation under each heading, and reveal which is or are the most influential factor(s), but will not, however, take some of the evidence offered at its face value.

The sales manager will, most likely, excuse low sales by sickness in the sales force and the trade being full of unsold stock, despite which the sales team has battled on heroically and won the firm a higher share of the few orders around than it has any right to expect. Unfor-tunately, while evidence of that quality needs verification, decisions have to be taken fast about whether or not to put the factory on to short time. The cost attached to getting the decision wrong, either way, is high. What do you do?

Starting with the resource closest to hand, the sales manager, you ask to be told quickly whether the cause is:

- competitors encroaching significantly on areas that we expected to protect;
- high retail stocks of our brand because:
  - it is selling out of the shops too slowly,
  - Marks & Spencer have promoted children's shoes effectively,
  - the public is demanding competitors' brands more than ours;
- a general slowdown in trade through:
  - the usual seasonal demand coming in late,
  - changes to school holiday dates,
  - less consumer spending,
  - a credit squeeze;
- poor trade perceptions of our brand or our service;
- mass holiday, etc, absences in the sales force.

You must have answers to these questions, and within a day or two. Otherwise the unsold stock could clog up the warehouse and absorb all the firm's cash. What needs to be done is to reduce the effects of millions of individual buying decisions among consumers and retail-ers to just a few main questions. Each bears directly on your business. Thus an almost infinite variety of possible avenues of enquiry has been reduced to a dozen or so.

That is an example of relevant and appropriate reduction of variety, which has rendered complexity comprehensible. Had the list of questions been shorter, it might have risked missing some impor-tant point altogether. As it is, while there is a possibility that some important factor will be missed, the list above does cover most of the field. That list is therefore short enough to be manageable yet long enough to cater for the likely explanations. It avoids sophisticated economic analysis for two reasons: time was short, and it was in any case unnecessary. It was unnecessary because acceptable surrogate measures exist for those aspects of economic activity which affect purchasing decisions of children's footwear. The retailers' reports to the sales manager are close enough, and certainly adequate for these purposes.

Clearly, it is vital that you know the cause of the problem so as to assess its seriousness, decide if a response is called for, and choose the best response. If you thought that the problem was lack of con-sumer demand, you might have devised an advertising and promo-tion package. That would have incurred considerable cost, justified if it was the only way to keep the factory running, but unforgivable if the true reason had been the simultaneous absences of all the star salespeople. In the latter case, the sales manager might learn a few lessons about scheduling absences.

Statistics

Statistics is a branch of mathematics which managers find useful in:

- showing up patterns in past behaviour;
- showing correspondences between different factors;
- providing a springboard for forecasting.

All these could conceivably be accomplished without recourse to special techniques, so why should statistics be so useful?

As has been stated already, the manager's main contribution springs from judgement. To be fully effective, it cannot operate solely on hunch and feel: facts have to come in somewhere. The most preva-lent and useful facts available to a manager are numerical, and numbers are capable of being manipulated by the unwary into giving misleading guidance.

In the old days, most managers who wanted to use statistical methods had to learn a lot of formulae and how to apply them. The difficulty which most of us seem to have with maths at school rose again to haunt them. While it can be interesting and useful to learn the detail of the calculations, most managers can avoid the number-crunching if they want to: the personal computer, or even the scientific calculator, will do the hard work for them.

Helpful though the computer is in doing the sums, it still needs to have the right numbers supplied to it, and the user needs to know which techniques to invoke in particular situations.

Statistics is a very broad subject, and most managers use only a very small part of its range. The areas of greatest use cover:

- probability
- distribution
- regression
- correlation.

To learn the ways in which these are calculated and the kinds of applications to which they are best put, the first-time manager can consult any textbook on statistical applications to management prob-lems, using those headings to search each index. There now follows a brief sketch of each.

Probability

Probability is expressed as a decimal fraction: complete certainty is represented by a probability of 1; a 50–50 chance has a probability of 0.5.

Tossing a coin brings about two outcomes, heads or tails. Unless it has been tampered with, the chances of any one toss resulting in heads is 0.5.

Likewise, the chance of a normal, six-sided die falling on any one number – say, a four – are one in six, or about 0.167. The chances of any one throw resulting in one of any two numbers – say, a five or a six – are twice 0.167, that is 0.334. The chance of any of five numbers being thrown – say, any number between one and five – is five times 0.167, or 0.835. (It really should be 0.833, the slight inaccuracy arising from the fact that 0.167 is an approximation to three decimal places of 0.16 recurring. But in an example like this there is little reason to worry about tiny variations.)

To change from one example to another, 50 marbles will be used, 20 white and 30 black. All go into a bag, and one is drawn out. The chances of it being white are calculated at 0.4, thus:

Probability of white

$$= \frac{20}{20 + 30}$$

$$= \frac{20}{50}$$

$$= 0.4$$

This also tells us that the probability of drawing black would have been 0.6: it had to be one or the other so that there was a probability of black or white of 1.0. Subtract 0.4 from 1.0 and the probability of black emerges.

Suppose that the marble which came out was, against the probability, white. If that marble is kept out and a second marble of unknown colour withdrawn, it will not carry the same probabilities. This is because the total number of marbles in the bag and their colour-combination are now different. The probability of white is now:

$$= \frac{19}{19 + 30}$$

$$= \frac{19}{49}$$

$$= 0.39$$

Furthermore, the probability of drawing a second white after the first can be calculated by multiplying the two sums together:

$$\frac{20}{20 + 30} \; \frac{19}{19 + 30}$$

$$= 0.4 \_ 0.39$$

$$= 0.156$$

That shows the chance of drawing two whites in a row as 0.156, or about one in seven. As is easily seen, probability is not a guarantee of behaviour, merely an indicator of what is likely to happen. In practi-cal terms it shows that, over the long run, a pattern similar to that indicated by the probability figure is likely to emerge. Toss a coin five times, and it might come up heads on four occasions. That does not mean that the probability on any one spin is four in five or 0.8. If it is done much longer, say for 50 times, it will come out very close to a 25:25 split. The more often an event occurs, the closer the cumulative results will be to the probability.

The use of all this to the manager is that he is unwise to forecast solely on the basis of instinct. Take the example of a development manager responsible for a new piece of equipment which uses a lot of unproven technology. It consists of 100 modules, each of which has worked in test conditions 19 times out of 20. Thus, he concludes, the probability of failure of each module is only one in 20. It hardly seems worth working out what the probability is of the whole assembly working, but just for fun he does so. He multiplies the 0.95 probability of each of the 100 modules working satisfactorily, thus:

$$0.95^{100} = 0.006$$

To his surprise he finds that the probability of the equipment working is 0.006, or six chances in 1000. This happens because the cumulative risk of one chance in 20, taken over 100 modules, is so great.

He rushes back to the drawing board, and raises the reliability of the modules. Also, he halves the number of modules which make up the equipment. Testing shows that the probability of failure of each module has now fallen from 0.05 to 0.02; thus, the probability of each working has risen from 0.95 to 0.98. Using the new number of 50 modules, the calculation of probability of the equipment working is:

$$0.98^{50} = 0.36$$

It is still a very unreliable piece of equipment; the probability of its working is only 0.36, or about one time in three. Nevertheless, it is a great advance on six chances in 1000. It would be just a small step to turn the calculation on its head to discover what combinations of reli-ability and number of modules would achieve a probability of an acceptable level of reliability. To stick with the 50 modules, if the reli-ability of the equipment is to rise to a probability of working of 0.95, the probability of each module working will have to rise to around 0.999, or one failure in 1000. Even then matters are hardly satisfac-tory: there will be a failure one time in 20 – not an acceptable perfor-mance in most contexts.

Distribution
Distribution records how events are distributed among a range of categories. They can concern frequency and probability.

A frequency distribution can be illustrated by people's shoe sizes. A few have very large or very small feet, and the majority are around the average. In statistical terms, there is a low frequency distribution of small and large sizes, and a high frequency of average sizes.

Figure 4.2 shows a histogram (or bar chart) portraying an imaginary frequency distribution of shoe sizes, based on a sample of 10,000 women.

A distribution such as the one shown in Figure 4.2 makes it easy for the manufacturer and shopkeeper to see the right mix of sizes to

The principles of management

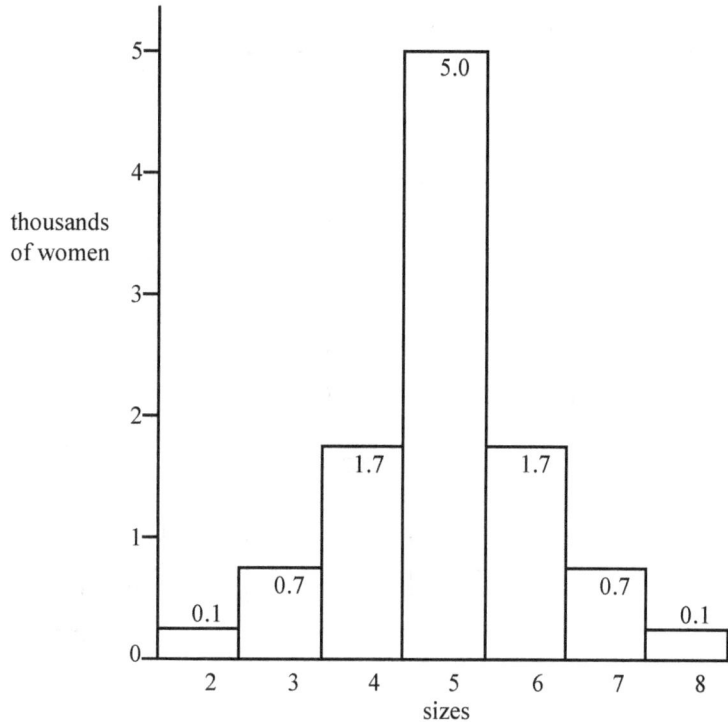

Figure 4.2 *Hypothetical distribution of shoe sizes*

make and to stock. In other words, recording of the frequency distribution has produced the basis for prediction. It is no great problem to see how the raw figures can be converted into probabilities, so that people not ordering 10,000 pairs at a time could also get their mixes right. Converted from a frequency distribution into one showing probability, the picture is as shown in Figure 4.3.

The retailer and manufacturer can see that half of their production and stock probably ought to be in size 5, since the probability is that every other customer will be of that size. Alternatively, they might decide to ignore the 'tails' of the distribution, sizes 2 and 8, where they stand to make only 2 per cent of sales: they could be more trouble than they are worth. That would imply that more than 50 per cent of the stock ought to be in size 5, and so on for the remaining sizes. Alternatively, they may feel that every other supplier cuts out the unpopular sizes, leaving a useful market segment of neglected consumers. Then again, they could remember that a lot of trade in

The first-time manager

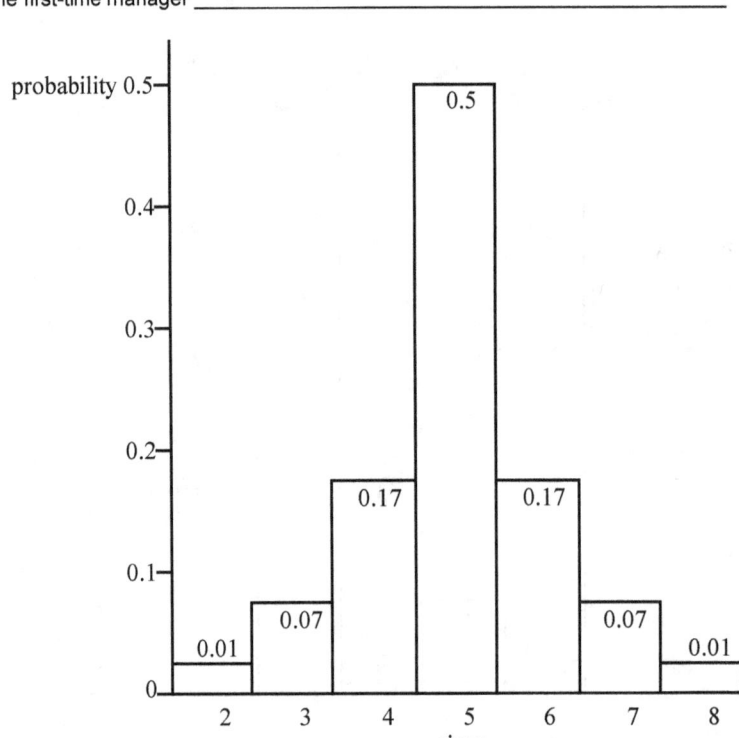

Figure 4.3 *Probability distribution from Figure 4.2*

smaller sizes comes not from adults but from schoolchildren, and decide to beef up order of the smaller sizes.

Whatever decision the shoe trader takes is of no importance to us. What is of concern here is that statistics and statistical methods have yielded information to help decisions. In no case has the distribution effectively dictated the decision, but instead it has provided food for thought and a jumping-off point for its user to decide what to do. Because the information was available, the decision will be of higher quality than it might otherwise have been.

The same sort of technique can be used in all kinds of business activities. An example is in quality control. Huge efforts can be made to eliminate faults which are very infrequent and easy to remedy. A look at the probabilities and frequency distributions is likely to prompt the useful thought of whether it might be better to cure the problem when it arises, rather than cutting out at much higher cost any chance of its happening at all. It can also help when deciding which slow-selling products in a range to discontinue and which to drop. In one case statistics can help to show how often the infrequent failure is likely to arise, and in the other, to show whether sufficient market exists to justify the effort of trying to sell more. Hunch could have come to the same conclusion, but it is a poor basis for such decisions.

The next move is to look in more detail at distributions. The measure of shoe size proceeds in clear steps, because that is how shoes are made. If instead the measure had been the length of feet, the steps between sizes would have been all but indistinguishable. In place of the steps on the histogram there would have been a curve. A distribution of that sort is called 'continuous'.

The continuous distribution which occurs most in nature and in human activity is known as the 'normal' distribution. Normal distributions come in all sorts of sizes, but they all have in common the same bell-curve shape. It might be tall and narrow, or wide and flat, or tall and wide and so on. Figure 4.4 shows two typical profiles.

The shape of the distribution is expressed by two parameters: the mean (in everyday terms, an average), and the standard deviation (which is calculated to a formula which scientific calculators and personal computers have installed in them). Normal distributions always have the same form. This means that, of the total area under the curve, there is always the same proportion at a given distance from the mean. That distance is measured in standard deviations. So,

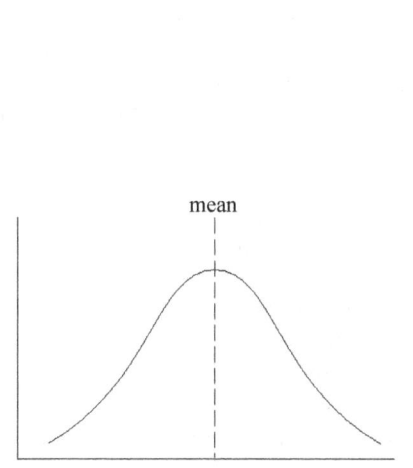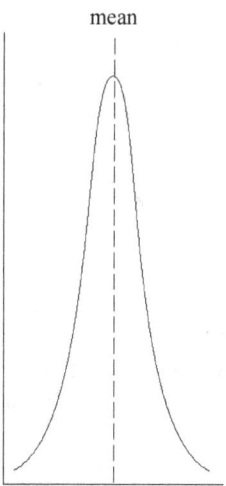

Figure 4.4 *Two typical normal distributions*

The first-time manager

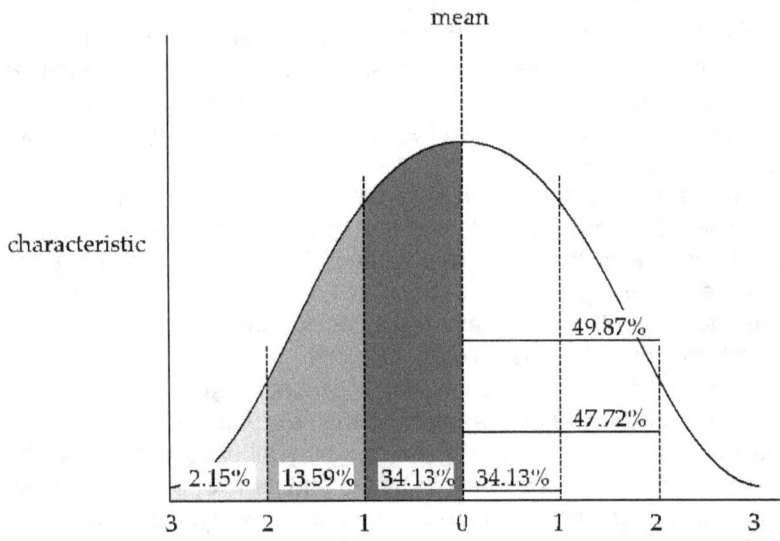

Figure 4.5 *Proportions and standard deviations*

if you have a mean and a standard deviation, and believe that the dis-tribution ought to be normal, you can predict what proportion of the total population will lie at which distances from the mean, as in Figure 4.5.

To the left side of the mean in Figure 4.5 are shown the proportions of the distribution at one, two and three standard deviations from the mean; to its right is shown the accumulation of those proportions. The same information can then be taken one stage further, as in Figure 4.6.

Figure 4.6 shows that at one standard deviation on either side of the mean, 68.26 per cent of the population is represented. If the dis-tance from the mean is doubled to two standard deviations, the pro-portion covered rises to 95.44 per cent. Thus, all but 4.56 per cent (100 – 95.44) is covered at just two standard deviations from the mean. Since that is so close to 95 per cent, the question might well arise: How far from the mean do I have to go to cover that propor-tion? A glance at the standard tables will show it to be at 1.96 stan-dard deviations on either side of the mean.

The practical use of this distribution is great. To return to the earlier example of shoe sizes, the normal distribution supplies

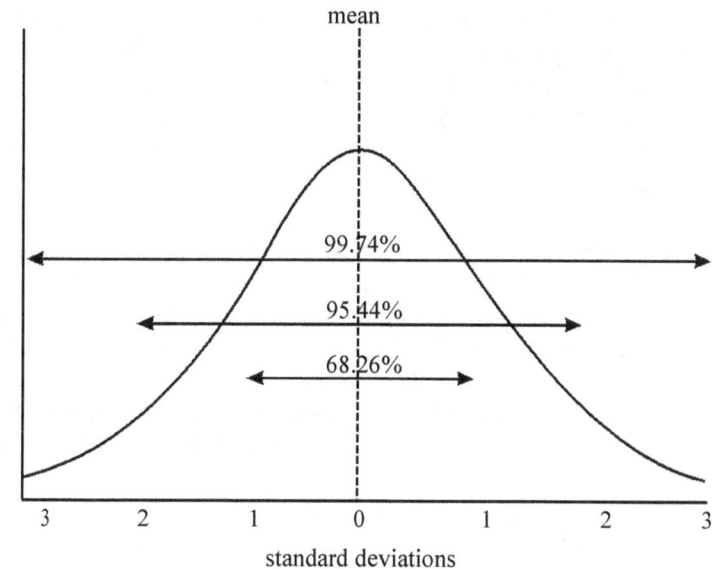

Figure 4.6 *Proportions either side of the mean*

answers to such questions as: What proportion of consumers takes (say) size six or more? What proportion of the market is satisfied by (say) the three most popular sizes? In essence, where is our time best spent? All are questions of considerable importance to the manufac-turer and retailer alike. The distribution's use is not confined to the broad marketing issues: it can be applied to orders received, cus-tomer patterns, stock items and time spent, as well as many more besides.

The great truth which the normal distribution uncovers is that there is a disproportionate reward for effort spent in different ways. One standard deviation to both sides of the mean covers only one-third of the width of the distribution, which is to say one-third of the ways in which you spend your time and effort. Yet that third of your time yields more than two-thirds (68.26 per cent) of the results. Apply it to many activities and it will show that a third of the work produces two-thirds of the results. (Shortly we shall explore an approach that refines these proportions and comes up with rather different figures, but the general principle is the same.) Whether or not the distribution is normal will govern the applicability of this proportion in any given case. The overall message remains: a minor-ity of activity produces most of the output. From there it is not a great leap to conclude that managers need to do two things, repeatedly advocated throughout this book: to minimize or discard entirely rela-tively unproductive activity, and to increase the share of their time and effort given over to the work that really gets the results.

One thing to remember is that the normal distribution does not cover 100 per cent of the population, just 99.74 per cent, so that the curve never quite touches the base line. It is not vitally important in most practical situations, but it should not be forgotten. Thus none of the predictions which are made from a distribution is ever completely accurate. This is not the place to go into detail, but forecasts made by these means should always be expressed as subject to a degree of uncertainty. The specialist textbooks go into these issues and supply the formulae; and most database and spreadsheet programs for personal and home computers will do the calculations automatically.

So far we have dealt with distributions in which the characteristics of the whole population are known. Frequently, in real life, that is not the case; we have information on only a few items, and would dearly like to predict the characteristics of the population at large. Again, distributions are a useful tool.

The first principle is that any samples we obtain from the population must be truly random. The statistician's definition of randomness is quite specific: each member of the population as a whole must have an equal chance of being picked.

Once the sample is assembled, it is important to know how well it represents the whole. That is largely a question of its size, not of what proportion it is of the total population. As a rough guide, 30 to 40 is usually the minimum for most purposes, though it is calculated exactly for a given confidence level. The more confident you want to be, the larger the sample must be. Thus questions of cost come in, since bigger samples cost more to deal with, both in time and money. One standard technique which has emerged from sampling tech-niques is the quality control chart.

Quality control charts
If a machine makes thousands of items or a call-centre takes thousands of calls, it is impossible – or, at least, extraordinarily expensive
– to test each one for conformance to quality standards. Thus some form of sampling is the only realistic way of checking. But that sampling has to be sufficiently representative of the whole output to make the exercise mean anything.

The principles of management

To produce a quality control chart (QCC), the ideal has to be defined first. In this example we shall use a simple cylindrical part. We could equally well have chosen an aspect of customer service during a contact with the hypothetical call-centre – whether or not a particular insurance product was offered, for example. The ideal here might relate to a dimension: say, a diameter. It is specified as a given size, plus or minus an amount known as 'tolerance'. (Sometimes tol-erance runs one way only, so that, for example, an item may be of a certain size or greater, but no less.) Next, the size of sample to be taken in order to conform to the required confidence level is calcu-lated. Two limits have thus been defined: the warning limit, which, if a sample exceeds it, triggers a further investigation to increase the degree of certainty of the information; and the action limit which, if exceeded, causes the machine to be stopped, reset and re-started. Where the tolerance is expressed as plus-or-minus, the QCC will look like Figure 4.7.

In Figure 4.7, the first three checks, taken at exactly half-hourly intervals, showed that the samples' averages were not of the target size, but none was outside the warning limit. The fourth check showed that the warning limit had been exceeded. That resulted in further checks, not shown on Figure 4.7, which proved this to be a rogue result. Thus, on this occasion the machine was not stopped and

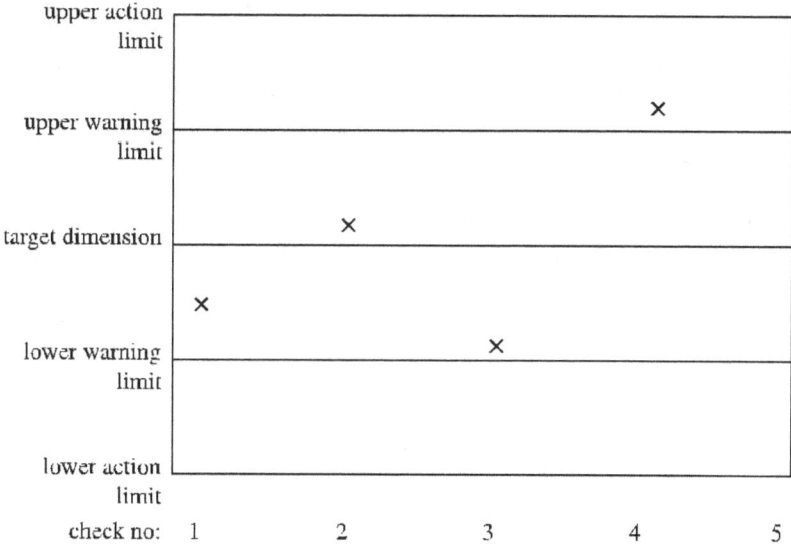

Figure 4.7 *Quality control chart*

costly down-time was avoided. The action to be taken at each stage is very much up to the manager responsible to decide, the important part of the message being that the degree of tolerable deviation can be calculated, as can the size and frequency of sampling necessary to give an acceptable substitute for testing the entire output.

Distribution: some further examples

A firm makes rather expensive gold contact switches for specialist electrical applications. The amount of gold deposited on the contacts is critical to both costings and quality. Too little gold and the contact will not perform, too much and the product makes a loss. The firm believes that the variation follows a normal distribution, and is trying to define its quality specification for gold deposits.

It is possible for the pattern of gold deposition to follow the distribution in Figure 4.8(1). That would be a quality disaster: a very large proportion of the output would fall below the target size.

Following the same pattern of distribution, the firm moves the mean well above the target size, as illustrated in Figure 4.8(2). That clears it of practically all risk of making the deposits too small, but would be disastrously costly. All the output would be above specification, some of it grossly so.

The firm then investigates some new, more sensitive equipment which will enable deposition to be more tightly controlled. That should produce the pattern of distribution portrayed in Figure 4.8(3). This still means that the minimum deposition will be achieved by practically all output, but this time at excesses costing much less. If this pattern is compared with that in Figure 4.8(1), it is seen that the means are in the same place, but that the standard deviations are very different.

Of course, there is a pattern which it would be even more attractive to follow. It is shown in Figure 4.9, and is clearly not a normal distribution. It is known as a 'skewed' distribution. If it could be achieved, it should ensure both that no product falls below the minimum stan-dard, and that the least excess occurs above the minimum.

Despite its asymmetrical shape, formulae exist to calculate such distributions as this, just as they do for the more regular shape of the normal distribution and its close relatives.

Regression and correlation

So far, questions involving only single variables – height, weight and so on – have been addressed, which can be arranged into one

The principles of management

(1)
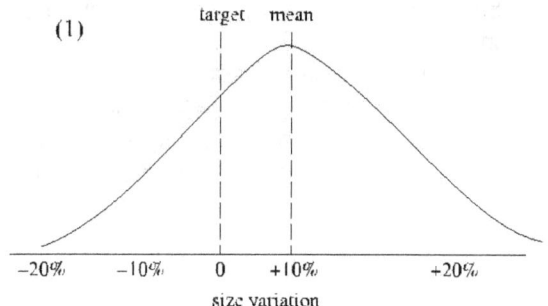

(2)
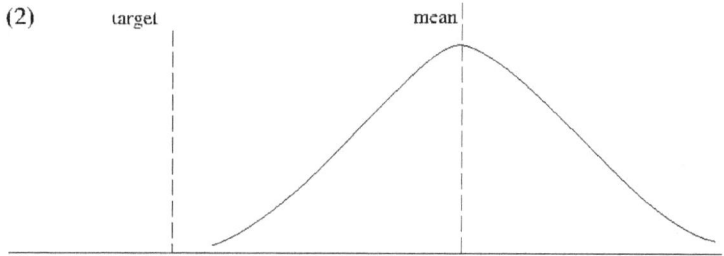

(3)
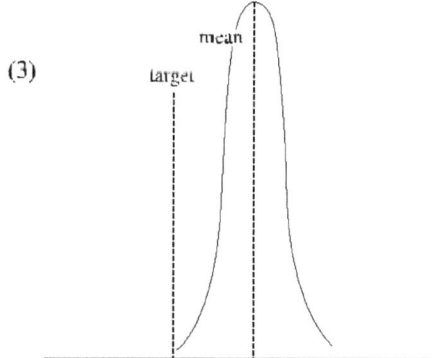

Figure 4.8 *The effects of different normal distributions*

distribution or another. Other types of problems exist, in which more than one variable is at work.

Often in problems of this sort patterns are sought as aids to understanding. As an example, a farmer feeds his animals to make them gain weight. The faster they do this, the sooner they can be sold and new ones be brought in, and the greater will be the return on his land,

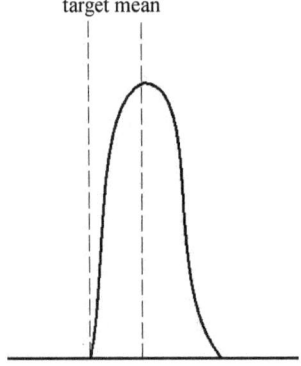

Figure 4.9 *A skewed distribution*

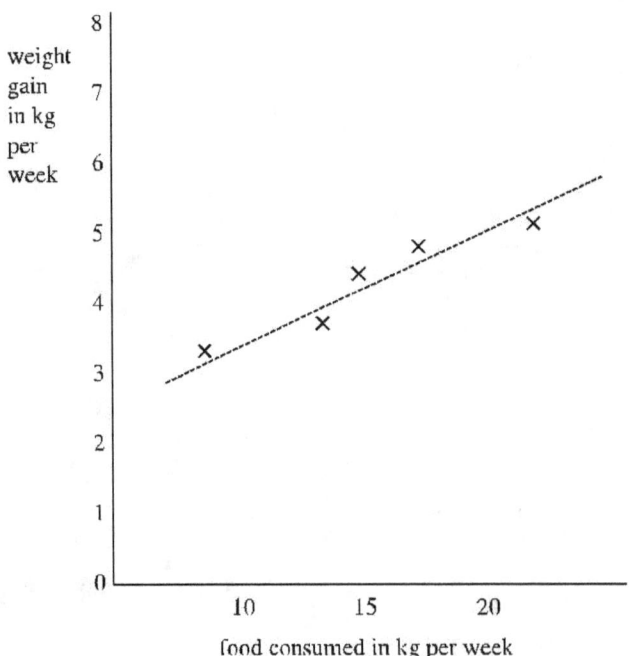

Figure 4.10 *Linear regression*

The principles of management

buildings and labour. He experiments, and produces a chart, shown in Figure 4.10.

The dotted line in Figure 4.10 is the 'line of best fit', and is not sketched in by eye. It is calculated by the process of regression analy-sis. Where one straight line is involved, it is known as linear regression.

Usually it is not enough merely to fit the line to the results. One also wants to know how good the fit is; that involves calculating the corre-lation coefficient. Where it is equal to one, the fit of the line to the points on the chart is perfect. Where it is lower it shows how close to – or distant from – a perfect correlation there is between the two factors under consideration.

Frequently there are more than two factors at work. In the case of the animal feeding example there most certainly are. The extent of veterinary care, the mix of foodstuffs, health, the use of growth addi-tives, the weather, the availability of drink, access to shelter, the extent of exercise – all have their influence, as well, probably, as many more.

The farmer is clearly concerned to know more about this, as he does not want to give £2-worth of food to make up for a temperature drop that it would have cost £1 to remedy by heating or insulation.

The technique used to relate all these factors is multiple regression. In this case it reveals the optimum mix of inputs to achieve the best output before diminishing returns start to set in. To show all the factors listed above would make for a very confusing illustration, so just one other factor appears in Figure 4.11 – the temperature in the creatures' housing. A very low temperature results in poor weight gain, as the animals use too many calories keeping warm; a high

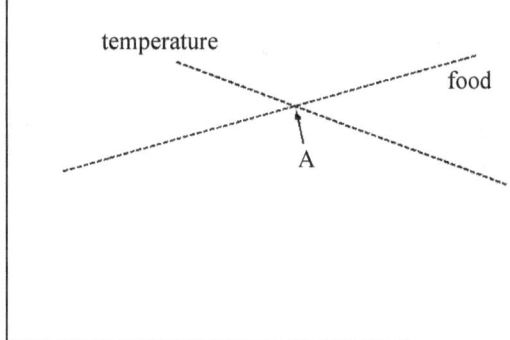

Figure 4.11 *Multiple regression with two factors*

The first-time manager

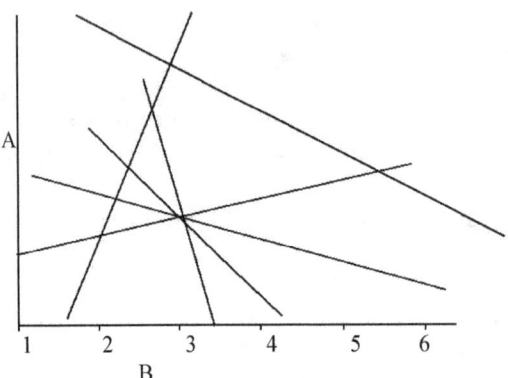

Figure 4.12 *Multiple regression with several factors*

temperature depresses appetite and hence weight gain. Once again, the farmer's experiments do not explore the extremes.

The point A marks the spot at which the food and the temperature curves cross one another, in other words, where they start to cancel each other out. At that point they are in equilibrium, so that is the point at which the temperature and feeding rate are held.

As has been stated, multiple regressions can appear somewhat complicated. Figure 4.12 shows one such. Despite its appearance, its message is easy to see. If A is what we are trying to maximize (say, weight gain), level three on the B scale is where its highest level is reached. We therefore pitch all the other inputs at their level which corresponds with B at three. There is no point in putting in more, as it will not give a worthwhile result. In a sense, we are boxed in at that point.

Pareto's Principle, or the 80:20 rule

As has already been said, most of any effect is accounted for by a minority of the inputs. This rule takes that idea further. It states that – roughly speaking – 20 per cent of the work done will account for 80 per cent of the output; the other 80 per cent of the work can therefore produce only 20 per cent of the results.

Applied to managers' work in organizations, this idea is enormously powerful. Of course, the split is rarely exactly 80:20, but it is usually near enough for the message to be valid.

As examples, four areas will be taken: stock control, customers, vehicle journeys and a manager's personal time. The aim is to show how the 80:20 rule can help in each case.

Stock
Holding stock costs money, and keeps cash tied up; thus the bare minimum consistent with an acceptable level of safety is all that should be kept. If 80 per cent of the sales are accounted for by only one-fifth of the items held in stock, the organization should be thinking seriously about whether the slower-moving products should be kept at all. Too often stocks of the slow movers are higher than those of the more popular products, simply because the same quantity of each is ordered for reasons of economy. Another reason for hanging on to these nearly dead products is that the customers expect it. If that is true, why don't the customers turn their supposed expectation into purchases? There can be valid reasons of this type, but tests of valid-ity are rarely applied, the same old pattern being good enough for another year in far too many organizations.

Customers
It also costs money to deal with a customer. If only 20 per cent of the customers account for 80 per cent of the sales, some of the remaining four-fifths of the customers could be dropped with no noticeable effect on volume, but a considerable effect on costs.

Deliveries
It costs money to send vehicles out on deliveries. If 80 per cent of the output is delivered by only 20 per cent of the journeys, why bother with the rest? Let them come and collect the goods, or, better still, take their unprofitable work to a competitor. That rids us of a cost and imposes it on him, giving us a double advantage.

Manager's time
The manager's time is his or her key resource. Some would say that it is the only one that really matters. If 20 per cent of the work produces 80 per cent of the results, he or she clearly ought to throw overboard, quite ruthlessly, some of the things done now, so as to free time for the really productive aspects.

To take that point a little further, to cut out the bottom fifth of the things done would double the time available to tackle the work that produces 80 per cent of the results. While that does not mean immediately producing 160 per cent of the earlier performance, one could quite reasonably look for an increase in effectiveness of 30, 40 or 50 per cent despite quite a noticeable slackening of effort.

The opportunity of such huge improvements is not to be sneezed at. However, there may be problems when the manager tries to strug-gle free from the cloying grip of relatively useless work. The notion of 'satisficing' comes in useful here. Satisficing involves intentionally setting out to do the bare minimum necessary, and absolutely no more. Applied to the less important work in a manager's life, it frees large chunks of time, as well as avoiding the charge of ignoring parts of the duties altogether. The savings in time can be quite staggering: if it takes ten minutes to do a minor report quite roughly, it could take an hour to polish it to near-perfection. By satisficing, the wise manager spends 50 minutes of that precious hour on really important work, while a less discriminating colleague spends all of it on an unrewarding task.

Written records

A final note in this chapter concerns the necessity for written records.

In organizations there is a need for actions and decisions to be recorded in writing and circulated to those affected. There is a further need for records of performance to be kept, for internal purposes. The law also imposes requirements for the creation and retention of accounting records going back over many years.

If little or nothing in these areas is recorded in writing, opinion will rule rather than fact. Recollection of agreements can vary alarmingly from one individual to another ('You said you *would*'; 'Oh no, I said I'd *try*'), even within minutes of the event. Thus good housekeeping dictates the creation, maintenance and agreement of written records.

There is a further aspect – of self-interest. The world being what it is, the first-time manager is particularly vulnerable if a senior manager chooses to deny a commitment for reasons of self-protec-tion. It is the senior, trusted person's word against that of the new junior. The only way the first-time manager can be protected from that form of ill-treatment is by producing a written record. An exchange of memoranda or letters is best. A scribbled note to your file, timed and dated, and written immediately after the event while recollection is fresh, is better than nothing.

Key points and tips

- Personal and departmental targets should be respected. They knit in with others that, taken together, add up to the organization's targets.
- Organizational planning is complex and takes time.
- If people are to own their targets they must be involved in their creation.
- Managers can be born but are more often made, via educa-tion and training.
- Thinking about causes and effects changes the flow of events into experience, which can be learnt from.
- Managers cultivate habits of thought that enable them to dis-sect and understand complexity.
- Basic statistical techniques teach managers a lot.
- Of all the tools managers use, the 80/20 rule is among the most powerful.
- Everything important should be recorded in writing.

five

Marketing

Marketing: what it involves

'Marketing' is a term misused and misunderstood more often than practically any other word in common business use today. To many people it is a polite word for selling, perhaps with a little advertising and publicity thrown in. While selling, advertising and publicity are important elements in the marketing process, they certainly are not everything that is involved.

Marketing starts from a particular view of what a business is for. The marketing view says that it is there to satisfy customers' needs at a profit to itself. To do this, it has to find out what those needs are, design products and services which will answer them, and set about supplying them. That has to be done at a price which is high enough to recover costs and make profit, and low enough to get the right amount of work – not too much, nor too little. Along the way someone has to go out and tell customers that the goods exist, get the orders, deliver and install, get paid, and then carry out after-sales services.

Mention of after-sales service suggests that the relationship contin-ues after the sale. So it should, for that is how customers, once attracted, remain hooked. It is a lot easier – and for 'easier' read 'less expensive' – to sell a second time to a satisfied user than for the first time to someone who does not know the organization at all. Indeed, the marketing process is a loop, which can be described by the diagram in Figure 5.1.

Figure 5.1 shows the overall picture of customer needs and the organization's characteristics marrying up to produce what the cus-tomer wants. Then the product is distributed to the customer, who is then told about it. The process is a loop, for once the purchase is com-pleted the customer will have new and different needs which could be satisfied profitably. They may be for service and spares, add-ons, and repeat orders for new installations.

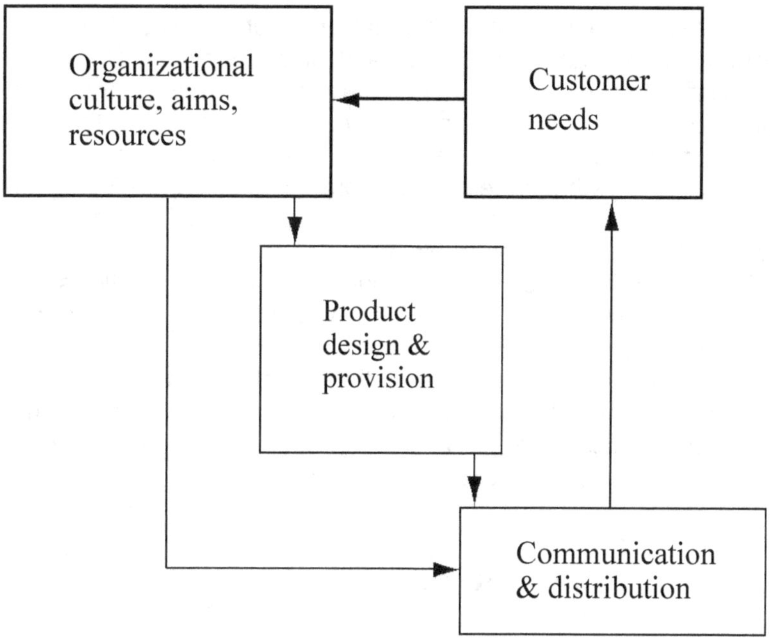

Marketing

Figure 5.1 *The marketing process simplified*

Listening to the market

A properly sensitive system for listening to customers' requirements will identify such opportunities. They will be spotted when the organization hears the answers to such questions as:

- Do the customers think we are doing better or worse than last year?
- Do the customers think our competitors are doing better or worse than last year?
- What are we, and they, doing right?
- What are we, and they, doing wrong?
- How could we improve?
- What ought we to improve?

That list is only a summary, but it is a good place to start from for the organization seriously interested in tracking its reputation among customers. From that simple list will flow many subsidiary ques-tions. It may be difficult for the first-time manager to grasp it in the early days, but even the most high-faluting market research is really trying to find the answers to basic and simple questions like these. It is difficult because some people seem to think it necessary to surround what they do with as much mystery as possible. If the first-time manager cannot see what sense there is in what is said, he or she should ask what it means. Far from being thought a fool, gratitude and admiration will flow from others present for they, too, had not understood, but did not like to ask.

Few organizations bother to organize their information flows in a disciplined and planned way. Those who fail to do so risk heavy pen-alties, for the organization that does not listen to its market loses touch with it; and an organization out of touch with its market is a classic candidate for failure. The market is constantly evolving, frag-menting, changing its pattern and coalescing again. To keep up with all this the organization needs information.

The place of marketing

Thus the role of marketing is central to the conduct of the business of any organization, public, private or charitable. If an organization fails to satisfy its customers' needs at a profit it will eventually fail altogether. If it fails to identify its customers' needs it has no real chance of satisfying them; and if it does not follow the evolution of those needs it will become increasingly out of touch and eventually irrelevant.

The term 'profit' may seem to sit oddly with mention of charities and some public bodies. To them, profit might not be expressed financially, but in terms of a movement towards their objectives. It might be recognized as cleaner streets, more families helped, or an important building saved. The benefits to the organization are impossible to express financially, but benefits they are, and they can be described as profits. Certainly, viewed as profits, they make sense in marketing terms. Indeed, one might see the outputs of the not-for-profit sector as profits for society as a whole, rather than a smaller group of shareholders.

The whole strategy and direction of the organization has to be market-led. Production, distribution and administration policies must be strongly influenced by marketing considerations. Staff selec-tion and training have to take marketing into account, or else the tele-phone may be answered rudely and the delivery drivers look scruffy.

Even at the lowest level of detail marketing obtrudes: the look of the company's letterhead and the decision over which grades of paper to use for which correspondence can, in some circumstances, be very important.

Marketing people

Really good marketing people have to possess a wide range of strengths and characteristics. Indeed, they need to be among the most versatile of managers. The reason is that they are required to possess the skills and gifts of numeracy, an informed literacy, aesthetic sense and an understanding of people and their behaviour which is at the same time both instinctive and rational.

Numeracy is necessary to deal with statistics and management accounting concepts. The marketing manager's literacy does not just mean the ability to read and write, but the ability to express himself well and persuasively as well as to understand the written work of others such as advertising and PR people. Design, both graphic and three-dimensional, is very important in marketing, and the aesthetic sense to distinguish good from bad is vital. Probably the most funda-mental is the understanding of people, for it is their motivations which decide, in the end, whether or not the organization's products are bought and appreciated.

The combination of many areas of competence in one individual may suggest examples from another age. Renaissance man was master of the sciences as well as the arts of his day. He understood and could perform the detailed, meticulous accumulation of evi-dence, the formulation of hypotheses and their testing, proceeding the while by a series of mostly small steps, each secured by the cer-tainty of absolute proof which the scientific method demands. By an infinity of such steps the whole of today's science was created.

In marketing, as elsewhere, it is important to know when to seek scientific information and when to apply judgement. The analytical side of marketing is extensive, but it does not outweigh the interper-sonal and creative aspects. Marketing needs new ideas: they can be prompted by information and analysis, but someone has to apply the vital spark of creative intelligence to bring the new idea into being. Marketing research never does more than provide the information which is the launching pad for ideas. Current techniques are not up to having the ideas as well. The emergence of computer-based intelli-gence could, eventually, change that picture dramatically.

The people side of marketing is important too. As well as in their role as colleagues, marketing practitioners encounter people as customers, both individual and in the mass. That statement could be challenged on the ground that the mass is no more than a collection of individuals. So it is, in one sense. But if the behaviour of single individuals is studied it yields less information than if attempts are made at categorization as well; categorization involves aggregation into masses.

Marketing and communication

The colleagues with whom marketing people deal are both internal and external. Those in their own department and elsewhere in the organization participate in conventional colleague relationships. To refer to suppliers such as advertising, PR and research agencies as colleagues may seem odd, if the special nature of relationships with them is not appreciated. Those agencies are much more than mere suppliers; they immerse themselves in the ethos and values of the organization in order to understand it as well as possible. This model is seen increasingly as virtual organizations multiply. These are orga-nizations that deliberately do not try to perform all business func-tions themselves, but farm out many of them to subcontracting partners.

Marketing's dealings with customers and consumers are central to its concerns. (Customers – such as shops – buy from the manufacturer or other supplier; consumers are the end-users. Tesco is Unilever's customer. The member of the public who buys Persil from Tesco is the supermarket's customer and Unilever's consumer. It is perfectly possi-ble for the customer to be the consumer as well, where the consumer is supplied direct by the manufacturer.) Marketing studies people indi-vidually in some depth, in order to discover how their minds work in general, and especially how they react to particular propositions. The large collection of individuals which constitutes the mass is also studied for signs of opportunities to create groupings. Such groups are called 'segments'.

The appreciation of aesthetics may seem to be a strange item to add to a list of desirable qualities in a marketing person. Its relevance is that aesthetics is an important element in communication, and com-munication is one of marketing's main areas of concern.

Words are one important medium of communication. The marketer deals with them in many forms, most notably perhaps in research reports, recommendations for action, advertising copy, instruction manuals and letters to users (especially the dissatisfied ones). Anyone unable to appreciate well-written examples of these forms of communication is ill-qualified for marketing work. Marketers do not have to be able to write well themselves – though it helps – but be able to recognize good and bad writing.

Visual images are another tool of communication. An eye for an image which works is essential (questions of beauty or ugliness are irrelevant here: the criterion is whether or not the right message is conveyed well). To appreciate a particular image's effect fully, the marketer has to be aware of what its impact would be in other media and other styles. Thus he or she needs an understanding of the strengths and limitations of all visual media in order to be able to do the job well.

Every product has a three-dimensional form. Whatever its shape, it conveys messages to the observer about what it can and cannot do. Those messages ought to be the ones which the marketer wants to be received. Thus he needs some appreciation of the effect which three-dimensional design has on people. A spade may *be* strong, but if it *looks* weak where the blade meets the handle, people will not buy it. A scent-bottle may hold the product quite securely, but if it reminds people of a jam jar it is unlikely to sell. An electric drill that appears to have been fathered by a rhinoceros looks as if it can survive the toughest of jobs.

It is essential that marketing personnel are at least competent in their dealings with people. They have to work with advertising agen-cies, PR firms, and a wide range of people from both within and outside the organization. Furthermore, because they have to make abstract concepts understood, they need to be able to express them-selves well. Leadership characteristics are also called for: advertising and PR people work best when they are motivated and excited about the opportunity to advance their careers by working on the organiza-tion's account. Sometimes these creative people have to be told that their work is not acceptable, and told in such a way that they really want to do it again and better.

The first-time manager

The marketing task

Planning

Like all management functions, marketing has long-, medium- and short-term aspects and perspectives. They can be described as in Figure 5.2.

The process of planning these events does not take place just once every five or ten years, of course. Most organizations have 'rolling' plans which, every 12 months, move forward by one year. Any orga-nization with any sense will not stick too rigidly to its planning cycle: a good idea or a new opportunity which appears unexpectedly will not be shelved for up to five years just because it was not thought of at the right point in the planning cycle.

The plans of the marketing department are one element in the total plan for the organization as a whole, the corporate plan. Other departments will submit their plans for finance, production and personnel, but none of them can really get going before the marketing plan is ready. A production plan which proposes levels of output for which there is as yet no sales forecast is rather pointless. Once some sort of sales forecast has been made, production people can get to work properly on their own planning.

Likewise, the personnel department cannot plan to train or recruit particular skills until they know what skills are wanted, in what quantity and when. They cannot decide whether or not to replace people who retire until they know if that contribution will still be needed.

Finance, too, has to await marketing and production plans. Once it knows the likely timings and size of cash flows, it can consider

Long-term	5–10 years	identify likely needs of the market, and how to satisfy them at a profit
Medium-term	1–3 years	set up the practical implementation of long-term ideas
Short-term	up to 1 year	practical implementation: getting sales, controlling costs, making profit, gathering information

Figure 5.2 *Long-, medium- and short-term marketing perspectives*

whether the outflows are temporary or permanent, and thus how they should be covered. There is only one major exception to that principle. It occurs where the organization's finances are likely to be under stress. In such cases the financial people will publish in advance the constraints which have to be imposed on stocks and sales. Their colleagues can then work within those limits, saving time, trouble and friction.

The way in which the marketing department goes about its task of long-term planning is a combination of the usual ingredients: science, intuition and judgement. A generalized view of the process is offered in Figure 5.3.

Information for the planning process

The materials which the marketer uses in this process are largely provided by others. Economists analyse trends and forecast what will have happened to people's and industries' power and propensity to spend in future years. Some industries will have disappeared alto-gether and new ones will have arisen. Much of that work is specula-tive, but if it takes ten years to build the power station you need to know by 2007 at the latest whether or not it is likely actually to be needed in the year 2017. Some long-range forecasting may be border-ing on guesswork (albeit informed), but if there is no other source of

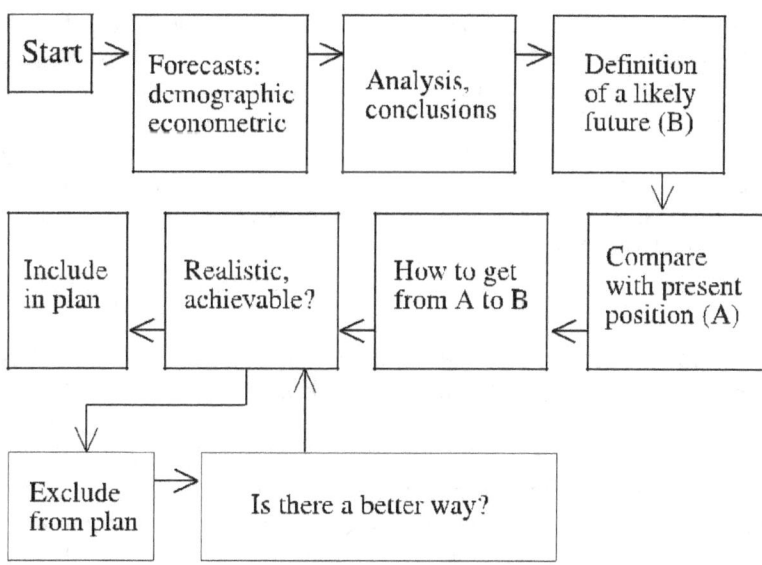

Figure 5.3 *Strategic marketing planning*

independent evidence it must not be ignored altogether. Of course, the forecasters' ideas are not swallowed uncritically, but are modified by personal intuition and judgement.

Demographic forecasts are on safer ground. They deal with the composition of the population. In 2005 it was easy to say how many children aged between 13 and 15 there will be in the year 2011, for all of them had been born. Applying a known factor for child mortality produced reliable forecasts for most of the 20th century, when the West was largely free from mortal epidemics and pandemics. More recently the picture has been confused by the emergence of possible new threats to populations which might, or might not, prove to be real.

Forecasts of lifestyle have always existed, but more attention has been paid to them of late. The idea behind them is that the products and services which people choose to buy are part of a package which, in total, can be described as a lifestyle. The marketer's task is to identify the lifestyles of different groups and to find out two things: unsatisfied needs, and ways of positioning the organization and its products to match them to the group's view of itself. An early – and by now universal – example of an obscure product which became a mass market lifestyle item is blue jeans. Originally a manual worker's workwear, it gained glamour by association with the Amer-ican cowboy and hence became the uniform of youth and, eventu-ally, staple clothing. Today much attention is paid to 'database marketing'. This assumes that one aspect of lifestyle can be a predic-tor of other tastes. For example, a person who regularly buys fine wines may also be interested in gourmet foods, or even in holidays in France. Thus, people on a database of customers of a wine-merchant can be approached to buy other products. These products may not be directly related (like the wine and food example above), for much effort goes into identifying the probabilities of the purchase of A being a predictor of the purchase of B.

Marketing research

Quantitative research, as the name suggests, deals with quantities and numbers, things that can be counted. It seeks to establish how many of us do, have done or will do (or not do) a particular thing, such as buy anti-dandruff shampoo. It is mostly conducted via interviews or questionnaires. From the aggregated results of all the answers given, the researcher can form a picture of how a market is made up. If the same research is repeated at intervals, change and the direction it takes can be monitored.

Qualitative research deals with the feelings which people have about their needs, and about products, services and organizations. By definition it cannot, and does not try too hard to, apply numbers to its findings. It can give a vivid impression of the views that people hold and the issues which they consider to be important. It is often conducted by the *group discussion method*, under which a number of people – up to 10 or 12, usually – talk about an issue, guided by an experienced leader. The participants are carefully selected to repre-sent a particular group which the organization is interested in.

Often an organization will use the two broad categories of research to complement one another. Qualitative research establishes the issues which people seem to find important, and quantitative infor-mation is gathered to test the true representativeness of the views expressed.

One error which inexperienced marketing people are prone to make is to become hypnotized by the apparatus, jargon and science of research. It is easy to believe that it provides all the answers they will ever need, and that nothing should be done unless there is posi-tive research support for it. For one thing, research needs interpret-ing. For another, it can only ever report on what is. It can never synthesize ideas or exhibit flair, two of the marketing department's more important duties. Only a human being can discern from research reports the possible existence of an unfulfilled need, and design an imaginative answer to it or indeed decide to ignore the reports altogether. The Walkman was launched unsupported by market research, simply because the boss of Sony at the time believed in it.

Just as these techniques apply to consumer markets, so they are used to find out what industry wants. Industrial research starts with a great advantage, in one area at least. Organizations which sell to the public can foresee their own needs, using the research techniques described here. Suppliers to those organizations are able to use the same sources of information to adjust their own marketing effort. If the public taste shifts to new products, the factories which make them will need new equipment. Organizations supplying those fac-tories with equipment can thus see what they will need to do – but only if they take the trouble to keep abreast of the information available.

Even for pure industrial companies, far removed from consumer markets, information is abundant. Even if, at first glance, it is not apparent, it is often in existence or can easily be generated. In industrial marketing especially, it is frequently unnecessary to build a better mousetrap; giving quicker delivery or better after-sales service can be the key to swinging the market your way.

Advertising

What advertising is for
The job of advertising is to spread a predetermined message in a controlled way to a specified audience. It is under control in so far as the message, how it is expressed and where it appears are all dictated by the advertiser. (There can be exceptions, as when the alcohol advertisers can hardly get on to TV at Christmas because the government has booked all the best spots for its drink-driving campaigns.) Advertising is solely about communication, a vital element in any marketing activity. Because its place is so important in some markets, and because vast expense can be involved, it becomes a topic of great interest at senior levels of general management. It is quite normal for big-brand advertising campaigns to cost tens of millions of pounds.

At the other end of the spectrum are those firms in which advertis-ing plays little or no part. They find that their communication objec-tives are best met by other means; thus the creation and control of advertising are by no means important issues for every marketing manager. However, a marketing manager who lacks experience and understanding of advertising is deficient, for circumstances can arise in which it could be the right tool for a particular job. Indeed, in recent years many organizations which were previously not engaged in advertising have started to employ it. Frequently they are the industrial suppliers who used to think that their sales force visits to customers and presence at exhibitions were all the effort necessary. More recently they have come to understand the way in which appropriate advertising can create a receptive atmosphere for the sales force, and pull more people on to their exhibition stands.

Advertising media
The main media available to the advertiser are:

- direct mail
- radio
- TV
- press

Marketing

■ cinema ■
Internet.

There are others – such as posters, directories and exhibitions which have their own specialized uses. Posters can help in mass markets where constant awareness of the product is desired, usually in support of a campaign on other media. Exhibitions are an excellent way of contacting the really interested potential buyer, for few people waste their time and money going to exhibitions on subjects that they are not committed to.

Direct mail involves sending letters and other sales materials through the post. Its objectives can be various: to fix appointments for salespeople to call, to solicit enquiries for catalogues, to obtain an order, to invite people to a demonstration, or any of a number of aims. The characteristic of most direct mail advertising is that it asks for direct action – filling in a reply-paid card, making a telephone call, etc – and that its effect is readily measurable.

The other sorts of advertising hope eventually to result in buying action, but their immediate purpose is to inform and persuade. Here, radio may seem to be at a disadvantage to television, but as someone once said, the pictures on radio are better. The way in which radio can create mental images is far from fully exploited by advertisers.

Press advertising is a far better developed form. It varies between the small classified ad in the special-interest magazine and a double-page spread in the *Sun*. Certain advertising tasks can be achieved only in press media. Its flexibility – from local and specialist media, through regional editions of larger publications, to full national coverage – is in its favour. So is its ability to deliver clearly defined segments of readers: well-off men, young women, etc. A further advantage is its life, as the reader can return time after time to a printed ad.

TV's great advantage is obvious: it moves and talks. It is a medium which is realistically available only to the larger advertiser, since the cost of air time is high, and it is easy to spend six figures making the film itself. And the ads have to be repeated, for not everyone watches the commercial channels all the time.

Cinema offers some of the advantages of TV but at lower total cost. However, the audience is strongly slanted towards the young.

Repetition of advertising has been touched on. It is a basic tenet of advertising that single ads rarely work. A fixation among marketing managers is the effort to measure and judge the degree of repetition necessary to achieve their communication objectives. A further consideration is the distinct creative opportunities offered by differ-ent media. The quality Scotch can be shown to advantage in a full colour magazine printed on art paper; the car can be shown in use on TV; and the excitement of the motor race will come over with great impact on the cinema screen. This can lead to the danger of stereo-typed advertising: only a few of the ads for quality Scotch, for example, could be solely for the brand advertised. In many ads a dif-ferent bottle could be substituted without causing a stir. Thus adver-tisers are constantly striving to convey their products' unique propositions in new and relevant ways. When it comes off, and it is consistent with all the properties of the brand, it can raise a good product's sales performance into the super-growth league. In that way effective advertising not only sells more product, but it also sup-ports prices against pressure for discounts, as well as building repu-tation which can be traded on in the future. The magic of it is that excellent advertising need cost no more than the mediocre variety.

At the time of writing, the Internet has yet to deliver on its prom-ises. These promises are very impressive, and will doubtless be met at some future date, if only for some groups of advertiser. That is why organizations believe it is important to be represented there, but for the time being few can truthfully claim it as a financial success. Once the percentage of transactions undertaken online rises to double figures, and the proportion of would-be purchases abandoned before completion falls to under half, it may be viewed differently.

Swallowed whole, that rather dismal conclusion might be mislead-ing. Many firms make really unintelligent use of the Internet, drag-ging their overall performance down, while others use it well, deliver excellent service and profit accordingly. Once the poor performers have raised their game or got out, the average quality of customers' experience will rise and, with it, their propensity to use the Internet.

Who creates advertising?

Few organizations attempt to create their own advertising, except in the recruitment field. Even there specialized advertising agencies have grown up. Most product advertising is created by agencies, who usually buy the space or time in media as well. Media buying always used to be part of the full-service advertising agency activity, but specialized media buying organizations have grown up quickly in the last few years.

The relationship with the advertising agency is complex, can be difficult, and is potentially rewarding or disastrous. If marketing people seem to spend a lot of time with the agency it is not just because of the beautiful people and the superb hospitality. They are probably doing a great deal of valuable work. There is a lot at stake, both in the expenditure on advertising itself, and in personal reputa-tion and career future. Most of the decisions are judgemental, and the scope for getting things wrong is therefore wide. While an unexceptional campaign may just fail to win market share, it is possible to create a bad one which will lose it. Then the damage done is far wider than simply that to the advertising budget.

Distribution channels

'Channels of distribution' is the marketing jargon for the route which an organization's products and services take from the producer to the customer. In the case of most consumer products, the majority go via wholesalers and retailers. There is also a flourishing business

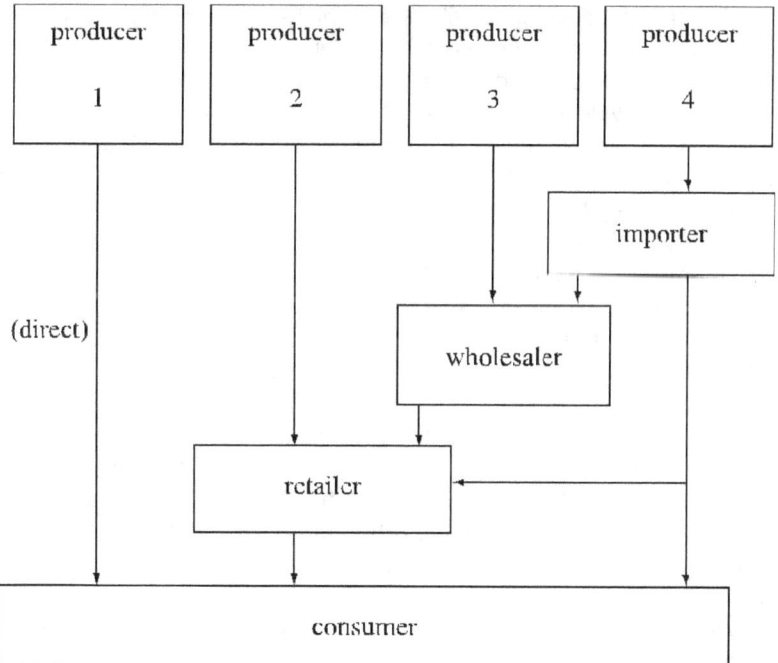

Figure 5.4 *Generalized view of channels of distribution*

done via mail order catalogues, as well as mail order direct from the maker to the user. The various routes are summed up in Figure 5.4.

In Figure 5.4 there are four producers, each with a different distribution policy. The picture given is representative of the options avail-able, though there is nothing to stop organizations from adopting more than one channel if they wish. There can also be differences in nomenclature, such as the fact that wholesalers in the motor trade are called 'factors'. Then again, the retailer need not be a shopkeeper, but could just as easily be a mail order catalogue operator or a website. Some wholesalers operate on full-service principles, others along cash-and-carry lines.

The choice of channels can be of great significance strategically. It sets the tone for many of the other marketing activities, as well as cre-ating major constraints and setting up great opportunities.

One example of this effect will show its importance. If an organization makes sweets, it has to decide how they will get to the shops so that the public can buy them. In only a few, specialized instances is that kind of product sold direct to the public, although sales direct to the catering trade may become important once the product's reputa-tion is established. If it decides to sell through high-volume outlets it will have to create large-scale advertising campaigns, for unadvertised products are rarely stocked. Such is the competition for shelf space in these shops that evidence of advertising intentions alone will rarely be enough. Buyers will need to be convinced of the rightness of the marketing thinking behind the product before they will take it on. After all, the buyer's job is at stake, too.

An advertising-intensive firm needs a strong sales force to get, and keep, its products in distribution. It needs a good marketing depart-ment to supply the ammunition the sales force needs. Thus the firm becomes marketing, advertising and sales led, with obvious effects on its organizational shape and character.

Alternatively, the firm could have decided to sell through low-volume outlets without advertising support. In that case, emphasis would be on product design, packaging, presentation at the point of sale, PR and sales skills. Without advertising support, the way it looks in the shop determines whether or not it sells, and good salespeople are needed to get and hold distribution of unadvertised lines.

Another alternative open to the firm is to specialize in own-label manufacture. That would again change its character. There would be no advertising, perhaps some product and packaging design work, some selling at a senior level to just a few large outlets, and great emphasis on the control of costs, and provision of service.

These three organizations are superficially the same: they are all confectionery manufacturers. But they will be very different places in which to work simply because of the diversity in their channels of distribution.

Selling and the sales force

Some people still persist in the belief that salespeople are born and cannot be made. It simply is not true. That supposition's only resem-blance to fact is that it helps if would-be salespeople are naturally good at dealing with their fellow humans. Most sales managers prefer to recruit the less colourful but disciplined and trained salesperson, than one whose ability stems solely from manner and charm.

Training is vitally important, for selling is a structured activity. Moreover, it has to be repeated frequently, since sales skills deterio-rate with resistance. The general structure of a sale is described by the acronym AIDA, which summarizes the stages through which every sale must pass. AIDA stands for:

Attention: engaging the prospect's active attention in what is being said

Interest: relating the proposition to the prospect's problem

Desire: wanting the proposition on offer

Action: acting on that desire, by placing the order.

While selling is an art, it is based on a body of theory and science, arising mainly from psychology. It needs all the help that it can get, for selling is a difficult task. It is concerned with getting someone else, voluntarily, to do what you want them to do.

The sales force, which has the job of putting those skills to work, may seem featherbedded. They are paid well, get company cars, expense allowances and incentive schemes. Office-bound colleagues may be heard to mutter that *they* don't need incentives to do their own jobs properly, so why does the sales force?

Two things are special about them. One is the competitive market for good salespeople. If company A does not cherish them, company B will soon recruit them. If all the good people disappear in a short space of time, sales can fall sharply and drastically. Suppose one-third of orders stopped coming in: it throws finance, distribution and production into chaos.

The second special factor is the conditions under which salespeople work. Not only are they under pressure to perform all the time, but unlike most of their colleagues they work alone. One of sales management's main headaches is keeping up morale while their people, frequently hundreds of miles from the company base, constantly experience rejection and frustration. A career in selling can be something of a paradox. Typically, it attracts gregarious people, who then work alone and are constantly rejected. This pres-ents sales management with some interesting challenges, and they find themselves permanently engaged in rebuilding damaged egos.

The two main reasons for employing a sales force at all are: 1. cus-tomers rarely buy things of their own volition, but tend to buy only what is sold to them; 2. the extra quantity that the salesperson sells, over and above the amount which the customer might have bought anyway, is what justifies his or her costs.

Physical distribution

Where tangible goods are concerned, the first issue to be faced is who will be carrying the goods: a contractor or the firm's own transport? The former, as a specialist who might be recovering the cost of a journey from more than one customer, ought to be more economical; the latter is more easily controlled, will work more in the firm's inter-est and in some circumstances could be cheaper. The decision between these two courses has become less of a one-horse race in recent years, with the growth of a diverse range of transport services. Only recently, guaranteed 24-hour delivery was novel; now it is commonplace.

Marketing's concern with customer service ought to influence the choice of method and the standards to be observed in the distribution operation. Sometimes distribution can make all the difference to sales. If many firms offer delivery in four weeks, the organization which switches to 48-hour waiting times ought to win. A close partnership between administration, production, warehousing and distribution will be necessary to make that turn from a promised breakthrough into a fact.

Product design

What the product or service does, how it does it and what it looks like are central marketing issues. They are also of no little interest to pro-duction people. Design ought to be based on:

- what the consumer's unfulfilled needs are known to be;
- what competitors are offering;
- what is feasible in technical and cost terms;
- the organization's overall strategies.

To that list of ascertainable imperatives the designer brings personal flair. Everyone recognizes flair when they see it, but defining it is not easy. Designers themselves say that it is rarely the result of a momen-tary flash of inspiration, but more usually it comes after many hours of disciplined thinking about the real nature of the technical, produc-tion and user problems involved. True insight is rarely instanta-neous, and true insight is the stock-in-trade of every useful innovator.

Pricing, positioning and the marketing mix

Deciding how much to charge for the product is often thought of as an accountancy decision, but it should not be. The accountants are highly qualified to calculate a product's cost, and to explain the profit and cash flow implications of a particular price, but they cannot set prices at all. The only relation which price (what it can be sold for) has to cost (how much it cost to make) is that it is preferable in most set-tings to see that the former exceeds the latter.

Pricing is a marketing issue, above all. It relates to what the customer wants, and how much he or she is prepared to pay for it. Nobody other than the marketing people has any idea of what that price is. They also know how they can maximize profitability by changing the product's 'positioning' and the 'marketing mix'.

Positioning has to do with the relationship between the product and its competitors. If the product is perceived by consumers as more or less the same as – or wildly different from – the competition, that ought not to have come about by accident. It should be as a result of a conscious marketing decision.

Marketers should be aiming for the maximum total profit. At a basic level, economics states that this can be achieved by selling a few at a high price or a lot at a low price, since demand falls off the more prices rise. The trick that the marketer tries to pull off is to defy the laws of economics by selling *more* at *higher* prices, for there real profit maximization lies. Just putting up the price is rarely enough, though the record is full of stories of where a price increase was followed by a jump in sales. Usually other factors have to be adjusted too.

This is where the concept of the marketing mix comes in. It embraces all the attributes of the product itself and of the services surrounding it. It recognizes that the proposition which the product presents is more than simply a bundle of functions, offered at a particular price. The extent to which any function is offered should come about, not by accident, but through calculation of consumer needs and the positioning it is intended to establish. Abstract values are included – indeed, they can be dominant in some markets – such as the tone of the advertising and where it appears, the style of the pack-aging, the perception of value relative to competition, the values which the product expresses, and many others besides. Crucial are the level, balance and effect sought from the various promotional expenditures.

Sales promotion

Sales promotion is a portmanteau term for all those activities, with the exception of the sales force and advertising, which seek to influence demand for a product. Its most direct elements are limited-period offers to trade or user, and thereafter its link with the core activity becomes more tenuous, in the form of media publicity in editorial matter, sales force motivation schemes, sponsorships and charity deals.

The more competitive fields of business place much effort, expenditure and ingenuity into this field. To keep pace with competitors is their minimum requirement, to exceed them and excel is the aim. Agencies specializing in sales promotion work exist for two primary reasons: few marketing departments can maintain the pace of innovation for very long, and the outsider's view can often bring more ideas to a hard-pressed marketing department than it could ever gen-erate for itself.

Trade relations

Largely the responsibility of the sales force, in this area they benefit from the support of publicists and promotional specialists. The trade can be reassured, just as much as a private individual, about a company and a product by means of favourable stories in the press. They may be harder-headed than the average citizen, but they are far from immune to influence.

The nature and scope of trade promotions are settled between sales (who have to implement them) and marketing (who pay). They both want long-term as well as short-term results, and at the very least do not want to run promotions which actually alienate the trade on which they depend – which has been done.

Public relations

Although PR has been touched on under a number of headings, it does deserve a section to itself since it has such potential to influence perceptions of organizations.

PR covers many activities, all directed towards two ends: improv-ing perceptions of the organization and its products among relevant groups, and limiting the extent of unfavourable perceptions when criticism is heard. Indeed, while most emphasis is placed on the constructive aspects of PR, its finest hour often comes when adverse stories are flying about. The trust developed with journalists in happier days then pays off, because the journalist telephones the PR person for *their* side of the story before filing copy.

Contrary to popular opinion, the aspect of PR which deals with media relations is based not on spin and lunches, but on truth. That there can be many interpretations of the truth cannot be denied, but the good PR person never tries to deny facts.

To the regret of many PR people they sometimes have to deal in trivia, especially when dealing with the tabloid press. The more interesting aspects of the job for many are where they are negotiating to place senior people into interviews. Think of the eminent people (excluding politicians and trade union leaders) whom you have seen and heard on TV, and of the ones you know of whom you have never seen. The difference is in both their attitude to publicity and the strength of their PR people.

PR also operates outside the media (though with half an eye on it). It seeks out influential groups who can help, or could cause trouble, and deals with them accordingly. A toy manufacturer, for instance, might try simultaneously to tell Health Visitors how its products help children to develop, and reassure consumer watchdogs about the care that goes into design and manufacture. It could also find itself called on to run a campaign aimed at Members of Parliament, EU functionaries or MEPs, to persuade them against enacting unhelpful legislation.

Marketing: a summary

Marketing's position in the organization is at the interface between its public and its own resources. It sets the agenda for the organization, or at least it ought to. Everyone else in the organization depends on the marketers to get it right, for without a market there can be no organization.

Key points and tips

- Sound marketing is central to organizational existence.
- Marketing is the means of meeting organizational aims by satisfying customers.
- Marketing is complex, involving quantitative, qualitative and behavioural issues.
- Communications are an essential element in effective marketing, and many media are used.
- Part of marketing is to choose how the product gets to customers and to oversee that process.

six

Managing Production of Goods and Services

Systems

Production is an important function, for if the output is not made there is nothing to sell. Making it is not enough: it also has to be avail-able at the right time, to the right quality and at the right cost. Thus the main concerns of production managers are:

- Quality
- Quantity
- Cost
  - using the least inputs
  - carrying the lowest stocks possible
  - occupying the least space possible
- Timeliness.

As has been seen, the marketing department operates to a large extent with 'soft' systems (systems which are so complex that nobody can describe truthfully and fully the cause-and-effect relationships).

'Hard' systems, by contrast, are a lot easier to understand. They can be very complex, but what is going on is usually knowable and measurable. An example of a hard system is one for accounting. In a large organization it may be extraordinarily complicated, but if you stop the clock at any point you can measure exactly what is in each account, what changes have taken place in a given period and why. Complex it may be, but a hard system is explicable and measurable.

As with an accounting system, so with a production control system.

If 5000 items come in and 200 of them are rejected, 100 damaged in handling and 10 lost, 4690 must emerge from the other end. The facts of what happened in the journey from the goods-inwards bay to the finished goods store are known or are ascertainable.

Thus the total system which production represents is made up of a number of sub-systems – paint shop, raw material store, press shop, assembly line and so on. They in turn can be broken down into further sub-systems. Within the paint shop there is a section for prep-aration, another for applying the paint itself, a drying section, inspec-tion procedures, and so forth. These can be broken down into individual job functions. The same principles apply to services as they do to tangible products: banks, insurance companies and dry cleaners break down in exactly the same way.

From this it will be seen that a map or family tree of the factory can be drawn. It starts with the complete factory, and subdivides it into progressively smaller functions. Or it could start from the bottom with the individual job functions, building up to the overall picture. Such a diagram would be complicated, but the flows within it – of materials, labour and cash – would be known. For instance, it would never show electrical sub-assemblies travelling to the paint shop, or finished cars back-tracking to the press shop. Nor would an airline's invoices to customers go via its training department.

The predictability of the hard system means that, while there are millions of ways in which such a system could go haywire, produc-ing the wrong things in the wrong quantities at the wrong time, the area in which the problem is being caused is identifiable. Just as in the finished car itself, a malfunction in one sub-system (wheels and brakes, transmission, electrical, etc) can cause faults in others and can be traced and put right.

The kind of problems experienced in an advanced production or service environment operating under great pressure lend themselves to computer assistance. In keeping track of the complexity, working out the implications and even taking simple decisions, IT helps a great deal. Stock control is an example. A retail chain trying to keep stocks as low as it can has a problem if it works from manual records of sales. The task of recording sales is laborious, then the delay between the information being available at the branch and being coordinated at HQ, and the working through of calculations of what has to be ordered, all take time. Those delays mean that buffer stocks have to be held, just to cater for information processing. If instead sales are recorded at the checkout by computer, the information can be in HQ within seconds, processed into branch re-orders from the warehouse and, if necessary, replenishment ordered from the supplier. The only human intervention is to check that the firm really does want to re-order, just in case it is a seasonal line coming to the end of its life for that year.

Hard systems which deal with great complexity and a great deal of routine processing of information are areas in which IT thrives. It does the number-crunching chores, aggregates information, compares with performance criteria, and identifies potential trouble-spots (such as potential stock-outs). Production managers are computer literate as a result. IT helps them to do their work better by helping them to spot where they are falling behind, and by meshing vast quantities of detail so as to replace estimation with measurements of results.

The management of people

In most organizations, the production function has traditionally employed the largest share of the workforce. The increasing application of automation has diluted this effect considerably in some industries, though for many it seems likely to remain true for some time to come. Thus its managers still need to possess skills in dealing with people. That does not mean that they are able to keep everyone happy all of the time, but it does mean getting the right results from them. For much of the time people may feel harassed if not actually overwhelmed, but if they can be shown how to cope and then to excel, past struggles will take on a rosy glow in retrospect.

Skills with people do not always come easily, to production managers or anyone else. An engineer deals with hard systems and with materials and processes with known properties. People are not like that. Their performance can vary, they can consistently underachieve, and they can fail to show up altogether despite knowing that their contribution is vital. To someone who has been immersed in gears, motors, metals and hydraulics, these unpredictable creatures can be a real puzzle. One of three reactions seems to follow from that:

- surrender in confusion
- treat people like automata
- adapt.

The last is clearly the most desirable response, though many do seem to get stuck in the groove of the second option. It is the best qualified who leave, and the least qualified who stay in such situations, so that the organization becomes populated by the incompetent and the inexperienced.

In larger organizations trade unions will probably be represented. This is especially true in the public sector, where union membership is deeply entrenched. Indeed, most public-sector employees may not approach their managers over pay and conditions issues, since agree-ments exist which allow them to be the subject of discussion solely between management and unions.

The HR department may contain specialists in negotiation, but they cannot operate without a production manager to tell them what to negotiate about, within what constraints and with what objectives. Even then the production manager cannot leave the HR to it, but has to be in on the talks to help to present cases, rebut assertions, and provide the detailed knowledge of the production system and its workings without which no real negotiation could occur. Certainly, the trade union side will not talk until they have prepared in depth, so that the management side has to do the same.

This wide variety of challenges calls for a special breed of person. In addition to the skills needed to run the technical aspects of the pro-duction process and to manage the people, they also need to be alert to potential problems, quick to respond to them decisively, energetic to cover all of the ground, wily and resourceful, tough-minded and fit physically and mentally.

Production planning

The management of production starts from someone else's figures. Production plans cannot be made in isolation, but come about in response to customers' needs. It is usually the marketing depart-ment's sales forecast which triggers production planning.

Late arrival of sales forecasts can be a potent cause of war between a marketing and a production department. Production needs to know demand levels early since it will be in severe trouble if it sources too much, or has too little, raw material, creates more or less manpower capacity than is needed, or hires storage facilities that prove to be unwanted or, even worse, cancels those that it really does turn out to need. While the early, unofficial version of the forecast does enable some planning to be done, its basis is dangerous since great changes in volumes and timings can come about as a result of the approval process. Even that is not as bad as the situation in an organization where no information is passed until the (late) official forecast arrives. There the production people have to work on hunch and past experience to plan their operation and hope that, when the proper piece of paper does turn up, it bears some resemblance to their working assumptions.

A situation like that ought not to arise in the first place and certainly should not be allowed to persist. That two sets of people are forecasting independently is wasteful. Where it does happen there is something seriously wrong with the way the organization is run.

The converse problem can arise when the marketing department is able to forecast in time and the production plan is unveiled to schedule, but the production department cannot make what has been ordered. There is some excuse in highly sensitive production processes with high failure rates, or where development is proceeding in hand with production, but none where the technology is simpler.

Once a sales forecast has been obtained by some means, legitimate or unorthodox, the production department can start its own plan-ning. It will look at current stocks to see first if anything at all needs to be made. In the case of some products it will not, for every firm has excess stocks of one product at least at some time or another. Sub-tracting stocks from demand shows how much needs to be made and when.

The next step is to look at stocks of components and materials to see if they will last. If more needs to be ordered it is unlikely to be available by return, but a lead-time has to be allowed for. Certain suppliers may be unreliable, and extra stock has to be held in case they deliver late. Then the capacity of the various departments of the factory will be looked at.

It is then that the problems are exposed. The production planner knows that 200 machines need to be made next month, the assembly shop can put together 50 a week, but two of the components will not be available until week 3: what does he or she do? The usual answer is to try all the internal juggling possible and, if that fails, to lean on the supplier for at least a few items to be made early. If that does not work, the marketing people have to be told either to revise their delivery date requirements or accept that promises will be broken. If they will not play, the last resort is to incur extra cost via extra shifts or the employment of casual staff from the third week onwards, or to subcontract some of the work to an outside firm. It rarely pays to pose that choice to sales staff, for their orientation towards customer service at almost any cost decides the question. Marketing people are supposed to be responsible for profit as well as sales volume, and their judgement ought therefore to be less one-sided. Ideally, they will take a balanced view of where the firm's best interest lies, whether in dropping today's profit to hold the customer or facing down the possible wrath of the customer at late delivery in order to preserve profit levels.

It is often very difficult indeed for production people to accommodate alterations to plans that have been laid weeks or months in advance. If this month's forecast of sales for each of the next six months is wildly different from its predecessor, the production people may well tear their hair out. If next month's restores the cuts made this month they will tear out the marketing people's hair as well. Yet that sort of situation is far from unknown. It can easily come about through, for instance, evidence of a few major customers' inter-est not coming out until later than expected, and the delay being interpreted as apathy. The apportioning of blame then starts – but who is to blame in a situation like that? Optimism over their inten-tions would have been misplaced, and the relationships could have become strained if the salespeople had chased more strenuously. It is unfortunate, but it just has to be accepted and dealt with by the pro-duction planner.

Production management principles

The basic principle underlying production management is that a con-stant level of production is the easiest to manage and results in the cheapest output. Changes in the amount produced cause problems and hence expense.

Figures 6.1, 6.2 and 6.3 show how levels of output can vary. Steady output is the cheapest to produce, and rising and falling output the most expensive. If demand from different seasons can be overlaid (for instance, air-conditioners and heaters), it can sometimes produce a near-perfect overall total quantity of production.

This has already been rehearsed as a reason for friction between production and marketing people. Marketing responds to the customers' needs, and this causes demand to vary over time. The

Managing production of goods and services

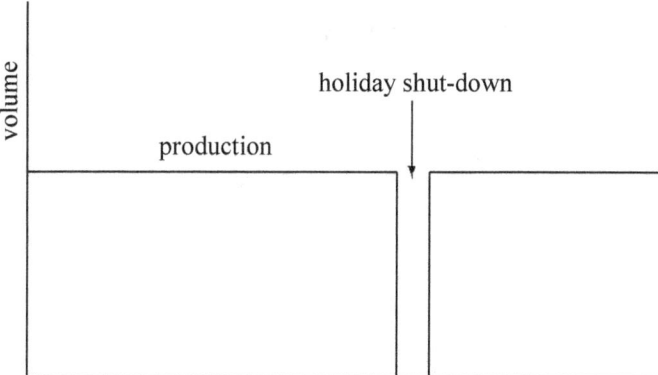

Figure 6.1 *The production manager's ideal pattern of production: steady output all year long*

corresponding messages are passed to production, who can become deeply frustrated. Many a production manager becomes prema-turely old through the effort to get marketing people to understand the realities of running a factory.

Marketing people ought to realize that constant chopping and changing of production schedules hits profits. They should also realize that large seasonal fluctuations raise costs. The marketing department should therefore pass, and keep to, three resolutions:

1. Not to change the level of production called for any more than is absolutely essential; to give plenty of warning when it has to be changed; and, when they cannot give enough warning, to ex-plain why;
2. To do everything they can to minimize seasonality;
3. To develop markets with a seasonal pattern which runs counter to the present one.

The first calls for a mixture of prudence and good manners. The second and third are common sense. If the present business peaks in the summer and falls away in the winter, products which answer winter needs ought to be developed. At the very least, techniques should be used to shift as much demand as possible out of the peak period. A major toy company which had access to cheap money from its American parent used these funds to allow dealers to take in stocks early but pay at the normal time. By carrying stocks when the trade wisdom said it was wrong, the dealers sold a lot more; and the

The first-time manager

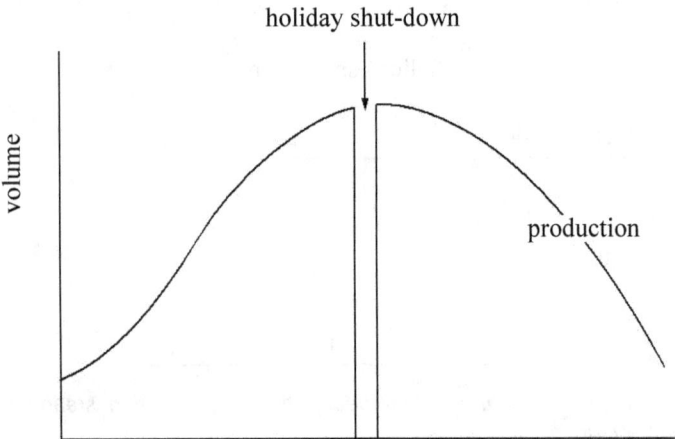

Figure 6.2 *The production manager's nightmare: production rising and falling with the season*

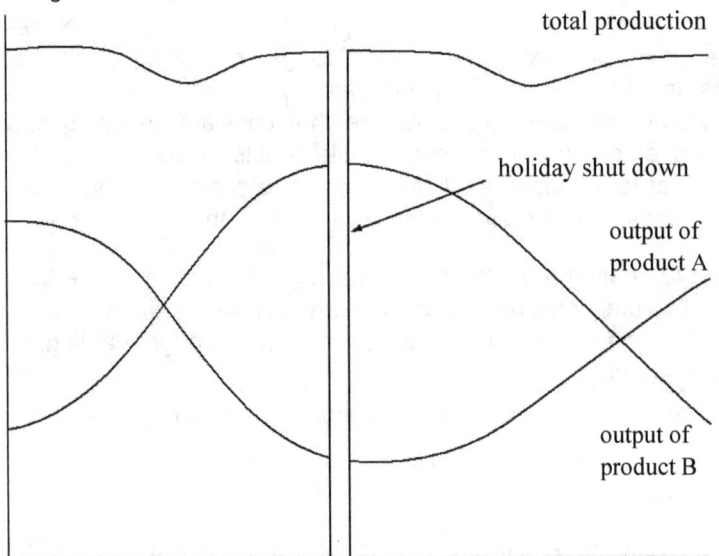

Figure 6.3 *The production manager's acceptable seasonal compromise: total production roughly level*

manufacturer found that he was selling half of his output in each half of the year, said to be an impossibility in the toy trade at that time.

In some industries 24-hour, seven-day production is the norm: some financial services operations (such as telephone banking), steel works and other continuous process industries are obvious

Managing production of goods and services

examples. In others, production stops at weekends and for holidays, but is continuous at other times. In many industries that intensity of use of assets is unknown. Some products have, by their very nature, to be made in batches, perhaps because their raw materials are avail-able only at certain times of the year, or because one day's production satisfies a week's needs, or for some other reason. In these cases it is important for the batch made to be neither too big nor too small. Too big, and it will incur costs of carrying the excess stock; too small and it will be less economical to make. The balancing act between these two considerations has been considered deeply by operations analysts, for the effect on profits of getting it wrong too often can be disastrous. The usual illustration of the calculation appears in Figure 6.4.

The economic batch size is that size of batch which coincides with the lowest total cost per unit. The total cost is, of course, the total of

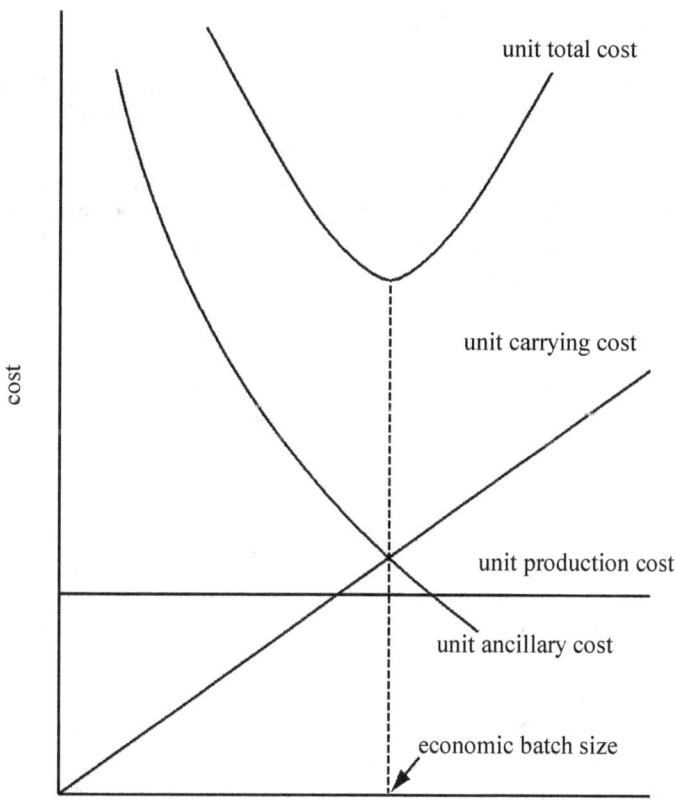

Figure 6.4 *Economic batch size*

the three costs: production, ancillary and carrying. Production cost is usually known to an organization, since it is such a basic item of information. Ancillary costs are those which arise from the creation of the order: paperwork, buying and clerical time, and the cost of setting up machinery. Carrying costs are those associated with holding and handling stocks: warehousing and internal transport in the main.

The cost of setting up machines, to take just one element of ancil-lary costs, is usually more or less fixed, whatever the batch size, within normal limits. Thus it costs less per unit the larger the batch is. By contrast, the cost of carrying each item of stock usually rises as the quantity increases: a few can be tucked away in a spare corner, incur-ring little in the way of handling and storage cost, but a larger quan-tity may necessitate extra transport, rented outside warehousing and a lot more handling. That, in turn, implies further costs arising from losses and damage.

The important issue highlighted by Figure 6.4 is no single one of these costs but their total. The whole point of the exercise is to arrive at it. In general, the unit cost is high if either a few or a lot are made, and at its lowest somewhere between the extremes. The point at which it is lowest dictates the ideal size of batch to make. The number actually made may be adjusted slightly to take account of practicalities: using up old raw materials, for instance, or making some extras to allow for rejects.

Managing the production process

Once the plan has been drawn up, someone has to put it into practice. That part of the job may involve scrapping much of an earlier plan. To do that without a descent into chaos it is essential to know where-abouts on the previous plan one is. To change from an unknown position to one which you rapidly lose sight of is an excellent route to disaster. Incredibly, there really do exist organizations which operate on that principle, but they rarely survive without a major change for very long.

To have control all of the time on all fronts, the production manager uses a variety of systems to record events and compare them with the plan. The events concern the timing and the quantity of movements of materials from goods-inwards stores through to the finished goods warehouse. The flows are summarized in Figure 6.5.

Managing production of goods and services

Clearly, this is a very simple summary of a very complex picture. Production managers strive constantly to ensure that it does not become confused. Many of the generalized boxes in the diagram can be broken down into further sub-sections. To illustrate that point, the rejects from the production process have been split into further divisions. They could have been broken down still more, to show the fate of rejects bought in from subcontractors, which will almost certainly be different from those generated by the firm's unaided efforts.

It is most unlikely that anyone will have drawn up a precise plan which embraces all these systems throughout the organization. However, there will be in the minds of people working in each section a clear picture of how their own part works and how it relates to others with which it interacts. Where no formal system exists, the people concerned will invent their own.

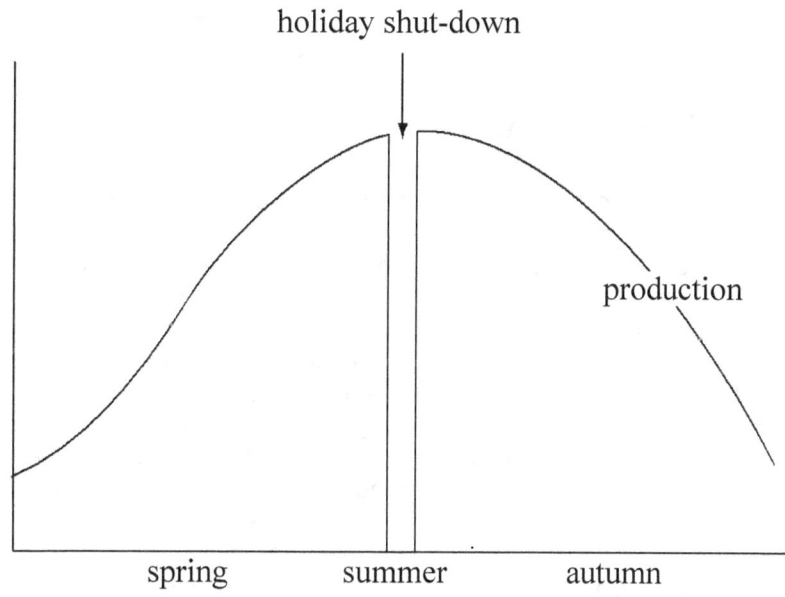

Figure 6.5 *Production flows summarized*

Individual ingenuity and initiative are not to be discouraged as a rule. As long as the home-made systems work towards the aims of the production department they should be used. The trouble with control systems which are devised informally and locally is that they can be fine for present staff and current conditions, but incapable of adaptation to meet changed requirements and conditions. Still less can they mesh with other informal systems in parallel, upstream or downstream sections. Thus the organization which allows its systems to grow informally is under a great threat which is com-pletely invisible. The organization runs smoothly and under control today but, as soon as new demands are placed upon it, it is unable to deal with them. The new situation requires a quick response, so man-agers call for information fast. Because that question had never been anticipated, the answer simply cannot be supplied in the form which the question requires. If a manager, applying the wider vision expected, had designed the system rather than just letting it grow, the chances are that it would have taken into account many more factors, and thus would be better able to serve the organization's true needs.

Group technology

During the last century there were remarkable advances in the way in which production was organized. One of the most important was the introduction of group technology (GT). While it was developed for engineering applications, GT has been used successfully in service industries.

Research had shown that the vast majority of production batches in engineering shops was for very small quantities. Yet all produc-tion areas were set up in such a way as to be ideally organized for long runs. The result was that, in some cases, as much time was being spent setting machines for a new run as was spent on the run itself. Since machines cost money whether they are working or not, this revealed a substantial area of waste. If a way could be found of reduc-ing set-up time and improving scheduling so as to lower the number of re-sets required to deal with different runs, considerable savings would be made. GT supplied just this.

GT works by, first, classifying the factory's products into 'families' with similar characteristics. The characteristics are merged into a the-oretical *composite component*, which possesses all the family's charac-teristics but which itself does not exist. The machines necessary to produce the composite component are then grouped together on the factory floor. Thus all the machines which produce the characteristics of the family are in one place. Those machines are then set up to make the composite component, so that all the characteristics are available to be made. What is actually made is then determined by which pro-cesses are *left out*.

By these means startling improvements in machine productivity of 50 per cent and more were claimed, even in factories which, by general consent, were efficiently run. The benefits did not stop there: firms are known to have reduced delivery times by two-thirds and stocks by one-third.

The basic principle of GT, that of setting up the production area to make the composite component, and then bypassing certain pro-cesses to get what you want, is an interesting inversion of the conven-tional approach.

Work study

Work study involves systematically observing and analysing how people perform their jobs. It is most often applied to production workers because of the ease of measuring what they do, and because that is what the technique was developed for in the first place. It has a bad name for being a means of making people work unreasonably hard, but applied properly it reduces waste of materials and effort, and raises output and quality.

Work study comprises two primary branches: method study and work measurement.

Method study people use the acronym SREDIM to describe what they do:

1. **S**elect the task which will be studied
2. **R**ecord how it is undertaken
3. **E**xamine the facts recorded
4. **D**evelop a better method
5. **I**nstall the new method
6. **M**aintain the new practice.

Work measurement is a close relative, taking the same course up to stage 3. Its fourth stage is to measure the time which the task takes. It is concerned specifically with time, so it then goes on to set out times that the new method should take. It often applies the technique of *activity sampling* – basically, noting at fixed intervals what is happening and generalizing from that sample of observations. It can be surprisingly illuminating, and overcomes many of the problems associated with following people with a stopwatch.

The two techniques together are very powerful. Method study looks at how the job is done, work measurement at how long it takes. Both go into enormous detail and have a variety of approaches asso-ciated with them. The main assumptions underlying work study are:

- almost certainly people are working inefficiently;
- without a critical and disciplined examination no improvement is likely to come about;
- the outside expert asking fundamental questions is the most powerful agent of change ever invented.

Stock control

Organizations need to control their stocks for these reasons:

- to make sure that they have enough of each item in the right place when it is needed;
- to ensure that they are carrying no more stock than is necessary;
- to trigger the decision to re-order at the right time;
- to ensure that products to be discontinued are run down in an or-derly way;
- to enable reconciliation between what is known to have been bought and used with what is actually in stock.

In a nutshell, the main functions of stock control are to keep the factory running and to keep as little money and space tied up as possible.

Control is applied to all forms in which stock is held, whether as raw materials or finished goods. The basic process follows this simple pattern:

What we started the period with	100
What we got in during the period	200 +
Total available during the period	300

What we used during the period   250 –
Left over at the end of the period   50

The figure in the last line becomes the starting figure for the next period, of course, and the whole calculation can thus go on to infinity. It will be done for all items of any significance, whether expressed in terms of value or importance to the production process.

To move from recording stock movements to a system of full stock control it is necessary to add two further elements. They are time, and target levels. Recording what happened in the past is useful in a number of ways, but it does not involve looking forward. Stock control takes forecasts for the sales of products, examines present stocks and those which are on order, allows for delays between ordering and receiving the goods, and works out when orders need to be placed and how large they should be. It is then up to the pur-chasing department to ensure that these orders are placed and exe-cuted. There needs to be close liaison between the functions of stock control and purchasing, to ensure that changes to lead-times are com-municated, to allow stock control to take account of delivery delays, and to tell purchasing when delivery promises have not been kept. In such circumstances, the production planners need to become involved. They may need to switch from making products whose components will be in short supply to those for which all the parts are available, and then to switch back when the missing items are deliv-ered. The rule of thumb is that the shorter the warning, the greater the disruption and cost involved in changing over.

The standard illustration of the stock control process is in Figure 6.6. When dealing with stock in general, the quantity on the ware-house floor is not necessarily the most useful piece of information to managers. Above all they need to know the 'free' stock figure, the amount which is left after current commitments have been met.

Many a first-time manager has learned this the hard way. Someone asks if there is enough stock to ship 1000 boxes to Thackeray's, who have just been on the telephone. He takes a quick look at the ware-house (the staff are all away at tea), sees 4000 there, and answers 'yes'. He did not know that 3800 of them were about to be shipped to Dickens's, a far more important customer who ordered a month ago. Such an experience both induces stress in sales managers and proves the first-time manager's lack of vision, and is not recommended.

Stock control is also concerned with what happened to the stocks which the organization has bought. That involves much paperwork

The first-time manager

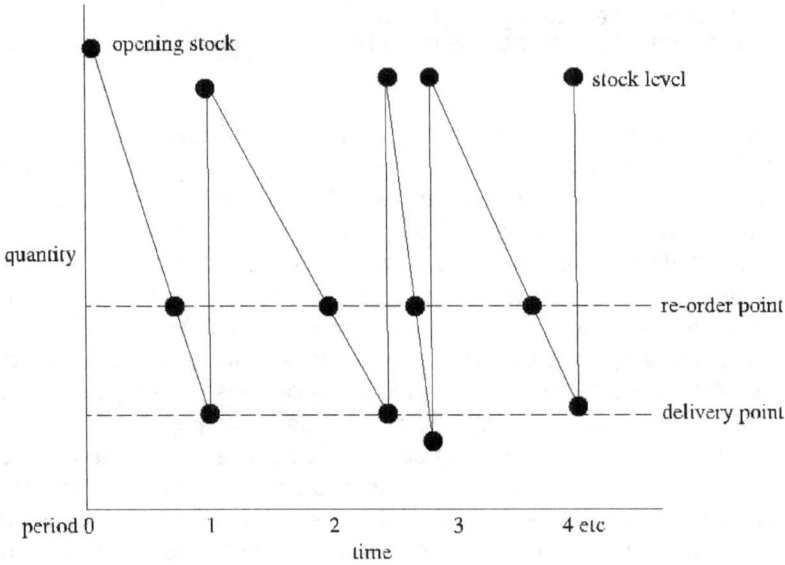

Figure 6.6 *Stock control chart*

and a close relationship with accountants. The Forces have an adage: nothing moves without a piece of paper. It ought to be stuck to rigidly by all staff concerned with the stewardship and movement of stock. The stock is not their property yet it is their responsibility; if any goes missing, they cannot shrug their shoulders but must account for it. If they are unable to, suspicion of either incompetence or dishonesty or both will fall on them. Competence and honesty being essential to their remaining employed, they ensure that they can account clearly for everything in their care. It is important that the first-time manager recognizes this, and works within the general rules for maintaining stock records as well as protecting his or her own back as far as any stock for which he is responsible is concerned.

In the complexity of a large organization it seems that if one or two items go astray they will not really be missed. That is true, as far as it goes. Few stocktakers ever manage to agree the stock records with what they can actually count. That is no excuse for making the dis-crepancy worse. So many people abuse the system that the first-time manager wins friends if he goes out of his way to show respect for it and the people who have to work it.

Just-in-time (JIT)

Such is the cost of holding and handling stocks of materials that some radicals began to ask why it was necessary at all. The answer was, clearly, that suppliers could not be relied on, and that sales forecasts are often inaccurate too. In some industries it is possible to do something about forecasting systems. In some circumstances it can be more expensive to hold a buffer stock of materials against a rainy day that rarely comes than to accept the cost of occasional stock-outs. The greatest scope for improvement might lie in suppliers' performances, they thought. If early, firm orders could be given, if suppliers could be introduced to management techniques which allow late changes to production plans, and if heavy penalties could be imposed in the case of late delivery, something could be done in that area too. From these ideas was born the notion of JIT, of receiving deliveries minutes before they are needed in the factory and doing away with stocks of the most frequently used items altogether.

One of the most visible early exponents of this idea were the supermarkets. Tired of building new shops with large store-rooms, they decided to make over virtually all of their floor-space to selling. Thus their sales and profits improved, and with them the levels of customer service they could achieve: a wider range of goods could be offered in the extra space. It meant that, instead of taking in deliveries several times a week, deliveries had to be made to the larger stores several times a day. It demanded a sophisticated system for record-ing sales and stocks so as to create quick re-ordering as goods sold out of the shops. It has thus led to a shift of responsibility for stock holding from supermarkets to their suppliers, one that their buying power has enabled them to enforce.

Purchasing and procurement

The function of getting the organization's requirements bought in a disciplined way and at least cost is obviously important. In some organizations it does no more than place orders and chase for deliv-eries, but it ought to be more powerful than that.

The first decision which an organization needs to take is who is permitted to place orders. Can anyone buy what is needed, or are all orders to be channelled through one person? In most organizations a little of each applies. Major items and those bought in large quantities are purchased centrally. Less significant items and some with special characteristics are bought locally. In both cases a common procedure should apply so that the order can be tied up with delivery note and invoice in due course. Under such a system there is no possibility of paying for the same item twice, or for items which were not delivered or not ordered in the first place. Those things do happen in poorly regulated organizations.

A good buying department will:

- look at proposed suppliers in great detail and in a detached and disciplined way, and assess them ('vendor rating');
- find and use sources of supply at least total cost to the organiza-tion (least prime cost may turn out most expensive in the long run); the Internet can spread the search worldwide;
- ensure that delivery does take place to time, and warn all concerned where this fails;
- advise on prices, availability and delivery times;
- verify invoices;
- develop and enforce terms and conditions of purchase;
- assist operating managers in all dealings with suppliers.

To some, this list – and particularly the last item – may make it look as if the buying department is trying to extend its influence for no good reason. In fact there are all sorts of sound arguments for having the technical and specialist people's dealings with suppliers checked by a professional who has sound knowledge of the law governing the buying and selling of goods. There is many a specialist, eager to press ahead with a project, who has unwittingly established an open-ended commitment to a supplier. A supplier who is naive or unscru-pulous may let that situation run until a sizeable bill has mounted up, which they have a well-documented right to collect.

Quality control and quality assurance

The control of quality is an area carrying huge implications for internal costs and external relations. If customers are to be happy with the product it must perform to the specification agreed or assumed, for at least as long as is acceptable. Quality control (QC) is therefore con-cerned with two related issues: quality (the extent to which the product is fit for its purpose) and reliability (the extent of its ability to continue to work to the quality standard).

Thus the word 'quality' has a special and specific meaning in industry. In everyday speech, high quality is more or less undefinable and is loosely associated with luxury goods. The term is used here in its special, industrial sense.

Quality breaks down into two further divisions: quality of design (the extent to which the design itself achieves the purpose) and quality of conformance (the closeness with which the output resembles the design).

Raising quality costs money by increasing internal costs. It may also save money, by lowering the tangible and intangible cost of dealing with customers. It can also make money, by (for instance) gaining for the product a reputation which creates extra sales. The lowest quality is cheapest to make, but fetches a low price and attracts many complaints, so it is rarely profitable. The highest quality achievable costs a vast amount to accomplish, but customers might be reluctant to pay for it so it, too, is not profitable. Somewhere between the two lies a point where a little less quality fetches a rather lower price, and a little more quality fetches only a slightly higher price. In other words, the return on the investment in quality is at its highest.

QC does not aim to eliminate customer complaints, but to control them down to a predetermined level at which supplier and customer can stand the damage. The idea of what limits are acceptable varies from product to product. If a lettuce is less crisp than expected, the customer shrugs his shoulders and resolves to choose more carefully next time. If a turbine blade from a jet engine lacks the right degree of crispness it could cause the deaths of hundreds of people. Even so, the jet engine manufacturers know that they can never eliminate error; they dedicate themselves to holding it down to a stupendously low level.

The extent of the precautions taken does sound as if they are aimed at error elimination, but these engineers are not arrogant and they are realists. The manufacturer keeps records of the sources of every one of the thousands of components used in each engine. The suppliers keep similar records, all the way back to the steel mill which made the material from which the turbine blade was created. This means that if a fault is discovered in one component in one of the engines in a Jumbo in Singapore, all the aircraft from around the world with engines containing components from the same batch can be grounded immediately for investigation. Many lives may have been saved by this system, which justifies its great cost.

Unfortunately, the world is full of organizations that maintain standards of quality which are far higher than is appropriate. This is not an argument for shoddy goods but a plea for the reduction of waste and thus of cost. Unnecessary over-specification costs every-one money and depletes scarce resources wastefully.

Excess quality often stems from engineers' and production peo-ple's professional pride. The same can apply to innovations in prod-ucts, which may be quite unnecessary from a marketing point of view, and can even add to unreliability. It is a fact that reliability stems from the use of simple designs with the fewest possible compo-nents and proven manufacturing methods. Components which are likely to fail can be double or treble banked, and the design can see to it that failure leads to safety (the vehicle's throttle drops to tickover when the cable snaps, rather than flying up to full power).

Testing is important in establishing reliability. What is usually found is that failures are relatively common in the early and late stages of a product's life. At the beginning the failures owing to faulty assembly or substandard components show up; at the end it is wearing out. Early failure is infuriating to the customer and embar-rassing to the supplier, so that many firms run in their products before delivery. Then most of the early failures occur before delivery and red faces are saved all round.

Many firms which are in a powerful position in relation to suppli-ers buy on the basis that goods will be accepted only if a certain pro-portion of a sample taken from each delivery passes a quality test. If too many of that sample are faulty, the entire consignment is returned. Such a deal sharpens suppliers' attitudes wonderfully.

Mention of sampling reintroduces the topic of statistics. They are the basis of the quality controller's basic tool, the QC chart, shown in Figure 6.7. This is a more detailed version of the one which appeared in general form in Figure 4.7. The samples taken are strictly of the predetermined number and at exactly the correct times. They are measured, and their mean plotted on the chart. If the reading strays into a warning area, further samples are taken to check on the first sample's reliability. If it moves into the action area, the machine is stopped and reset.

Levels for action and warning are calculated statistically (by *standard errors*, for anyone who is interested). This application of statisti-cal techniques is extremely useful in cutting the cost of inspection within a predetermined level of risk that the sample taken might not be representative.

Quality assurance (QA) is a quite different approach. It starts with

Managing production of goods and services

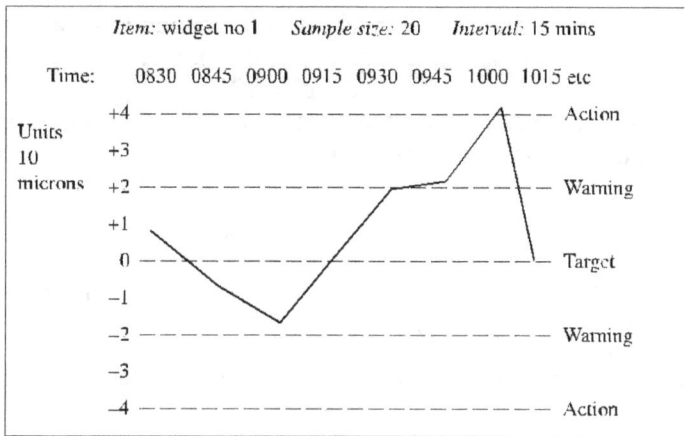

Figure 6.7 *Quality control chart in detail*

the idea that quality control is foolish: it allows mistakes and then sets a police force to spot them. Why not eliminate them in the first place, doing away with the need for inspection altogether? QA depends on training the staff to understand the importance of quality and giving them the time and means to supply it, encouraging them to be self-checking.

Value analysis

Value analysis (VA) is a close relation of QC. QC concerns itself with the design's achievement of its purpose and the closeness of the fin-ished product to its design. VA looks at function, that is to say at the 'purpose' to which QC relates.

VA does not start by looking at what is being done now. Its interest is in the function which the product is intended to perform, in order to see if that function can be performed more cost-effectively than by the present method. Usually a product performs more than one func-tion, but there is generally a single purpose which stands out clearly as the main reason for its existence. Attention is paid to that in the first place. A very precise statement of function is made, pared down to the minimum. Far from being an exercise in pedantry it is meant to result in the clearest and most economical statement of what the product is for.

From that statement the value analyst proceeds to look at other ways in which the same function could be achieved, in the hope that one will come up which is more cost-effective.

It is worth spending a moment to consider what is meant by the term 'value'. Value is a concept which can be thought of in three ways:

Exchange value: what a buyer will pay for a product;

Use value: what the buyer will pay for the practical function which the product carries out;

Esteem value: the extra which the buyer will pay over and above the use value.

It is readily seen that the first is the total of the other two. The way in which they combine can vary dramatically. Consider two cars; one a Mercedes, the other a Ford. The use value of each is more or less iden-tical, but the esteem value of one is far higher than that of the other. Thus the exchange values are markedly different. The same exercise can be conducted in every field in which products and services are bought and sold.

So far it may have sounded as if the value analyst is merely a theo-rist. Not so. VA's most frequent contribution comes via design improvements within products, stimulated by asking of each internal function:

- Does this have to be done at all?
- If so, must it be done this way?
- Is there a better way?

Rarely is VA a solo performance. It can be started by one person but it requires the involvement of people from production, marketing, accounting and design departments, and sometimes even outside suppliers.

Variety reduction

A good way of increasing costs is to make a wider variety of components or finished products than is actually necessary. Some sales departments and the weaker marketing department will encourage their production colleagues to make virtually a different product for each customer. Every change in production incurs cost, and changes should therefore be kept to a minimum.

The problem is that any range of products has a tendency to grow in number. Therefore determination is needed to restrict growth to what is demonstrably desirable. As with finished products so with their components. Common components should be used as much as possible to create the variations in output; it can be difficult to perform the balancing act between satisfying the different needs of a variety of market segments while minimizing variety in manufacturing.

One of the best examples of that last point is a leading car manufac-turer. In Europe it offers over 100 varieties of cars from fewer than a dozen bodyshells and engine blocks.

The same principle is evident in financial services. A standard set of covers for all sorts of risks is combined into a simple insurance policy. This is customized in the call centre for a particular client by eliminating or modifying the elements until the customer feels they have exactly the cover they need.

Premises location

The choice of where the office, laboratory, call centre, warehouse or factory should be put is made in the light of a large number of factors, uniquely combined for each industry, each organization within it and each location within an organization.

Usually the first consideration is whether or not to expand the existing facility. Labour is certainly a crucial determinant for many organizations. Raw numbers of unemployed are not enough, otherwise organizations would be flocking to the worst blackspots. Skills and the capacity to learn, with a supporting educational infrastructure, are recognized increasingly as being of prime importance.

Clearly an organization must investigate factors other than grants. Among them are housing, schools and the general environment. If these are not attractive to key staff the chances are that they will decline to move, wrecking – or at least severely damaging – the entire exercise. From the point of view of the organization's operations, it needs to know about the passenger and freight transport service, suppliers, telecoms system capacity, sites with the right characteristics, and the attitude of the local authority regime. In special cases there might be political and safety considerations, not to mention accessibility to the MD's home, and whether this location fits in with the organization's other sites and its markets.

Usually one of the most influential factors is the cost of getting materials in, and finished goods out to customers. Unlike so many of the other factors it lends itself to numerical analysis. There are some very clever computer programs which will guide a firm to pick the best location for its operations.

Premises design and layout

The last thing anyone designing a new facility should do is to think what it ought to look like from the outside. The floor layout should be designed first, and in meticulous detail. Only when everyone is quite sure that the layout will work should any thought be given to putting walls and a roof over it. That is a slight exaggeration, for people will enquire about economical roofing spans before designing layouts which can be built over only at prodigious cost. It is also a statement of an ideal for most organizations, since they have somehow to fit their operations into an existing building. Here compromises will be needed, but there is usually more than one building to choose from. The trick is to choose the building which enforces fewest compro-mises and confines them to unimportant matters. Once the building has been chosen you are more or less stuck with it, so it is important to get as close to the ideal as possible. Indeed, when organizations are putting up buildings for their own particular needs they often create something which is over-specified. That is because they have an eye to the future. The commissioning organization may place only light loadings on floors, but does not specify that the building should meet just their own needs. They build to more exacting standards because if their policy, products or processes change, they do not want to undertake costly and inconvenient alterations. If the worst happens and they need to sell the building quickly, a general-purpose build-ing should be more in demand than one with only a specialized application.

It is easy to underestimate the space which will be required by not allowing enough for unused space. The gaps between desks or machines may look great, but when people, work-in-progress and materials are moving around they can prove inadequate. Increased height in a building raises not only the construction cost, but also that of keeping the building lit and heated. The relation between these matters and safety is obvious, but there are other effects which justify the use of special advisers. For example, a lighting tube flashes imperceptibly at a speed so fast that it looks like a steady source of light. If it does so at the same speed as a piece of machinery rotates, it can set up a stroboscopic effect which makes the machine appear to be stationary. Someone puts a hand on the moving part, and there is a horrible accident.

The availability of services within the building also deserves foresight. Requirements will change, and provision made today for future access to electricity, water, gas, telephone and data circuits and so forth will be far cheaper and more convenient than breaking into them afresh at some later date. That point – forethought and pro-vision for the future – applies to every aspect of the building's design. Otherwise the fixed requirements for waste disposal, vehicle turning areas and access points may be so inflexible and costly to change as to scupper future plans for development.

Within the building the layout is the single most important consideration. Poor layout leads to inefficient communication, and even to complete confusion. The first rule is to have a one-way system. Pro-duction may start at one end of the building, flow straight on and eventually emerge from the other end, having turned neither left nor right. Or it might start in one corner, run all round the building in a curve, and out at the preceding corner. It could also mix these approaches, but as long as it flows in one direction only it follows the first principle.

The second principle is that the route should be as short as possi-ble. The least distance between machines (as long as it is safe), and the less handling, the better. In this context it ought to be remembered that premises exist in three dimensions: there is air space which can be used as well as floor area. Indeed, many a consultant has saved a client the cost of an expensive extension by making better use of the height of the existing building.

Next the question of flexibility is considered in relation to future changes. Clearly, equipment should not be sited so close to walls that it cannot be maintained properly, or so as to obscure service points, safety exits and so on.

Safety of people is very important, and comfort is closely related to it. To aid it, gangways should be wide enough for emergency equip-ment to pass, and clearly indicated on the floor. They should never be obstructed. Rules about smoking should be explicit and understood by all: many organizations allocate a special area to which smokers must go before lighting up. That is not a means of oppression, but a sensible precaution against a known fire risk and a way of protecting the health of others. Advice on safety matters in general is freely available from the officials of the Health and Safety Executive and fire and building regulations departments. Like most officials, they would prefer to get the problems ironed out at the planning stage, rather than having to take enforcement action against a dangerous installation.

Make or buy?

Often a management is faced with having to decide whether to buy in parts and components for their range of products – or even a com-plete piece of equipment – or make their own. The criteria are usually:

- the degree to which current capacity is utilized;
- relative costs;
- strategic importance to the organization;
- quality performance of vendors versus own production;
- vendor reliability.

If the premises are half-empty and the product is one which it could make, the decision almost makes itself. That would probably apply even where the made-in cost was higher than the bought-in price, because the internal cost will include an element for overheads which will otherwise go unrecovered.

Subcontractors can be unreliable in delivery times and in quality. Many a firm was set up on the assumption that it would buy in made parts and confine itself to assembly, but was forced by suppliers' poor performance to make the parts itself. Even where the policy is to buy in, a firm will sometimes make a part of its requirements itself for strategic reasons. If lack of the part could halt production altogether it is quite usual to source it from more than one supplier, including in-house manufacture, so that a fire, strike or other mishap at one will not close down the organization's entire production.

Research and development (R&D), and new products

Production people are always influenced by R&D matters, and are sometimes responsible for them. R&D covers a number of basic functions, the main ones being the improvement of existing products and methods and the development of new. R&D is therefore rarely conducted in a vacuum, but involves input from departments responsi-ble for production, marketing and also accounting and others. Marketing have to be happy that changed specifications will at least not harm customers' and users' interests. Accountants and work-study people want to ensure that any expected savings will not be illusory. Buyers will advise on availability and get quotations for any new parts and materials. Employees will need to be told about the change and why it is necessary, and trainers will have to ensure that people understand any new methods. In some situations the law could even be involved, if methods or materials are hazardous. Insurers and patent experts may be consulted, new maintenance schedules created, and many more people required to contribute.

The reasons for R&D projects can be diverse. They can stem from desperation at falling sales of existing products, from caution which dictates the spreading of risk, from ambition to beat competitors and many more reasons – including the desire to exploit the unexpected opportunity which luckily presents itself.

One area which industry often overlooks is the output of the academic research world. Theses, papers and research reports are pouring out in a vast and growing stream. In the academic culture, information is for publishing almost irrespective of its commercial worth, although that altruism is coming under increasing pressure as funding fails to grow at the rate of spending. Anyone in the organiza-tional world will find it worthwhile to search the literature for work related to his own field of interest. It can be painstaking and plodding work, but the help of an academic librarian cuts it down appreciably.

Whatever the way in which R&D is organized it is vital that it serves the needs of both production and marketing departments: marketing for new products and improvements, production for better methods and materials.

Maintenance

Plant and buildings have to be maintained or their useful lives are considerably shortened. Moreover, they may become dangerous if neglected.

Maintenance takes two forms: routine maintenance for protective reasons and the emergency repair after a failure. The former is planned for and undertaken in an orderly way to fit in with times when machines are normally idle. The latter is, by definition, unexpected. Nevertheless provision has to be made for it.

As with other production matters, cost is an important aspect. It is foolish to look at the cost of maintenance in isolation. Rather, the whole-life cost of equipment should be considered, which includes the cost of maintenance as well as that of purchase. Once it has been decided which machine to buy, the cost of maintenance to the neces-sary standard is merely a consequence of that decision and not an independent issue.

To be sure that maintenance is being conducted to schedule, each piece of equipment should have a log in which all maintenance, breakdowns and usage are recorded. Logs should be inspected regu-larly by the manager responsible, who should also carry out spot checks to see that what is said to have been done has actually been done.

Where sudden failure occurs the production department has to decide whether or not to halt production completely, or whether the unserviceable machine can simply be bypassed while the shift is completed. As soon as it is available to them, the maintenance team descends on it and keeps on working until it is put right. The cost of paying them to work round the clock may be high, but it is usually a lot less than keeping an entire factory or department idle during working hours. For that reason the contracts of employment of main-tenance people usually require flexible working. Some firms do not keep their own maintenance team, or they restrict it to particular activities. They use outside specialists to make repairs, often from their equipment suppliers. Whether or not that is more economical over a year than keeping an in-house team is usually decided by the number of breakdowns, the length of time each repair takes, the cost of idle time, and the repair gang's response-time, cost and general reliability. This is especially true of IT systems, where the supply of hardware, software and maintenance is often contracted out.

The law

The law affects the production department in many ways. The two areas of greatest concern to the operating manager are to do with health and safety and with the protection of employees' rights. Thus emphasis is often placed on production people understanding their duty to work in a safe manner, and on production managers – super-visors included – realizing that defined procedures have to be fol-lowed if people misbehave; they cannot just be fired at will.

Where it is involved with buying, the production department is concerned with the law of contract. The same body of law affects what it provides for the customers to buy. In addition, if it behaves in an actionably negligent way the production department places at risk the funds and reputation of the entire organization.

Some people regard the law as a nuisance which limits their right to behave as they wish. That attitude contains the seeds of the very cause of the law's intervention in the first place. The first Factory Acts were brought about solely by the sense of outrage felt by decent people at the behaviour of Victorian manufacturers. The latter defended their actions in a number of ways, including the argument that, if people did not like the conditions, they could go elsewhere. In other words, the factory owner had a perfect right to behave abominably and it was up to the staff to vote with their feet if they objected. More recently, controls on polluting effluents have been introduced for one reason only: that manufacturers thought that they had a perfect right to dump their muck on other people's doorsteps. Thus, if the organization does not want the law to interfere with its opera-tions it ought to make sure that it is not behaving offensively. Because they fear that legislation could prove inflexible and unpleasant to contend with, many industries have set up self-policing arrange-ments. These generally comprise a voluntary code of conduct and a disciplinary system for dealing with offenders. Where they are effec-tive, most people within and outside the industry would agree that they are preferable to getting Parliament involved. Nevertheless, the lawmakers must never lose sight of the fact that it is the threat of leg-islation that keeps these arrangements effective.

The first-time manager

Key points and tips

- Good production managers usually come up through a hard systems environment and are able to make the transition to managing people as well.
- Ideally, levels of production will be constant throughout the year.
- Production runs on quantification, timing and location – learning how many, when and where.
- All managers can usefully employ the methodical ways of seeking improvements that originated in production settings.

seven

Finance and Accounting

To many outsiders the art and science of accountancy is a closed book. Two factors may be responsible for most of this effect: the increasing complexity of the legal requirements for disclosure and taxation, and the great skill with which the accountancy profession has limited entry to its ranks. This has been done in part by progres-sively raising the educational requirements for acceptance into training, which may be no bad thing. There are two obvious conse-quences of the resulting shortage of fully trained accountants: sala-ries are ever increasing, and more and more people are training via less conventional methods.

Along with the rise in demand for accountants, membership of the leading institutes is growing. The three main ones are the Institute of Chartered Accountants, the most prestige-laden body of them all; the Chartered Institute of Public Finance and Accountancy, which specializes in issues of public-sector accounting; and the Chartered Institute of Management Accountants. Management accounting, or cost accounting as it used to be called before it extended its influence beyond the costing arena, deals with the day-to-day task of keeping the organization going, part of which involves forecasting. Together with the company secretary (served by the Chartered Institute of Secretaries and Administrators) they cover the whole spectrum of the organization's financial and legal concerns.

What accountants are for

The primary attitudes and skills which a chartered accountant brings to an organization are:

- an understanding of finance: where money comes from, at what price and on what terms;

The first-time manager

- an understanding of systems for financial control;
- knowledge of how the law relating to accounting and taxation must be applied;
- prudence, clear-mindedness and a grasp of the totality as well as the detail of systems.

The first three items on that list are predictable, but the last is no less important. Indeed, it reflects the greatest contribution which accoun-tants can make to organizational decisions. To the hard-driving sales manager or the energetic production supervisor looking for big savings, the accountant can look like a real nuisance, seeming to lack vision, and only picking holes in what the other wants to do. The annoying thing is that the accountant's considered criticisms are usually perfectly accurate. They need to be, for often they are the only thing standing between survival and organizational suicide. Of course, there are accountants who are overcautious and so concerned with minutiae that they cannot see the big picture, just as there are airline pilots, jockeys, musicians and surgeons with the same charac-teristics. However, a manager usually comes unstuck when ignoring an accountant's advice.

The first-time manager, in particular, can learn a great deal at the knee of an accountant and will rapidly see how the influence of the accounting department reaches through the entire organization from top to bottom and from side to side. That pervasiveness helps to explain why accountants so often become chief executives. Theirs is the only department in an organization whose trade is the under-standing in financial terms of what all the others are up to, and the

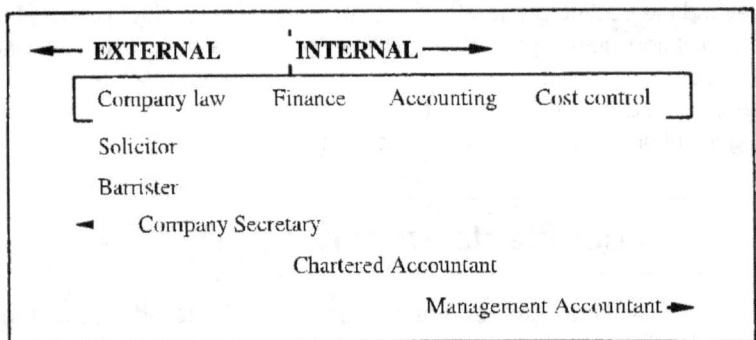

Figure 7.1 *The spans of professionals' authority within a private-sector organization*

medium in which they work – money – is that in which efficiency and effectiveness are most often measured.

A company accountant will say that the job covers several broad responsibilities and activities. As with other departments, they involve internal, departmental responsibilities as well as interactions with the wider world:

The accounting department
Invoicing and credit control
Paying debts
Maintaining statutory records
Negotiating with tax-collecting bodies
Organizing and facilitating audits

For other departments
Facilitating the setting of targets
Advising on and operating costing systems
Capital investment appraisal

For the organization at large
Recording and reporting individual and overall performance
Aggregating individual targets and performances to agree with overall aims and performance
Forecasting the financial position
Producing statutory accounts
Designing, installing, operating and maintaining systems to enable all this tohappen on time.

In addition, if the accountant has responsibility for sourcing finance, he or she will also represent the organization to banks and other financial institutions, and support the finance director and chairperson in their representations to City analysts and journalists.

It is most important that the accounting department has at least great influence over – and preferably total control of – the systems used by operating managers to conduct forward planning and to assess their future financial performance. The main reason for this is obvious: the organization cannot be run on a series of unrelated and incompatible home-made systems. The systems used by each depart-ment must be welded into an organization-wide whole. Further-more, amateur systems do not always take into account all the factors which a professional recognizes, and they are therefore usually inac-curate, sometimes dangerously so.

This point highlights one of the accountant's prime effects on an organization. It is to introduce and maintain a consistency of approach to financial matters. So strong is belief in the value of con-sistency in the way results are calculated and reported that investors look with great suspicion on firms which change the basis for accounting in their annual reports. They may argue that they are trying to reflect reality more closely, but the hard-bitten investor knows from experience that such changes are too often made to cover up a mediocre performance. Any financial director will resist pro-posals to change accounting conventions needlessly, and it will take very strong arguments to convince him or her of a need. So the first-time manager who rails against the unfairness of the reporting system in reflecting results will usually do so in vain. The best course of action may be to do one of two things: to keep and publish parallel records on a more realistic basis, or to give the organization results which show up as good on the reports. The first approach may be laborious, the second cynical or realistic, depending on your point of view.

The accountant's obsession with consistency is not pedantic. It comes from a commitment to the idea that figures for the current period ought to be capable of direct comparison with those from any other period in the organization's existence (inflation makes that dif-ficult enough, but the accountant would argue that this is no reason to make it completely impossible). That, in turn, springs from the allegiances which the accountant has. The first loyalty is to profes-sional standards, and the second to the employer. If asked by the employer to compromise on what is right, the accountant would rather resign than comply. It is upon that structure of allegiances that the credibility of the figures which accountants produce rests. A company in trouble might prefer to conceal rather than disclose its difficulties, but the fact that this is not easy to do is what creates confi-dence on the part of shareholders and lenders.

This issue surfaces during audits. By law every limited company of any size has to have its annual accounts audited by an outside firm of professional accountants. Fascinating clashes of interest can occur when the auditing arm of the accountancy firm questions the propri-ety of actions undertaken at the instigation of its colleagues in another branch. In order to minimize this, the auditors are usually consulted over any proposed changes before they are implemented. If they draw the line, the proposal is usually killed. Unwise directors try to pressure the auditors to look leniently on their creative accounting, but such attempts are very misguided. If the initial rebuff is not enough to bring the effort to an end, the auditors may feel that they have to resign. Among investors that is seen as a most damaging event. Appointing a different firm because it has quoted a lower price is one thing, but losing the auditors by inviting them to behave improperly is quite another.

While on the subject of audits, there is a common misunderstand-ing about their purpose. They are not designed to uncover all possi-ble misdemeanours: that is the task of the Serious Fraud Office, not an auditor. Auditors are watchdogs who check by sampling that correct conventions are being applied and proper records are being kept.

The accountant worships at four altars:

- accuracy
- clarity
- timeliness
- consistency.

There is one great truth which no honest accountant will try to conceal: *important areas of accounting are largely expressions of opinion, and it can be misleading to offer exact figures without a full statement of the assumptions which produced them.*

Unfortunately, all that most people ever see is the bare figures. A few points to explain the problem appear in Figure 7.2. They are meant to give a general indication, rather than an exhaustive discus-sion of one aspect of the issue.

Accountants are perfectly familiar with these points, of course. They have no real alternative to taking refuge in the fact that every-one else is reporting results on the same questionable basis, so that any individual set of figures is as good (or bad) as those of the herd. It does not stop the thinkers of the profession from being deeply con-cerned about the misrepresentation involved and from trying to evolve methods which show more accurately what is going on.

The three great points of weakness of our system of accounting are:

- everything is expressed in terms of money;
- the only issues recognized are those with a clear money value;
- reports look at the organization solely as a going concern.

To be able to measure an organization's achievements in terms of money is important. To do it solely in those terms is ludicrous, and about as sensible as judging the worth of a person by income alone. It would be even sillier to report only those achievements which lend

COMPANY PROFITS AND DEPRECIATION

A company's profits are calculated by subtracting costs from the value of sales. But what are the 'costs'? Accountancy convention treats depreciation as a cost. It therefore solemnly writes down the value of freehold factories and each year subtracts an amount from profits to allow for their depreciation. Yet in many areas they have risen in value. Only when a revalu-ation of property is undertaken is the nonsense corrected, but that is done infrequently and has a disproportionate effect on the profit reported for the year in which it is done. On the one hand, firms are reluctant to revalue since the City will expect them to produce a higher return on the higher value of assets which it discloses; and, on the other hand, they are eager to, since the take-over sharks are forever seeking firms with under-valued assets.

To take another example, motor vehicles are written down quite rapidly, often at 25 per cent each year. Everyone is famil-iar with the case of the chairperson's Rolls-Royce which main-tains its value in money terms, and of the little-used office manager's car which is sold for a lot more than its value on the books. The over-allowance for depreciation is revealed when they are sold, but meantime profits have been understated. Some will say that the way in which the fleet of vehicles is pooled for depreciation calculations offsets the effect of a mi-nority of vehicles which are over or under depreciated. That may be so, but where is our precision now?

Thus the idea of depreciation, like so many other accounting ideas, is thrown by changes in the value of money in relation to assets, and by movements in the value of assets relative to one another. This important cost, like so many others, turns out on examination to be based more on opinion and convention than any objective valuation. If costs are opinions, profit has to be an opinion itself.

Figure 7.2 *Company profits and opinion*

themselves to money measurement. Yet those nonsenses are at the heart of the conventions of accounting. Perhaps that is not the fault of accountancy as such, but more a default on the part of those who ought to lay emphasis on other aspects as well.

An organization might be training its people to levels of competitiveness well above those of its domestic counterparts. That would be an expensive and necessary prelude to domination of home and overseas markets. Yet the accountants will report that the training expenditure has made it less profitable, with no way of recording the gain to the firm's ability. If the same money had been spent on a fancy but unproductive office block, flashy furniture and new cars all round, the accounts would have recorded the gain to the firm's wealth in great detail.

Likewise, the assumption that the firm is a going concern produces some questionable reports. Firms do fail, unfortunately. Such a firm's assets may be written down to nothing by depreciation, but be worth huge sums on the nostalgia market. The delivery truck bought in 1921 and laid up since 1939 is valued at nothing in the accounts, yet is worth tens of thousands of pounds.

The purpose of these words must not be misunderstood. They are not an attack on accountants or accountancy, but a plea to non-accountants to put in the work necessary to understand the conven-tions which their accounting colleagues use. A degree of understand-ing is vital, for accountancy views should not be allowed to dominate decision-making. By understanding something of the conventions the first-time manager becomes better-equipped in three important ways:

- to understand the accounts and accountants better;
- to see the strengths of the accountancy approach;
- to see the shortcomings and failings of the accountancy approach, and thus to question its validity in any given situation.

If a first-time manager is in an accounting function he or she will do well to read carefully chapters other than this one. The content of this chapter and more will be covered in professional training. Accoun-tants can unwittingly cause more trouble and be of least help when they overlook the fact that so many of the most important areas of organizational life are not susceptible to numerical treatment.

The accountant and the financial world

The ideal of every organization would be to keep going by means of funds it generates from its own operations. Very few private sector organizations with any ambition to grow can achieve that position, and in the public sector they tend to absorb rather than create funds.

In the private sector finance comes in two forms, equity and loan. Equity is part of the permanent funds of the organization, and is raised by the sale of shares and the retention of profits. In return for their money, shareholders expect some degree of control to be given up by the management. In the case of ordinary shares, it introduces new shareholders who may or may not agree with the directors' ideas of how the organization ought to be run. If enough of them feel sufficiently aggrieved, they can dismiss the board of directors. Ordi-nary shareholders are the real risk-takers, who get a share of any profits but are the last to be paid out if the firm fails. They get their benefit in two ways: dividends (share of profits) and capital appreci-ation. The latter takes place usually as a result of the firm's earnings rising so that other investors can see that the shares are worth paying more for.

There are also non-voting types of equity investment, such as pref-erence shares, which carry a rate of interest instead of a share of any profits; it has to be paid whether or not the profit is there to support it. The 'preference' in their name arises from the fact that they are paid out before ordinary shareholders in the case of failure.

Loans are not free from obligation. Usually they will be secured on both some tangible asset and on the stock and the cash coming in as invoices are paid. Thus, whatever form finance from outside the firm takes, it is usually accompanied by a loss of control.

Loss of control means that top managers have to keep the finan-ciers happy or risk being replaced. The financier is looking first for security, that is, not to lose the investment. Once assured on that point a return will be sought. The form which that return takes varies with the investor. Some make their money by buying and selling quickly, others by relying on income and capital growth from a more or less stable portfolio of carefully chosen stocks. The first type wants flashy performance now, so that shares will rise a few pence and enable a profit to be taken fast. The second is more likely to be sympa-thetic to ploughing-in of revenue to produce long-term growth, for example, via training programmes.

All this places great pressure on company chairpersons to run round the City explaining what the firm is doing and why. That work results in a lot of the press stories about company performance which read as if they come about through divine revelation. If it keeps the share price up it makes the firm difficult for a predator to afford, and makes it cheaper for the firm to take over others by offering share cer-tificates instead of cash to the sellers. These are very serious matters, for the serious take-over specialists have tracking systems following every movement in the shares of their intended victims.

In the smaller organization the accountant will take on much of the job of representing the organization to its owners and backers. He or she will probably be company secretary as well, and as guardian of its legal and fiscal propriety is well suited to the task. The owners may be a small group of individuals – perhaps the family of the founders – and represent a very different set of interests from those exhibited at a large firm's AGM.

The accountant's dilemma

There is a whole series of balancing acts which the accountant is called upon to perform. If colleagues fail to understand what they are and why it is important to resolve them, much internal dissension may be caused.

The more important dilemmas involve clashes between:

- accuracy and timeliness;
- paying suppliers or conserving cash;
- putting liquidity at risk or chasing customers for payment.

Accuracy clashes with timeliness in a most obvious way. If informa-tion is to be useful it must be provided in time to be understood and acted upon. That often means that it has to be produced at speed, and speed can mean inaccuracy. Every report has two parameters: the degree of accuracy necessary and the latest time by which it can use-fully be supplied. In some cases a painstaking effort is needed because accuracy is more important than time: an example might be an investigation into alleged fraud on the computer system. In another situation speed might be all-important, a 'quick and dirty' reading being far more useful than a precise analysis that takes days to prepare. Into that category fall most of the requests for *ad hoc* help made by managers to enable them to see how things are going. They are really looking for a broad indication of whether or not things are going to plan, so that if the rough figure shows that things are more or less all right, they can turn their attention elsewhere; if it suggests that things might be going wrong, they can get more precise informa-tion on the area which seems to be the source of the trouble.

When it comes to the decision about whether to pay a supplier or to hold on to the cash, the accountant's first instinct is to keep the money. This cannot be done indefinitely, and any undue delay would damage the relationship with suppliers on whom the firm depends. The safety mechanism which stops the accountant from withholding payment for too long is the pressure from colleagues whose suppliers refuse to make further deliveries until the account is up to date. Certain large organizations, who believe that their clout allows them to get away with almost anything, delib-erately hold on to such payments for at least three months. Few suppliers expect to be paid on delivery, but after six or eight weeks they feel that they ought to be paid. Thirteen weeks feels too much like exploitation, and they seek customers elsewhere. The irony is that the attempt to use suppliers' money to fund its own operations drives the big organization's best suppliers away; and those who continue to sell to it raise their prices to compensate for the delay in payment. Does such a policy really pay off in the long run? Its attrac-tion is that the money not paid out is equivalent to money not bor-rowed, so that interest costs are reduced, but the savings may prove to be illusory.

If the organization hits an emergency shortage of cash, for a time few suppliers would get paid. Those who did would be the bare minimum of suppliers without whose goodwill the organization could not function. They include the utilities and vital raw materials suppliers. Others could complain but they would not get paid until the crisis had passed. If it proved terminal, those suppliers would remain unpaid for at least a couple of years while liquidators dis-sected the corpse. A sudden change in payment habits can spell trouble, so credit managers watch out for such signs.

This brings us to the third of the accountant's dilemmas, that of bal-ancing the need for liquidity against the danger of alienating custom-ers by chasing them too hard for payment. In the normal course of events a compromise is worked out, with the salespeople represent-ing the customer's point of view. If the credit manager should suspect that the collapse of a customer may be imminent, immediate action is taken. The customer is threatened with a writ or a winding-up petition, pointing out that this will be published in the media which credit managers read, and will trigger a flood of similar actions from other suppliers and hasten the downfall. That is not vin-dictive, it is simply making sure that if anyone is to be paid it is the credit manager's own firm.

That series of actions would be taken only by agreement with the sales department, who will have the responsibility for re-establishing the relationship if the customer survives the crisis. They also have a hand in setting the limit on the amount of credit allowed to custom-ers, a flexible figure which is adjustable upwards if it hampers the development of the account, or downwards if the customer begins to look shaky.

Basic accounting concepts: cash flow forecasting

This is the first of a series of sections which looks at some of the ways in which accountants do their work.

The main immediate aim of any organization must be to survive. The factor which governs survival (discounting voluntary discontinuance) is liquidity, the ability to pay bills as they fall due. An illiquid organization may be rich, but the fact that its wealth is held in the form of (say) land means that it cannot pay its bills. Some of the wealth will have to be turned into cash before the creditors can be sat-isfied, and that takes time. The staff, the tax collector and all the sup-pliers need to be paid in money, not title deeds.

Other issues of importance are profit and profitability (which are related but different). *Liquidity* will be dealt with first.

To the surprise of most people, accountants treat liquidity as being of greater importance than profit. They are quite right to do so, for an unprofitable firm can survive for quite a long time under normal cir-cumstances, but one which is illiquid fails immediately. The item in the accountant's tool kit which enables prediction of liquidity is the cash flow forecast.

In principle, a cash flow forecast is very simple: most nine-year-olds have no trouble in understanding it, so the first-time manager should find it very easy indeed.

The aim of the cash flow forecast is to work out what the bank balance is likely to be at the end of each of a specified number of periods of time in the future, say, monthly for the next year. The point of that is to see if, by operating in the way it plans to, the firm will run dangerously short of cash. If the forecast says it will, the action planned can be reviewed to see what changes to operational activity will bring about a less hazardous cash situation.

The calculation involved is simplicity itself:

- start with the cash in the bank now;
- add the cash which ought to come in during the period (it is assumed here to be a month);
- subtract the cash likely to be paid out in the same period;
- the result is the cash which will be left over at the end of the month, if the earlier assumptions come true; this becomes the opening balance for the next month.

The process is then repeated until 11 more periods have been covered. To anyone who has ever completed a stock record, that process is familiar. Stock records start with the number of size 12 widgets in stock, add on those expected in, subtract those which will be used, and arrive at a month-end total. That figure becomes the opening balance for the following month, and the process is repeated. In the case of stock, a predetermined reorder level triggers the placing of replenishment orders, without which it would run out. In the case of cash, there is no certainty at the start that the supply will be exhausted, since the reservoir is being constantly topped up by incoming payments from customers. Instead of looking to see *when* the firm will run out of cash, the accountant is trying to find out *if* it will and if so, *when* and *to what extent*. If the extent is major, extra finance will be needed or the plans will have to change to a less cash-hungry mode of operation. If it is minor and temporary it could be covered by slowing down payments to suppliers, or a bank over-draft, or both.

A cash flow forecast for a large organization is a complex-looking document, but the principles it follows are exactly those outlined above. The crucial point to remember is that a sale is recorded as such the moment the invoice is raised; it does not become *cash*, in the form in which it can be spent, until someone pays the bill – and that could be months later. Many commercial failures come about, especially in the small firms sector, because people think that they can spend against invoices issued, whereas they can in reality only against cash received.

The profit and loss account

The standard document which reports profits is the profit and loss account (P&L). A P&L is another basically simple document. It applies to a period of time, usually a year, and is created thus:

Total value of invoiced sales,
Subtract what was paid for things sold,
= Gross profit.

Subtract all the other expenses of actually running the firm,
= Operating profit.

Subtract cost of finance,
= Net profit before tax.

Subtract tax due on net profit before tax, = Net profit.

In that simple breakdown there appear four different definitions of 'profit'. Thus one of the first things the first-time manager learns is that the word profit must not be used unqualified.

Profitability is something else again. It is the measure of return on some resource. The profitability of a new investment is the rate at which it earns a profit. If it cost £100,000 and earns £40,000 a year, its profitability is 40 per cent. Typically, organizations are interested in ranking their activities in order of profitability, the more easily to dis-tinguish the most rewarding from the least. Their calculation or cal-culations of profitability will be based on the scarcest or most expensive resources: there is nothing to stop the calculation from being performed many times on different bases. To take an example, a precision engineer with a highly skilled workforce may have invested heavily in computer-controlled machines. Two key figures are of interest: the profitability of the very expensive investment and the profitability of the highly paid workforce. This leads to investigating in detail what the return is per pound invested, and per hour that the workforce operates. Investigating the profitability of individual customers or groups and types of customers may also be interesting.

The balance sheet

The two standard documents used for reporting company results are the P&L and the balance sheet. The P&L shows what profit has been earned, which is an important part of the story of what has been done with the owner's money. The owner also wants to know what all the money is tied up in at the end of the reporting period: that is what the balance sheet shows.

In order to create a balance sheet, the organization freezes its trans-actions at a particular moment and records the position of all its assets and liabilities – the wealth it owns and the money it owes. That position is different both immediately beforehand and immediately afterwards. For that reason it is frequently described as a 'snapshot' of the organization's funds.

The fundamental message conveyed by the balance sheet is twofold:

- how much money has been raised and from where;
- where that money was tied up, or where it was lost to.

Strictly speaking, the quantities shown on a balance sheet represent wealth rather than money, but since accountancy depends on the use of the money measure for everything (see earlier in this chapter), that wealth is expressed in monetary terms. Two acres of industrial land is wealth in anybody's terms, and therefore has to be shown in the owner's balance sheet. Unfortunately it cannot be shown as such in any accounting document, so it has to be converted into its estimated value, say £2 million. That enables the different forms of wealth to be totalled, whether they are in the form of stock, materials, equipment, vehicles, buildings, money owed due or cash.

All this involves a certain amount of estimation, as has been men-tioned already. It also means that the accountant's eyes are closed to ways of looking at values which can be much more relevant in some cir-cumstances. The idea of the 'going concern' has been touched on. It means that things are valued for accounting purposes on the assump-tion that the organization will continue in business. Thus a half-com-pleted car which is part-way through the factory is assumed to be saleable for a price which reflects the work put into it. If the firm really does continue in business that is the only realistic way of valuing that item, but suppose it is only days away from liquidation? The accountant would continue to value everything on the 'going concern' basis, even though the half-completed assemblies cramming the factory floor will be saleable only as scrap in a week's time. In such a situation, of course, nobody would delude themselves into thinking that the 'going concern' values are what the factory could be sold for. Under these conditions two parallel sets of valuations are done: the conventional one, and in addition a realistic assessment of what everything would fetch if the worst happened. The only valuation which means anything in the end is the price agreed between a willing buyer and a willing seller.

Mention of those different forms of assets introduces the distinction between fixed assets and current assets and their counterparts on the other side of the equation, long-term liabilities and current lia-bilities. Assets are things owned by an organization or individual on which a money value can be placed under the conventions of accounting. Liabilities are their mirror image: the debts owed on which a money value is placed. In brief, fixed assets are the ones which the organization intends to hang on to and to use, like buildings, vehicles and equipment. Current assets are those which it means to sell or otherwise recover the value of within a year, like stocks or debtors (money owed by customers, on the whole). As for liabilities, the short-term (current) ones are due for settlement within a year and the long-term ones are those which fall due later than that. In practice, many long-term liabilities remain outstanding for the entire life of the organization.

The layout and meaning of a balance sheet are illustrated in simple form in Figure 7.3.

It is easy to jump to the conclusion that certain categories of asset are always treated as fixed assets. Machinery might be an example. The key to classification lies in the owner's intent. If a manufacturer, it may be to keep and use a machine for a number of years, so that it is certainly a fixed asset to that enterprise. A machinery dealer, however, would sell it as quickly as possible. Thus to that firm it is an item of stock-in-trade, and thus a current asset.

At this stage it is worth stopping for a moment to consider what the balance sheet is saying. Its message is:

'We own fixed assets worth this much; add on the current assets, to see the value of all the assets we own; subtract from that what we owe in the short-term, and see the total value of the investment in the firm; you can also see what it is tied up in. To see where the investment came from and in what form, look at the long-term liabilities.'

	Heading	Usual contents
	Fixed assets	Plant, machinery, land, buildings, vehicles, equipment
(+)	Current assets	Cash, stock, money owed to us
(=)	Total assets	(ie everything we own)
(−)	Current liabilities	Debts for stock and day-to-day supplies, tax due shortly; short-term loans (eg overdrafts, which can be called in without notice)
(=)	Net worth	(ie what we are worth when our immediate debts are subtracted from what we own)

[This completes the first part of the balance sheet, which shows where the money put into the organization is tied up. It is followed by the part which shows where the money came from.]

	Long-term liabilities	Income from sale of shares; reserves created by profits (or reduction in worth caused by accumulated losses); long-term loans; longer-term tax liabilities

[Net worth and long-term liabilities are equal to each other. They have to be, since one shows where the money is now, the other shows where it came from.]

Figure 7.3 *The balance sheet simplified*

When the balance sheet is put together with the P&L, some useful information emerges. The degree of risk of the firm failing can be pinpointed, as can the profitability of the assets, two factors of considerable interest to owners, managers and other employees. There is much else besides, a great deal of which is revealed by *ratio analysis*, a simple technique which involves examining the relationship between different items on the balance sheet and the P&L.

The first ratio which anyone looks at is the so-called '*acid test*' or *liquidity ratio*. That examines whether the firm is in a position to pay its bills as they fall due. It takes the items which are cash (or almost as good as cash, such as debts owed to the firm) to see if they total enough to meet the current liabilities. If they are in a relationship of at least 1:1, all is assumed to be well for the immediate future, although there must always be questions about who the debtors are and how old the debts. Doubtful categories would include money owed by people who have absconded or firms which have failed, as well as debts which are in dispute for reasons of non-compliance with contract terms or because nobody can substantiate an invoice with a signed delivery receipt. Some companies' accounts contain a horrifyingly high proportion of such debts. One manager who went to work for a small group found this out at first hand. He tells the story of finding about £2 million owed to the firm, of which over £800,000 had been in dispute for over two years with half-a-dozen large customers. Thus nearly half the money that the firm ought apparently to be able to collect was simply not available, and unlikely ever to be collected.

The next test is the *current ratio*, in which current liabilities and current assets are compared. The point is to see if the firm will fail in the medium term. Accountants' experience shows that there ought generally to be at least £2 of current assets to £1 of current liabilities, to allow a comfortable margin of safety.

Being satisfied that the firm does not seem to be in imminent danger of collapse, the accountant might then look to see what return it is earning on the money invested in it. There is no single 'good' rate of return, since return ought to comprise two elements: the cost of the use of money (interest rate) which is more or less the same for all businesses, plus an amount which reflects risk. Since the latter is very variable between companies and markets there can be no all-embrac-ing convention.

The large and sophisticated organization is perfectly aware, of course, that these criteria are being used to judge its published results. For that reason many organizations choose to massage their year-end figures without actually lying. This is done by such tech-niques as placing a ban on buying stock or on capital expenditure for the last few weeks of the year. That allows stocks to fall and cash to build up, thus making the firm look more liquid. The trouble which that causes is twofold: once it has been done at all the trick has to be repeated every year, and it introduces inefficiencies which will affect next year's profit figures. Nevertheless, managements feel that they are driven to use such expedients by the constant pressure for results placed on them by the City.

Gearing

Gearing is a term which the first-time manager will encounter at some time. Gearing relates to where the long-term funding has come from, recognizing that loans are different from risk capital in the form of shares. The figures from which it is derived are all in the long-term liabilities part of the balance sheet. Gearing is the product of another ratio, that between the fixed capital, in the form of shares or owners' investment, and long-term loans. Its significance lies in the organization's exposure to risk versus its ability to exploit favour-able conditions quickly. If times are good, money costs 10 per cent and a 30 per cent return can be earned on it, it makes sense to borrow as much as you can and maximize earnings. If times are bad, the firm which makes no operating profit need not pay its shareholders (for that is one of the risks they take), yet it still has to pay interest on any loan. Thus in the good times earnings from heavily borrowed firms will be good, in bad times they will be poor – or even lead to the lenders calling in the loans, so that the firm collapses. Accountants like to see £1 of loan to £3 of equity (such a firm has a gearing of 33 per cent), or at most £1 to £2 (gearing of 50 per cent). A firm which has gearing of 10 per cent is said to have low gearing; one which is geared at 80 per cent is highly geared by anyone's standards.

The final word on the topic of ratios is that there is a multitude which can be calculated. The point is not just to do the arithmetic, but to select those which have meaning in the context of that firm's cir-cumstances. They should produce information on the firm's internal position, its likely future performance and its relationship to compa-rable and competing firms as a way of judging its management. Par-ticularly revealing are changes over time.

Sources of funds

Recognizing the importance attached to the question of organiza-tional liquidity, companies are increasingly showing a further table in their annual reports, a sources of funds statement. Accountants and others in the know have always been able to work this out for themselves from the other documents, but this labour-saving approach is welcomed by all. The first-time manager will do well to pay attention to that report, for it discloses early signals to changes in the health of the firm by way of that vital measure, liquidity.

It is a simple piece of arithmetic. In essence, it takes the balance sheets for the start and the end of the year, and calculates the changes in the size of each item. A reduction of stock, for instance, is represented by an increase in liquidity, a reduction in cash a decrease. The question which it answers is: 'Where have changes in funds come from in the year, and what have they been tied up in?'

Costing

This is a subject on which books the size of door-stops have been written. Cost accounting is an important discipline in its own right, as well as a key element in the art and science of management accounting. Its concern is to identify what the true expression is in money terms of everything done in the organization, so that nobody deludes themselves about the implications of their actions. It is a vital aid to management, and probably its most important contribution comes in telling what the organization's products really cost.

The cost accountant starts by classifying costs into categories. The first level of classification is by function, for example, whether a cost properly lies with the production function or the distribution func-tion. Within these functions it establishes cost centres, places where a group of people works together (or any other useful unit) for which costs can be gathered. They might include the training department, the London warehouse or the retailing division.

Next comes the idea of the 'cost unit', the unit of output to which all these costs are to be attached. For a civil engineering firm it might be a particular motorway contract, or for a food manufacturer canned beans size A2.

All the costs which a firm incurs fall into three categories: materi-als, including sub-assemblies and components; payroll; and general outgoings like premises, fuel, depreciation, utilities and interest. Further, they are either 'direct' or 'indirect'. Direct ones are clearly identifiable as belonging to a cost unit – the distribution depart-ment's diesel, for instance. Indirect costs cannot be readily identified as having an 'owner', such as the rental of the fax which everyone uses, or the interest on long-term loans. Having said that, the cost accountant is constantly at war with the imprecision which indirect costs suggest, longing to find a home in a cost unit somewhere for every one of these motherless waifs. Nevertheless, the common sense with which these people are liberally endowed says that there is always an irreducible minimum which no existing cost unit ought to be asked to absorb, and for which no cost unit can reasonably be created. Cost accountants are therefore under constant pressure from the managers of cost centres to share out a cost which they feel ought not to be borne entirely by them.

Some of the biggest problems faced by the cost accountant have to do with apportioning indirect costs to the individual products or cost units. The distribution department is a cost centre in its own right, but its costs can be met only by the profit centres (yes, there are those too) which actually sell the firm's output. If a parcels carrier were to deliver every item sold, there would be little problem: each case of product would be charged for individually and the costs could be allocated accordingly. When the firm's own lorries make the deliver-ies the share to be borne by each product is less clear-cut.

Firms therefore apply some convention, based on the limiting factor. If the product is feather quilts, it will be the space on the lorries and each product will be charged a proportion of the costs based on the volume shipped. If it is steel strip, the limiting factor on the lor-ries' loads will be weight. Thus the share of costs will be the share of the total weight delivered. Where, as so often happens, the products come in a variety of densities, the choice of system for allocating cost can be crucial.

As an example, a firm makes two products: boxes and blocks. The same number of units is sold of each, but one block is five times the weight of a box. The block is also a quarter of the volume of a box. The characteristics of the distribution task are as follows:

	Boxes	Blocks
Weight (kg)	2	10
Volume (litres)	20	5
Number sold	1,000	1,000
Total weight (kg)	2,000	10,000
Total volume (litres)	20,000	5,000

Thus the firm has to ship 2000 items a year which weigh 12,000 kg and occupy 25,000 litres. It costs £50,000 a year to run the delivery function, and the cost accountant has to consider how best to allocate the cost. He does some arithmetic:

	Boxes	Blocks
Cost per unit if apportioned by:		
Weight:	£8	£42
Volume:	£40	£10
Numerical share of deliveries:	£25	£25

This shows that the cost per unit could vary wildly, depending on the costing basis selected. This is important because the one selected could dramatically alter the pricing of the product and thus its chances of survival in the market-place and in the firm's range of products. Thus the wrong decision here could even result ultimately in the closure of a factory, with all the appalling effects that can have. In the end, under this example, the accountant would probably plump for a cost per unit based on some combination of volume and weight effects, but the decision is neither clear-cut nor easy. This highlights the difficulty associated with the technique of *absorption costing*, the method which tries to load on to each product a share of central overheads. What may have originally been fairly arbitrary decisions over how indirect costs are to be apportioned can assume major importance when decisions are being taken over which prod-ucts are too unprofitable to continue with. It can be downright dan-gerous when pricing is under discussion, and it is inflexible in the face of variations in the underlying assumptions about costs and vol-umes.

To address that difficulty the idea of 'contribution' was developed. Instead of trying to share out all the indirect costs, just the direct costs are allocated to each product. They are subtracted from the selling price to produce the contribution (ie to indirect costs and, it is hoped, profit). The total of all the contributions over the year from all the products is then set against the total of the indirect costs, and any-thing left over is profit. Clearly that is a lot simpler and more flexible, but it does mean that even greater vigilance is needed. It is vital that there are good systems for tracking the actual contribution compared to plan, since a loss of volume from a high contributor could, if not spotted and acted upon, plunge the firm into loss.

The test of costing decisions is with hindsight, when it becomes clear whether or not the product is over or under costed, and whether or not the volumes expected were sold at a price which allowed recovery of the actual indirect costs of running the business.

A general principle in accounting is that, if total profit is to be maxi-mized, the profit on each unit of the scarcest resource must be maxi-mized. In other words, the bottleneck which is stopping things from expanding or speeding up has to be identified. The most profitable item or mix of items which can be sold is that which produces the greatest return from the use of the bottleneck resource. If the lorry fleet is the limiting factor, and suppose that the firm makes £20 profit on all items in its range, it will make the biggest profit by cramming the lorries with the smallest item of all and delivering none of the biggest. In that way it maximizes the number of £20s it makes. More often that profit will be expressed as contribution, since it is not yet, strictly speaking, profit at all. The scarce resource varies from organi-zation to organization, but knowing which it is and squeezing as much out of it as possible is an important management task.

Thus there is no one costing system suitable for all firms in all situations. Even the custom-built system is likely to be just the best compromise available rather than perfect in every detail, despite the fact that an enormous amount of thought will have been expended on its design.

The mention of contribution brings in the idea of *marginal costing*. A firm needs to know what is the lowest price for which its products can sell without actually incurring a loss. That knowledge enables it to set a floor price below which no sale must ever be made, and to negotiate against if there is ever the opportunity to fill some vacant capacity at a low selling price. The marginal cost of a product is the cost of selling one extra item once all the indirect costs have been covered by the rest of the output. Its use must be carefully controlled since, if the other costs are not fully met, the marginal cost will cer-tainly not meet them.

Another concept which the cost accountant has constantly in mind is that of *opportunity cost*. It is the idea that one of the costs of doing what we are doing now is the sacrifice of the opportunity of doing something else. In practical terms, if a firm does something which earns it £20,000 instead of something which would earn it £30,000, the opportunity cost of that decision is £10,000. Or if research expen-diture rises by £100,000 it is at an opportunity cost to all sorts of activ-ities, including to shareholders' dividends, of £100,000.

Break-even analysis

A firm knows that its capacity will sometimes not be completely filled. The level of sales may be able to fall some way without eliminating profit; the question is, by how much?

The break-even chart illustrates this clearly, and also shows how

Finance and accounting

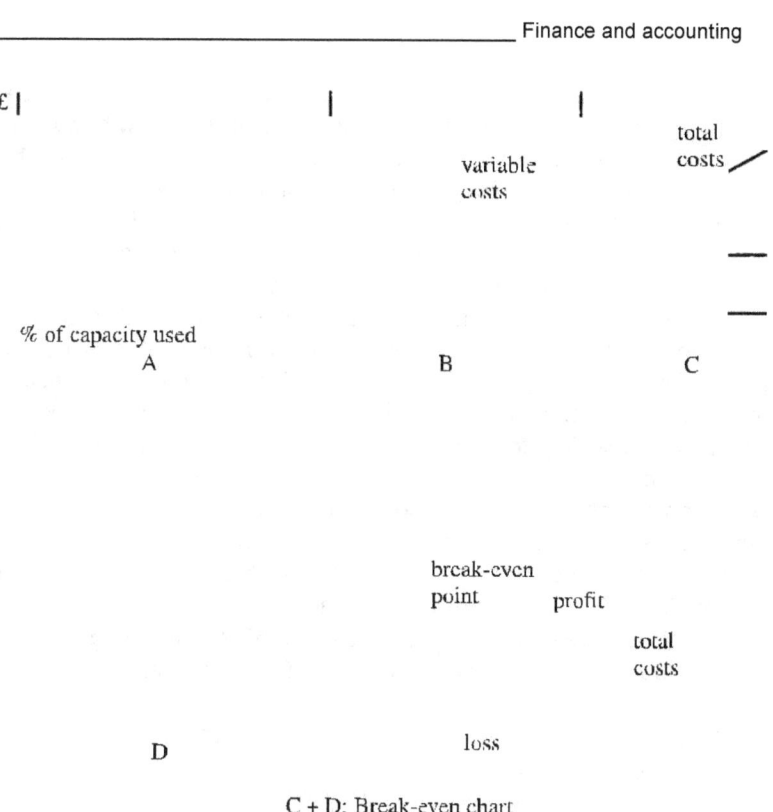

Figure 7.4 *Break-even analysis*

much profit or loss will be made at different levels of output. Figure 7.4 shows that It comprises three elements: the levels of fixed costs (similar to the indirect costs discussed above), variable costs (similar to direct costs) and sales. Fixed and variable costs are combined to show total costs, and when this is compared to the income from sales the level of output at which the firm breaks even can easily be seen.

Budgeting

One of the accountant's main jobs is to help with the setting of budgets and monitoring performance against them. A budget, in these terms, is a financial plan which shows what revenues are expected, what expenditures have been allowed for and hence what profit or loss is anticipated. As has been mentioned, the entire process usually starts from the creation of a sales forecast, and goes on to working out the cost of servicing that level of sales. To a sales manager, for example, the financial budget lays down two important goals: the value of sales which the rest of the organization expects the sales department to achieve, and the amount of expense which it is expected not to exceed in the course of gaining them. There will also be operating budgets which translate the value of the sales figures into volumes of particular products. The figures will be no strangers as the sales manager has been instrumental in their creation. It is a prime principle of budgeting that the managers who have to carry out the plans create the budgets. If budgeting is left to some central function, the operating managers can scarcely be blamed if they refuse to accept responsibility for achieving them. A budget which nobody is trying to achieve has no reason to exist, for the whole point of it is to create an overall plan for the period concerned which, ideally, everyone achieves exactly. Of course, there are always over-and under-achievers, but the existence of the budget enables top management to see whether or not variances are important.

Budgets are created for all the cost and profit centres, to give those responsible for them a precise statement of what they are expected to achieve. They are also fed with reports from the accountants which show at the end of each month how they have done against the plan. Each manager reviews performance with his or her boss at the end of each month and formulates ideas on how to deal with any variance from budget. This happens at all levels right up to the top of the organization. If the managing director is sitting on an organization which is persistently under-achieving, the chairperson will eventu-ally run out of excuses and will then come under pressure from investors for replacement by someone who will turn the results round. If the chairperson does not respond in the way the sharehold-ers desire he or she, too, could be dismissed.

Thus the budget is the single document which serves to point everyone's efforts in the same direction, causing the organization to work as a cohesive whole rather than as a collection of individuals each with their own personal aims to achieve.

Project evaluation

When the manager is confronted by the possibility of spending money now for an expected return later, the accountants become involved in evaluating the project. Given that one of the scarcest resources in any organization is usually money, they are concerned that only the projects which give the best return should attract investment.

The three usual ways of looking at investments and their likely returns are ones which compute the speed at which the investment will be paid back, a computation of the annual rate of return, and a calculation of the project's discounted cash flow.

The *payback* method asks: 'How long before the initial investment is paid back from the savings or extra profits which it will generate?' In a small organization in which most of the investments will pay themselves back in a year or so this might be acceptable. It is not ade-quate elsewhere, as will be discussed.

The *annual rate of return* asks a similar question: 'What annual per-centage return on the investment do the savings or extra profits yield?' Again this method is deficient in the case of the project from which the savings will not recover its costs more or less straight away.

The problems with these approaches spring from two sources. One is that both of them place the same value of savings made today as those made in a year's, or five years', time. To offset the change in the real value of money an inflation factor can be applied; the effect is real enough as can be seen from this table:

Present value of £1, discounted at 3 per cent pa

Today	After:	1 year	2 years	3 years
£1		97p	94p	91p ... and so on

Even where a discounting factor is applied, the methods are deficient. They fail to distinguish between the profit arising from the investment and the cash flow pattern which it implies. As we have seen, it is perfectly possible to bankrupt yourself in pursuit of a profitable project which runs you out of cash. Thus the primacy of cash flow must be recognized in any evaluation of investment projects.

To allow cash flows to be taken into account, as well as the time-value of money, the method known as discounted cash flow (DCF) was developed. To take a simple illustration, an investment of £10 will create savings of £2 a year, and annual inflation of 5 per cent is expected. The DCF calculation looks like this:

(Values are Year 1 pounds)

Year:	1	2	3	4	5
Outflows	£10				
Inflows	£2	£1.90	£1.80	£1.71	£1.63
Net flow	(£8)	£1.90	£1.80	£1.71	£1.63
– Cumulative	(£8)	(£6.10)	(£4.30)	(£2.59)	(£0.96)

Thus the organization has to be able to fund an outflow in today's money of £8 this year: if it can do that, the benefits are shown in future years. If it could not do it then it will look elsewhere to invest. The payback method would say that it will be paid off in four years. The rate of return calculation shows that the investment is earning 25 per cent a year. By contrast DCF has shown that the initial outflow still has not been recouped after five years: indeed, it will not be recovered fully until part-way through year 6. The advantage of this method becomes most apparent when the outflows go on for quite a while before any return comes in, quite a familiar pattern for many in big industry. DCF paints the flows in full Technicolor horror, so that there is no confusion between the glowing reports of potential profit and the certainty of imminent cash outflows.

No single technique tells the manager or the accountant all that they need to know, but DCF comes nearest to universal acceptance.

Key points and tips

- In all organizations the accounting function is powerful.
- Accountants strive to present a 'true and fair view', but some of their craft's conventions make this difficult.
- Much of the basis of accountancy is opinion.
- Accountancy does not reflect the full reality of an organization's position. Improving a machine's capacity is reported as a wealth-enhancing investment; improving the capacities of staff via training is shown as a wealth-diminishing ex-pense.
- Cash, not profit, keeps organizations going from day to day.
- To understand how organizations work, managers need to understand the basic accounting documents and conventions.

eight

Human Resources

Why HR departments exist

Where HR work is seen in its true light, the people in that function are excellent: is it the commitment to effective but humane management which creates an insistence on a superb HR department, or is it first-rate HR managers who earn respect for the contribution they make? Certainly colleagues' valuation of their work will colour the judgement made of any HR department; but the commitment to excel-lence in that department has to be made by top management in order for it to come about. If HR work is seen as a low-level activity, the chances are that the jobs in that department will be low-grade and will attract people who would be relatively ineffective in any function.

The true work of an HR department is not practised often enough in Britain today. It is to enable the organization to get the best perfor-mance, short- and long-term, out of that contrary and difficult – but completely indispensable – resource, people.

Most operating managers will confess in moments of frankness that they are not quite sure why their organization bothers to employ an HR department. They see their HR colleagues as a bunch of refu-gees from real life, who have fled from the world of action, responsi-bility, accountability and precision which the operating manager inhabits. In their place the HR manager erects, they believe, a smokescreen of waffle about human relationships and personal development, founded on pop psychology.

The good HR manager resists the implied suggestion that little or no account need be taken of people's legitimate human needs. Indeed, such a person sees this talk as conclusive evidence of the size of the task of bringing the truth to these unbelievers. He or she will feel at no disadvantage to colleagues, having been proved in the heat of battle as an operating manager. To this person two challenges are apparent: to become such a useful and helpful staff manager that col-leagues will actively seek advice rather than having to be force-fed it;

and to introduce the floggers and hangers to the sides of human nature which respond to encouragement and help. Tackling either is a major task, to undertake both is either heroic or foolish. None the less the good HR manager tackles both and succeeds.

The HR department and discipline

In some organizations it is easy for staff and line functions to become confused. The line (operating) manager is directly responsible for recruiting, motivating and disciplining staff. The employee cannot be expected to be responsible to a manager for output and to the HR department for disciplinary issues. Therefore no worthwhile HR manager would dream of getting between employees and their boss. Nonetheless, HR has responsibilities to the organization. They would remind the manager of the company policy, the letter of the law and considerations of best practice to ensure consistency and fairness in the way employees are treated. Thus they might be con-sulted about any decision to dismiss and be present at an interview towards that end, but ought not to carry out the dismissal itself.

It is in the disciplinary area that HR people have some of their most unpleasant experiences, but they owe allegiance to the organization which pays them to put their technical expertise to work in its inter-est. An operating manager has problems with a subordinate and invokes the disciplinary procedure (every firm must have one). It may be in the operating manager's mind to get rid of a difficult employee, but to do it within the rules. He or she looks to the HR department to collude in dismissing this person. If the HR manager suspects that there may be more personal animus than evidence of poor work, he or she is in a difficult position. Ideally, the manager would be shown the error and would reform: the people, the depart-ment and the organization would gain from a switch out of negativ-ism and into a positive concern to help the employee to contribute properly. On occasion, an analysis of the situation by the HR manager will bring about this change of approach. Regrettably it does not always work. In some cases the operating manager is in a position of vastly greater power than the HR person. The HR manager may then have to choose between standing up for beliefs or selling out principles in order to stay employed.

An extreme example was chosen in that illustration, where someone stood to lose their job. The pressures to conform to the operating manager's requirements are just as strong where mere manipulation is concerned. The HR manager may be expected to join in bullying or persuasion in order to get someone to do something he or she does not like the sound of. Increasingly the extension of human rights and the compensation culture make this risky.

The HR department's proper contribution

The departmental power balance is in better equilibrium where the organization recognizes from the top that HR issues have the importance that they really do carry. For a start, the organization's culture reflects the strong concern to develop and enable rather than coerce and enforce. Then a superior type of manager will be recruited to run the department, which might even be represented at board level. It will not only be supported in its efforts to raise the general standard of the management of people throughout the organization, it will also be positively required to do so. Such is the strength of the cul-tural dimension that no manager will take any decision without con-sidering its implications for people. To ensure that they are thought through fully, those thoughts will be laid before the HR people to get their reactions. Everything will be done to ensure that the organiza-tion gets the best possible return on the vital human resource.

HR departments which operate in the latter type of environment find themselves moving in a virtuous circle. The support which the culture gives them lends weight to their views; the better quality HR people apply to work for that organization; line managers receive service which develops their respect for HR work; and the culture recognizes even more strongly the importance of the HR department's contribution.

What the HR department does

Its overall role
The guidance which an HR department gives to line managers improves their handling of their people, and thus helps them to become better, more rounded managers. By encouraging a manager to think of the wider effects of actions on people, the HR operator is acting as midwife to the line manager's self-development. Dealing

with real issues at one's own desk, assisted by an expert, is no less valuable a way of learning than going on courses.

Recruitment

The specialist contribution of the HR department is particularly valuable in helping the organization to recruit, train and retain good people. Those broad headings encompass many individual activities and the exercise of a number of skills.

The job of finding good people starts well before the recruitment ads appear. The first step is to ensure that the organization presents a face to the world which is attractive to the kind of people it wishes to employ. In that task the HR department may work closely with PR people. Just as the way the organization looks to customers is too important to be left to chance, so the enlightened HR operator will try to ensure that all potential employees have a favourable impression of the organization as an employer. It will lay particular stress on certain groups of key workers without a good supply of which it could not fulfil its aims. In deciding how to project the organization, a study of its competitors for the same scarce manpower resources will be held, for nothing like this can be done in a vacuum.

Communications

The HR department is therefore often in the position of conducting its own communications campaign on behalf of the organization to potential employees. The message cannot fail to be picked up by existing staff as well. That is no accident, for it does no harm to bring home to them that they could find worse employers. It also highlights the need to stray as little as possible from the truth about working conditions.

The techniques employed include

- placing articles by employees in suitable media;
- sponsorships and support of charities, professional institutes and industry organizations;
- encouraging academic study of the organization;
- presence at careers exhibitions, in suitable directories, on the firm's website and other media.

Articles for the media can be on virtually any aspect of organizational life. The staff who write them gain in professional standing, and the organization gains by association. They might even be articles by the HR department itself. Under the same general heading is the offer to the media of expert interviewees who can be called on at short notice to comment on anything from the effects of the Budget to technical advances in the industry.

Community involvement not only shows the firm in a good light but it allows the wider world to look at its people as human beings as well as office-holders. The bodies and activities with which the organization chooses to associate itself in this way need to be picked with care. They ought to be consistent with the image which the organization wishes to project, and should harmonize with its values and practices. It reinforces perceptions of leadership to see an organi-zation involved with the sponsorship of students at college, with the development of professional institutes and trade organizations, and helping appropriate charities.

Sponsorship of academic study can take a wide variety of forms, from endowing a chair at a leading university to allowing students to use the organization as a guinea-pig for their projects. Academic involvement should carry a warning for the unwary, for once intelligent, motivated people are let loose they cannot be stopped from asking the questions which employees know are too sensitive to be referred to publicly. So if the MD's spouse really does take all the decisions about the colour the products should be, design students ought to be kept away, if the HR people value their jobs. Unless the spouse in question is a professional designer, of course.

It must always be remembered that the values of the academic world are such that the results of research are published openly (though names can be withheld), whereas consultancy is confidential. To be anonymous in research publications is small consolation to the one manufacturer of grommets within 50 miles of Manchester who bares all, and finds itself described as a 'grommet maker in south-east Lancashire': anonymous, but identifiable. Two sides of the same question are involved here: the findings of the research could make the organization look foolish, although it will draw its attention to things that urgently need putting right; and the fact of allowing the researchers in suggests a certain self-confidence tempered with humility. Organizations hope that the latter is the effect that will dominate, reinforcing perceptions that it offers a sympathetic environment in which to work.

The organization's communications specialist, whether suited in marketing or HR, may be expected to take on communications with existing employees. Internal newsletters enjoy a variable reputation, depending on their true function. Broadly, they fall into one of two camps: vehicles for keeping staff in touch with developments, and massage for senior egos. The second invites derision or creates cyni-cism; the first can be truly worth doing.

External relationships

Perhaps the most obvious instance of image communication is at careers exhibitions, especially those on the 'milk round', on which recruiters visit the major universities to try to attract the brightest performers to join their graduate entry programmes. Professional help from specialists in communication is usually called in so as to create the very best appearance and overall impression.

The good HR department realizes that every single contact with its potential recruits may be a matter of routine to the managers concerned, but is considered very critically by the recruits themselves. For that reason they are painstaking about the form of words used in telephone conversations, face to face and in letters by themselves and their staff. This is a particularly sensitive issue when people are being refused an interview or are having their application turned down. The person who is treated unthinkingly at that point may form an unfavourable impression of the organization. That may not matter too much for the immediate future, but in ten years' time he or she may be a highly desirable catch, or buying for a major customer.

Recruitment advertising, interviewing and selection

Recruitment advertising can be directed along a number of routes. It can comprise ads placed by the organization itself, or ads placed on its behalf by recruitment agencies. Those agencies can also be briefed to examine the lists of potentially mobile staff which they hold. The technique of headhunting can be added where a key and probably senior appointment is being considered. Once again great attention will be paid to detail. Where agencies are involved the briefing to them will be carefully prepared and delivered. Their enthusiasm for the organization as an employer will be developed.

Once the advertising begins to attract replies, the response mechanism goes into action. All the means of handling replies will have been planned in advance, and the criteria for selecting interviewees agreed. This must all be done carefully yet at some speed, for an application which goes cold can be difficult to reactivate.

Interviewing is an art and a science all on its own. Good HR people will be trained not only to ask the right questions but to listen to, judge and follow up the responses. The HR department will be able to organize the structure and method of interview, and to ensure that the employing managers (the HR department's clients) stick to them.

Following interview a decision has to be taken. Are any of the candidates worth recruiting? Which ones? What offers should be made? Should the second choices be told now, or should we wait until acceptance or rejection of the offer made by the first-choice candidate? These and other issues the HR specialist will advise on. Not the least decision is whether or not to re-interview a shortlist in greater depth before deciding finally, though that would preferably have been decided as part of the initial planning of the process.

After a candidate has accepted in principle there will be negotiations over the details of the terms of the employment contract, pension rights, relocation expenses, company vehicle use and so forth. Again the HR department will be involved. Then the new recruit joins, and one of the earliest contacts on the first day is with the HR people who will exercise their standard induction procedure for new staff. That process is not accidental either, but is designed to cover in a logical order all the things someone needs to know as a new member of the club.

Performance review

The employee, once recruited, will have performance reviewed by the boss from time to time and progress monitored by the HR depart-ment. The procedure for this will have been designed by the HR people in consultation with line managers. The point of performance review is that it helps the individual to know where he or she stands and to take appropriate action to improve their performance; the reason for monitoring it over a period is twofold. It enables tracking of the development of the individual, and it allows general conclu-sions to be drawn about the effectiveness of departments and of the organization as a whole in creating the pool of skills and talent which it needs now and will need in the future. If there is strong disagree-ment between the employee and their boss about the conclusions the latter is coming to, the right of appeal to a higher level exists. That might be invoked only after the HR department's attempts to arbi-trate had failed.

The head of a section or of a department is called upon to be pecu-liarly unselfish. A good member of staff is relied on, but must be encouraged to aim for promotion, which may well mean loss to another department. It is important that some mechanism should exist to ensure that good people are encouraged to help the organization as well as themselves by exploring their potential to the full, rather than leaving in frustration to take up opportunities else-where. That is why the HR department has to become involved in both career development and organization development. It looks ahead to foresee future needs for people, and looks at the present people to assess their suitability and potential. It therefore becomes instrumental in shaping the pattern of jobs which the individual manager is invited to take on.

Staff planning

HR managers are responsible for ensuring that there will be an ade-quate supply available at the right time of people with the right char-acteristics to deal with the challenges expected to confront the organization. It would clearly present major difficulties if, for instance, a major organization experienced a hiatus of talent suitable to staff its operations properly. To ensure that they get early warning of potential problems of that sort, organizations employ staff plan-ning techniques.

In essence this is a stock control exercise: who there is to start with, plus who will be recruited, less who will leave or retire, equals who will be left. The workforce can be split in several ways for this exami-nation. Individual departments and disciplines will be looked at, as will particular levels across the organization as a whole. Any gaps revealed by comparison with the forecast of what numbers and skills will be needed can be met by either recruitment or training. The situ-ation does not stand still for, unlike those classic subjects of stock control, widgets, the human resource develops and changes throughout its life-span. Nevertheless, a sophisticated model can be built to take account of at least the major variable. It does not obviate all the difficulties, shortages or surpluses, but it does make many of them foreseeable and thus easier to deal with in a calm and controlled way.

Training

Training is another area of concern to HR managers. Its purpose is to establish suitable levels of performance in the workforce and to maintain and amend them as requirements change. Change is the one fact of organizational life that is certain, and as an inescapable consequence organizations have to be prepared to train. Some people at all levels will be the sort of self-motivated individuals who get on with adapting themselves to the changes they see going on around them. Many people do not have that sort of motivation, so the organization finds that it has to take the initiative to identify training needs and design suitable responses. The range of training methods and vehicles to deal with different situations is vast, and requires special-ist knowledge if they are to be employed properly. The HR depart-ment does not carry out these evaluations and selections entirely alone, but in conjunction with its client departments.

Teams and personalities

HR managers also know that organizations are run not by individu-als but by teams. Teams operate throughout organizations at all levels. By definition, they consist of different individuals. It may be that two or more members of a team are at one another's throats, so that any good work that might have been done is submerged beneath the infighting and quarrelling. There is quite a good chance that if the selection of team members is left to chance, there will be more fric-tion. Instead the HR department tries to understand the personality type and motivation of people likely to become involved in team work and advise those assembling them on how to avoid destructive tensions. For that reason the person best qualified to do the job is sometimes passed over in favour of somebody who will fit better into the set-up. That does not mean that teams must always be bland. There is a strong case for including that uncomfortable character who voices the unpopular view and dares to think and say the unthink-able. It avoids the tendency to 'groupthink' which crops up in many teams. There are occasions when it is right to introduce such an element in order to jolt a team into action. The point is that these teams ought to work best when they have been deliberately designed for the task they are to undertake, rather than thrown together willy-nilly.

The HR department therefore has wide-ranging responsibilities in relation to the organization as a whole and to the individuals within it. Its work is never-ending, for no sooner has it dealt with a problem in one area than another pops up somewhere else. Overlaid on those short-term effects are the longer-term results of great shifts in society. One which has greatly affected whole organizations' philosophies of how they relate to their people, and hence to the work of HR depart-ments, is that arising from the explosion of part-time working. An-other is the shift from the integrated organization to one that outsources as many functions as possible. The work of adjusting HR policies to the constant shifts in the organization's development in relation to internal pressures and the outside environment is a continuous task.

Employees and the law

The main areas of regulation with which HR departments are concerned today are:

- contracts of employment;
- employment protection;
- health and safety.

Health and safety legislation imposes a blanket insistence that work should be done in a safe manner and that all employees in every industry work safely. Along with that come many detailed requirements on employers, from the labelling of containers to the appointment of safety representatives within each department. Most of the burden of understanding the detailed implications falls on HR departments, which interpreted for colleagues and ensure compliance.

Written confirmation of the terms of employment became required legally in the 1970s. The written details of the contract have to contain specified information on all the obvious matters like pay, hours, place of work, holiday entitlement, holiday pay, periods of notice and so forth. Good practice ties all those details in with company rules, job descriptions and grievance procedures.

The wise employer confirms to the employee in writing what the job comprises, to which post the job reports and which posts report to it. That document is referred to as a job description. There will also be company rules defining privileges, duties and unacceptable types of behaviour. Infractions must, by law, be dealt with by a formal disci-plinary procedure. This will probably involve a temporary black mark on a person's file for small offences (such as lateness), right through to instant dismissal for bad behaviour such as working unsafely, violence or theft. The sensible HR manager always invokes suspension so as to allow tempers to cool and evidence to be gathered before a decision about dismissal is taken.

Just as the employer must set up these formal procedures for disciplining the workers, so employees must have, again by law, the right to take up formally any grievances in connection with their employ-ment. Grievance procedures generally expect difficulties to be resolved between the employee and his or her immediate superior, with appeal to higher levels if they cannot agree. Employees' rights increase almost by the year. Common sense and civilized provision for protection against specific wrong, such as unfair discrimination, has been joined by human rights legislation. Since it springs from the mainland European tradition and is ultimately interpreted by a court founded in that tradition, its effects can be expected to be great and far-reaching.

The ultimate arena for settling most employees' disputes with an employer is the industrial tribunal. It comprises three people, usually with a solicitor in the chair. Evidence is taken informally and awards can be made against the employer of costs and damages, or reinstate-ment of the employee. Alternatively the employee may have to pay the employer's costs. No case reaches the industrial tribunal unless ACAS (Advisory, Conciliation and Arbitration Service, a govern-ment body) has tried and failed to bring about a settlement by negotiation.

Employment protection is such that, after working for one year for a large concern (two for a very small one) an employee cannot be rightfully dismissed arbitrarily. Furthermore, there is no qualifying period if the dismissal is on grounds of race or sex discrimination or pregnancy. He or she could be made redundant according to strict rules which test that the job, not just the individual's tenure of it, has been abolished. It is not that straightforward for the employer, who is required to make a reasonable offer of work elsewhere, or pay compensation.

The risk that an employer might be called before an industrial tri-bunal stresses the need to keep records. All that falls to the HR department to create, and often they have to maintain the records, although they will usually train the operating departments to keep them themselves. In tandem with recording events in relation to peo-ple's employment goes the need to train all levels of management from supervisor upwards in the duties which they and the organiza-tion have under employment and safety legislation. Thus, in addition to the other demands on them, the HR people have to be lawyers, administrators and trainers. Theirs is a demanding and fascinating calling.

How you can help your team to develop

Where an organization lacks a HR department the manager's people still need developing, but it becomes a DIY task rather than some-thing to be left to experts. Also, even where a competent and effective HR department exists, the team can do much to work with that department to make sure it is equal to the challenges it faces.

Probably the most important issue in these circumstances for the first-time manager is defensive: to ensure that he or she does not give cause for the firm to be summoned to an industrial tribunal. The law surrounding employment is already complex and becoming more so by the year, so that it is beyond the scope of this book to give compre-hensive instruction. The three things a manager unsupported by experts should do are:

- read an up-to-date book on employment law for managers;
- persuade someone senior to take on a part-time expert adviser (who might, but need not, be one of the firm's legal advisers);
- get the organization to subscribe to Croner's *Employment Law*, a compendium updated monthly which gives detailed guidance.

Earlier in this chapter the main involvements of a typical HR department were listed:

- recruitment;
- communications;
- external relationships;
- recruitment advertising, interviewing and selection;
- performance review;
- staff planning;
- training;
- teams and personalities.

Now that employees have been granted so many rights in law it would be courageous of the first-time manager unversed in legal matters to take on the whole of that list personally. Perhaps the best thing is for the manager to be aware that this whole area is a mine-field, and to move with great caution and only under expert guid-ance. Common sense and a sense of fair play are, regrettably, no longer enough. Nevertheless, there is much scope for the manager to make a real contribution by personal initiative, provided that the most dangerous areas are avoided. These include all aspects of recruitment and selection, performance review and staff promotion, trade unions and staff planning. That leaves us with training, teams and personalities, and one or two others that are relatively unimportant in a smaller organization.

Teams and personalities are dealt with elsewhere in this book from several points of view, meaning that only training remains under the spotlight. Even this can be dangerous unless it is interpreted nar-rowly: whom you select for training and how you go about it might be seen as unfair. Thus here we confine ourselves to training as such. We assume that the decisions on who is to be selected for training have been made and pass the legal tests for fairness.

Although training can scarcely be defined as a problem, planning it can be approached using Figure 9.1, the universal problem-solving model in Chapter 9. Before you go to that model to consider specifics, let us consider what 'training' is. In essence it comprises helping somebody to raise their level of performance in a job. To be of real use, it needs to address specific skills, rather than something more general.

For example, you may wish to raise performance in the general area of customer service, but you cannot train people in 'customer service': that is too general. To do it effectively you need to identify the elements of the package that make up customer service (how quickly the phones are answered, promptness of response to e-mails, quality of telephone responses and so on). That final item, the quality of telephone response, itself needs breaking down further. What are its components? Perhaps they include speed of answer, manner of speaking, politeness, handling of customers' frustration, accuracy of information given, honesty, assertiveness and record keeping. Next, you need to set a benchmark for good performance, which you require to be observed for each element of customer service. Then the gap between current performance and what is desired needs to be measured. This is the gap that your training must be designed to bridge.

Training, like motivation, is not something you can just impose on people. It demands their active and willing participation. It also needs to be pitched at their level: not too low, not too high. The key thing for the manager to grasp is that training takes far longer than one might reasonably expect. The reason for this is that it involves change: change of attitudes, methods and aims. Human beings are averse to change, so we need to be given time and space to shift our positions.

Another consideration is that different people learn in different ways. Some learn from having a go, making mistakes and trying again a bit differently. Others like to stand back and think about the new arrangements, piecing everything together in their minds before doing anything practical. Others like to understand the reasons why before they commit themselves. Some are a bit of each.

A training session using simulations

One of the best ways of training is to run simulations of the real thing, then for participants to discuss the results openly. In the customer relations field, let us say you want to improve telephone technique, and decide that your best operator will share best practice with the rest of the group. For that person to describe what he or she does is useful, but best of all is for colleagues to listen to simulated conversations with difficult customers. You do not need expensive equipment, nor to set up a conference call so that everyone can listen in. For the outline programme below you need between 90 minutes and two hours.

First you need to brief everyone on what will happen. Run through the programme, explaining each item, then ask for questions. The first task for the trainees is to prepare what the difficult customer will say. Set the trainees the task of working in three or four groups to produce lists of statements from customers who they have found hard to cope with. From this they create an outline script of the points they wish to make, and agree a manner in which to make them. This might take between 15 and 25 minutes. Each group appoints a person to play the part of the customer.

In the middle of the room, simply place two chairs back to back. Seat the person playing the customer in one and the call-taker in the other. Neither should be able to see the other, though they must be able to hear one another clearly. This gives a reasonable simulation of telephone contact, with its complete lack of visual cues. Observe and take notes so as to be able to give feedback later. If you have any doubts about the ability of the call-taker to handle what may prove to be a challenging assignment, assume that role yourself and encourage all the participants to take notes for feedback.

At the end of each simulated call, thank everyone for their work. Ask everyone to note down what they thought was good in the way the call was handled, and what, if anything, they were less happy with. After two minutes ask them to call out their positive feedback, and list each point on a flipchart. Add any further points you noticed but that were unmentioned.

Now review the positive responses to the simulation. Recognize and praise what was done well, and get agreement from the whole room for it. Now call for the negatives, asking the call-handler for his or her views and feelings first. People can be surprisingly good critics of their own performance, and often are far harsher on themselves than others would dare to be. Next call for any negatives that the call-handler did not give, then add any of your own. Be sensitive and gentle. People not used to this sort of thing can be badly hurt by what seem like trivia. Use a light touch, but avoid joking.

The other groups can now follow on. Do not worry about hilarity. As long as people are not acting so as to sabotage learning, laughter can be tolerated; indeed, it is usually a sign that things are going well.

You may wonder why I have not suggested introducing the benchmarks advocated earlier. It is because I feel both that trainees have enough to concentrate on anyway in a session of this sort, and that this is, after all, a simulation for sharing good practice, not an assessment of performance. In my view the benchmarks can usefully be employed in simulations, but perhaps to familiarize people with the standards that they require. From that, staff come to be better placed to understand how to observe them in the real world.

Once every group has conducted a simulation, you need to capture the learning that has taken place. Ask the participants to form groups of three to six members, and spend 15 to 20 minutes noting on a flipchart the points that came out of the simulations for them: what to do, what not to do, how we can make sure we do it right. They should write large, as they will show their charts to the whole group.

Each group in turn displays its flipchart and talks through it. Typically, they will be very similar. Some bright ideas will emerge from the third part of their brief, 'how we can make sure we do it right'. Again, add any points of your own, and thank everyone for what will probably have been a fun session. The job is not over yet, though.

Circulate sheets of paper headed 'anonymous feedback', with sec-tions labelled 'What I have learnt', 'What I liked' and 'What I would have liked to be changed'. Ask people to fill them in and leave them on the table by the door as they leave. Assure them that anonymity ensures that they can be completely frank, and that you need to know their true feelings if you are to get things right. Make a point of not watching the order the sheets are left in, so that you really cannot tie a sheet up with a person.

Your final task is to make a written summary of 'how we will get it right' and circulate it to those attending. Try to keep it to one side of a single sheet. If you judge the event a success, you might go on to look for other training areas for which you can usefully run this sort of event.

> ### Key points and tips
>
> - Better-trained and better-motivated people will produce better results from the same resources. Hence the view that people are the key resource.
> - It makes sense to direct specialized attention to the management of any important resource, hence HR departments.
> - The relationship is that managers manage, HR specialists ad-vise.
> - HR proposes policies to ensure labour-market competitiveness, consistency and legality.

nine

Five Key Skills

In this chapter we look at five things a first-time manager will be called on to do at some time, possibly very soon. Three address vital matters of dealing with other people in groups, and two deal with the manager's own mental processes. They are:

- solving a problem;
- managing your time;
- chairing a meeting;
- giving a presentation;
- running a staff session.

The first three are self-explanatory. The fifth may seem more mysterious, but is quite straightforward. It concerns facilitating a working session of your group in which you are all trying to solve a problem that confronts you collectively. The example I have chosen is an arbi-trary one, of speeding up turnround (of what, we do not know, and it does not matter) by 25 per cent. The manager here has the choice of either deciding alone, perhaps with a bit of consultation of staff, or involving the staff in the entire decision process. I advocate the latter, as I believe it is both easier and a very great deal more effective.

First, we deal with solving a problem.

Solving a problem

Problems come at the manager in all shapes and sizes, presenting themselves in a never-ending flow. This is to be welcomed since, as Sir John Harvey-Jones pointed out, a manager without a problem is a manager without a job. However such reassurance may ring hollow to a manager who feels as if he or she is already drowning in a sea of difficulties when along comes a further downpour to swell their number. There is, however, a way to deal with problems.

Essentially the message is this: dealing with problems can be

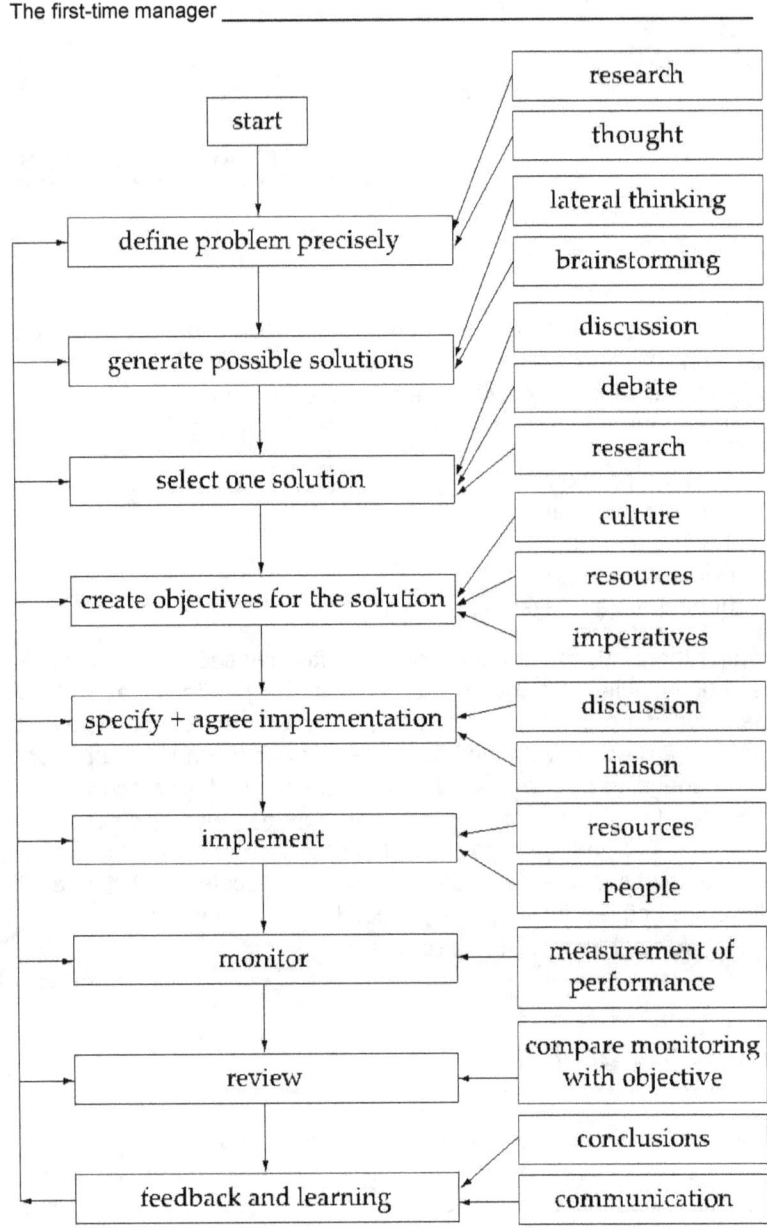

Figure 9.1 *The universal problem-solving model*

turned into a routine. Far from reducing the quality of solutions, following a routine will ensure consistency and thoroughness. In order to turn something into a routine, a model of behaviour needs to be available. The universal problem-solving model looks like Figure 9.1.

While following this model will not itself solve problems for you, it will ensure that you approach all problems consistently and cover all the ground necessary. Sometimes you can afford to seem to skip a stage (please note the 'seem') because you have special knowledge, but in general this model is a good servant. It also helps with communication: if you have to explain what you propose and why, or why you took a particular course of action, pulling this model out of the file will help you to put your case across clearly and lucidly.

Let us look at each of the model's stages in turn.

Define problem precisely

Problems are not always what they seem; sometimes the reported problem is only a symptom of a deeper, underlying problem. As any doctor will tell you, relieving symptoms may give a welcome respite but will not last; curing the problem is the only way of getting rid of the symptoms permanently. Alternatively, the 'problem' may be no such thing, merely a result of misrecording or miscommunication. To arrive at the precise definition you may need to do some probing (grandly titled 'research' in the model) and give perhaps quite a lot of thought to what is going on.

Generate possible solutions

There may be a long list of ways to address the problem, but only a few may be practicable. Or maybe only one approach springs to mind. Either way, it is good to be suspicious of only a small pool of solutions. While it might prove to reflect reality, it might equally well indicate a lack of imagination. Even (or especially) where a single, obvious solution presents itself, there is often merit in thinking creatively to extend the choice.

Select one solution

The manager may involve others at this stage as well as at others. Further investigation may be required to establish the true suitability of the solution selected, and much debate and discussion may surround this stage. It is important to remember that, up to the point at which you pass this stage, you can always turn back and try again. After this, you are committed to making the solution work.

Create objectives for the solution
Remembering that the solution is selected in the hope that it will make things better, we need to set up a test to show whether or not it really does. For that, some objectives must be created towards which it will work. These objectives will be conditioned, not only by the nature of the task, but also by several internal factors. Notable among them are culture (objectives that offend the local sense of propriety will fail), resources (objectives requiring unrealistic levels of resourcing will fail) and internal imperatives (setting an improvement target of 5 per cent will be unacceptable if the organization as a whole is aiming for 10).

When writing objectives it is important to make them SMART. SMART is an acronym composed of the initial letters of specific, mea-surable, achievable, relevant and timed:

- Specific: not vague or general;
- Measurable: without measurement there can be no knowledge of achievement;
- Achievable: unattainable goals are a waste of time;
- Relevant: must be related directly to the task in hand;
- Timed: must give timings by which results are to be achieved.

Specify and agree implementation
A simple solution to a small, self-contained problem might easily be implemented within the team. More complex matters might involve several members or all of the team, and perhaps people in other departments too. It is clearly pointless to declare a solution launched without first checking that it is understood and accepted by everyone it will affect.

The specification does need to be written, or all kinds of trouble can arise. Written specifications can be given to others to enhance their understanding. They can also be kept on file to resolve disputes; without the file copy it is one opinion against another, possibly months after the event when memories have faded.

Implement
Here the human dimension, never deeply buried, comes to the surface. People will be expected to undertake implementation. To do this they need to understand what is required, know how to do it, know how to deal with snags, and have the resources necessary. The wise manager will keep a close eye on events, handling problems as they arise and disseminating information about best practice.

While that might seem to be the end of the process, it is not. At least, that is true in the better-managed organization.

Monitor
In order to conduct the review, which is the next step after this, infor-mation needs to be gathered. The information will relate to the objec-tives, especially the elements of measurement and timing. A specific point is made here in the model as otherwise there is a risk that, in the press of business, no one will remember to collect the information. If that is done, nobody will be able to say whether the solution actually achieved its aims and the manager will look foolish, not to say incompetent.

Review
Comparing the outcome (from 'monitoring') with the aims (from 'objectives') reveals the extent to which the solution is on or off target. While the information may be interesting to the point of fascination, it is of no practical use until the next stage is undertaken.

Feedback and learning
The results of the review are fed back to each stage of the process in turn, starting at the bottom. The reason for this is twofold. First, if the solution has failed to deliver, the organization needs to know at what level it got things wrong, and working up the hierarchy until the level is reached where the mistake was made reveals this. Second, if the solution has succeeded the organization needs everyone to know at all levels of this process, so that they add this to their understand-ing of what works.

Only now is the process complete.

As a final point in this section I would advocate that managers adapt this and other general models for use in the specific context of their organization. Models are not sacrosanct, and since time out of mind craftspeople have modified standard tools to serve a particular purpose or suit an individual's hand. Having models is extremely useful, for it avoids the need to treat every situation as if it is the first event of its kind in history. That simplifies life. Refining the models in the light of experience ensures that they are adapted to changing cir-cumstances and the manager's own development.

Managing your time

Most people get about the same ration of time in a working year. From that ration some produce great results, others mediocrity. What makes the difference? Most often, the reason lies in the way they chose to use their time.

This is a topic on which a lot has been written. Of that which I have read, little seems of much use to me in my life which, in fairness, may be more a comment on me than on the writers concerned. To my mind there are two clear imperatives: to apply time where it will have the greatest effect, and to decide the sequence in which you do things.

Deciding where to spend the bulk of your time is easy. Think back to Pareto and the 80/20 rule, discussed on page 104. Applying that to the way you use time will mean devoting most effort to the 20 per cent of activities that produce 80 per cent of your results. As for the sequence in which things are done, Figure 9.2 is a simple tool which places tasks into four boxes in a simple matrix.

What Figure 9.2 is saying is that things are either important or unimportant, urgent or non-urgent, and you can post them in whichever box is appropriate. Box 1 is obviously what you do first, box 2, second and so on. Indeed, items in box 4 might never get done at all. If so, that might be a healthy sign, showing that you really are spending time where it is most needed. Of course, neglecting items from other boxes while you tackle those in box 1 often means they climb up the order of priority. That is fine, for when they appear in box 1 they will be dealt with. More importantly, you have not been diverted into

	IMPORTANT	
URGENT	yes	no
yes	1	2
no	3	4

Figure 9.2 *Classification of work to be done*

looking at possibly fascinating but ultimately unrewarding activities close to the end of the pecking order.

That might seem like very little on such an important topic, in which case, do read one or two of the many books on the subject. In terms of reward for time invested, however, I believe, I hope not arro-gantly, that the few minutes spent reading this will outperform the return from the hours needed to read entire books.

Chairing a meeting

Probably the single greatest source of the frustration that managers heap on their staff is meetings. Meetings are held for which there seems to be no clear aim, to which the wrong people are invited, which reach no clear decisions, where for every five people in the room there are six opinions on what was said, which take decisions without considering the implications. All this adds up to a great diversion of effort, waste of time and creation of annoyance. Yet the answers are simple. The effective meeting will:

- be well planned;
- be attended by the right people;
- last no longer than is absolutely necessary;
- deal only with the business in hand;
- result in a single view of events and decisions;
- take decisions that stick.

Well planned

First, the manager will have thought why the meeting is needed, and will have considered other means of reaching the desired outcome and rejected them. He or she will write down a clear definition of the aims of the meeting. Next, the people necessary to attend will be identified and contacted. Their preparedness and availability will be confirmed. An agenda will be written and circulated well in advance, with reminder e-mails going out a day or so in advance of the event. The right sort of venue will have been selected and arrangements for any catering made.

A conventional agenda has the following structure, although prac-tice will vary from one organization to another:

> A meeting will be held in (venue) at (time) on (date) to discuss (topic), chaired by (name) of (department).
>
> Agenda:
>
> 1. Apologies for non-attendance.
> 2. (If this is one in a series of meetings) Confirmation of the min-utes of the last meeting.
> 3. (If part of a series) Matters arising from the minutes of the last meeting.
> 4. Issue A.
> 5. Issue B.
> 6. Issue C (etc).
> 7. Date, time and place of next meeting.
> 8. Any other business, by leave of the chair.

Attended by the right people

Not only should the right people be there, they ought to be the only people there. Too often extra people are called in 'in case they are needed', spend their time doodling, and resolve never to attend one of this manager's meetings ever again.

Last no longer than is absolutely necessary

The meeting starts with a clear statement by the chair of the purpose of the meeting and its proposed duration. The agenda might even carry times by which each item is to be completed; this does tend to keep discussion focused. Someone is deputed to take notes of key points and decisions, to form the basis of a summary for later circula-tion. At the same time, it is crucially important to ensure that every-one has a chance to contribute. Anyone who is saying nothing on a topic should be asked what he or she thinks. People can remain silent despite having strong and possibly correct beliefs, in which case the organization is the poorer for not knowing their views. It is a wise chair who makes the effort to elicit them.

Deal only with the business in hand

Since everything in an organization is connected to everything else, it is theoretically possible for any discussion to involve consideration of every issue in each department. A good agenda will cover only what needs to be discussed, and a sound chair will confine discussion to those items. If something of real import does arise it can, if the chair agrees, be raised under 'Any other business'. By that time the aim of the meeting will be accomplished without the diversion of attention to other matters.

Result in a single view of events and decisions
Immediately after the meeting, the person taking notes will write up a confirmation of events and decisions, agree it with the chair and circulate it immediately. Depending on the culture of the organization it might take the form of notes or follow the more formal convention of meeting minutes, following the structure of the agenda:

Minutes of a meeting held in (venue) at (time) on (date) to discuss (topic), chaired by (name) of (department)
Attendance: Jane Pink (chair)
Jim White (secretary)
Jo Blue
Tim Black
Angela Brown
Mike Green

1. Apologies for non-attendance

Dick Grey was unable to attend as he had been called away at short notice to Siena.

2. Confirmation of the minutes of the last meeting

The minutes were confirmed as a true record and signed by the chair.

3. Matters arising from the minutes of the last meeting

Minute 13/4: Dick Grey had confirmed that the figure was 25, not 35 as had been thought.

Minute 13/8: Angela Brown now has the colour chart and it is out for consultation with staff.

4. Issue A

(Whatever has to be reported, for example) Jane Pink reported that ballpens were being stolen from counters at an alarming rate. Losses were running at up to 10 a month, 25 times budget. Various ways of addressing the problem were discussed

> and it was agreed that a ball of string and a book of knots would be purchased. Tim Black volunteered to do this by the end of the week.
>
> Action: Tim Black
>
> 5. *Issue B*
>
> (Ditto)
>
> 6. *Issue C (etc)*
>
> 7. *Date, time and place of next meeting*
>
> The next meeting will be held at (time) on (date) at (place).
>
> 8. *Any other business*
>
> There being no other business, the chair closed the meeting at 3.05 pm.
>
> Signed: Jim White (secretary)

Decisions that stick

The process of taking notes and circulating minutes immediately does remind people of what took place and their agreement to certain actions. Those with action points against their names will usually respond quickly. If by any chance there is disagreement about the minutes, the opportunity exists for people to air them with the secre-tary and chair while memories are still fresh. By contrast, minutes that come out weeks later, with action points not highlighted, are more often ignored.

Giving a presentation

This is a task that can reduce competent, confident people to a quaking mass. Experienced presenters, who might once have been like that themselves, simply cannot understand why. The process is simple, straightforward, and within the gift of anyone able to plan and speak. The key, as with so many things, lies in planning.

Contrast two ways of giving a presentation. The first involves no preparation and little idea of what it is meant to achieve; except for a great extempore speaker, this is doomed. The second speaker prepares by working methodically through a checklist of what needs to be done, then delivers according to a plan. This is likely to succeed. In the first case the performance is more like that of a brilliant debater; in the second, a theatrical performance, where the playwright creates the script and the actor delivers it. Indeed, a presentation undertaken by the method I shall propose could theoretically be created and delivered by two different people.

The first stage is to plan. For this you need to know:

- who the audience is;
- what the aim of the presentation is;
- where it will take place;
- when it will be given;
- the circumstances of delivery;
- the equipment and media available.

We shall now look at these in more detail.

Who the audience is

We all use different tones of voice and different vocabulary accord-ing to whom we are addressing at any time, even though the message may be the same. Consider the differences in how you would greet the following: an old friend not seen for some time; your boss's boss encountered at the theatre; the teenage daughter of a neighbour met in the shops; an old teacher at a school reunion; one of your team met in the park. They would all be different. A greeting is fairly free from content: that is, you are not trying to convey pieces of information nor to persuade, yet in each case your approach would be tailored to the audience. When the aim is to put across an argument or some facts, the tailoring becomes even more necessary.

Thus, when writing the script, have in mind a couple of representa-tive members of the audience and write as if speaking directly to them alone. If the audience is mixed you will need to decide what further aims you have, over and above the formal goals of the presen-tation. Is addressing all of them equally important? If so, write simply and clearly so as to be understood by the lowest intelligence in the room. Do you not mind particularly about some audience members, as long as you get across to one particular group? Script just for that group and let the rest go hang; but be careful not to appear arrogant.

As a general rule, all audiences can understand scripts that:

- use short sentences;

- use everyday words, generally those that came to us from Saxon rather than Latin and Greek;
- use the active rather than the passive voice ('we have sold more', not 'sales have risen'; 'we must try harder' not 'greater efforts must be made');
- do not try to impress by using abstruse vocabulary (which is itself an example of abstruse vocabulary, words that are not part of normal, everyday speech);
- use visual aids intelligently.

People familiar with academia may question this advice, recalling research done a few years ago at a conference where the same argu-ments were put twice in different papers. In one, the paper was written in clear English. In the other case the same things were said far more obscurely. The audiences were asked to rate each paper for intellectual content. The clear winner was the paper that nobody could understand. Some might contend that this says more about academics' gullibility than the theory of communication.

What the aim of the presentation is

Now that you have identified your target audience, you can move on to what you want to bring about. Exactly what is the presentation intended to achieve? Write this down, consider it carefully and even ask colleagues to criticize your aim. The reason for this degree of rigour is that you will constantly be returning to the aim in order to check that everything in the presentation works towards the aim, and that anything that does not do this is excluded. If the aim is not clearly and comprehensively defined, the presentation can only go off on the wrong direction.

Where it will take place

There is a world of difference between an informational session aimed at updating your team, while they sit at their desks and one delivered in a conference centre to several hundred people. While the nature of the audience is the main influence on the style of the presen-tation, the venue is also important. Your audience will expect you to be more formal in every way in the more formal setting.

When it will be given

A presentation to be delivered at 8 am on a wet Monday in February will first need to warm the audience up, perhaps literally as well as metaphorically. Attention to and involvement with what you are saying will not start off at a high level. On the other hand, one given that same night while the port is circulating following dinner may require you to discourage vocal contributions from the floor in order to be heard at all. This issue relates back to what was said about the audience: when you begin is related to the state they will be in, straight off the plane and jet-lagged, tired beyond caring after an 18-hour day, or full of excitement, alert and well rested at an event they enjoy.

If you have a choice, particular times are to be avoided. Immediately after lunch, while everyone is dozily digesting, is the worst slot. Other poor ones are when people are looking forward to the end of the session – just before lunch, before dinner or coming up to the conclusion of a meeting. If you are in a position to influence the time at which you go on, this might be worth remembering. The craftier reader will also have spotted that if there is bad news to convey it might be best to deliver it during one of the graveyard slots.

Video conferences with other parts of the world need to take into account the time of day in participants' home countries and the way of life there. The point is obvious when related to a New Zealander to whom your 3 pm is 2 am, but even within Europe habits vary. While all good Swedes might, for all I know, be tucked up asleep by 11 pm, many Spaniards are only beginning to think of going out to dinner at that time.

The circumstances of delivery

This touches on the issues of 'where' and 'when' that I have already covered. Remember that 20 minutes is the maximum time for which most people can be expected to concentrate; since that is the maximum, 10 or 15 minutes is a more desirable duration. Further dimensions to the context of your presentation could be influential. Examples include whether or not the press or public might be present, any overall theme to a conference to which all speakers are required to conform, and events within the organization or in the world outside. I remember on the evening of 11 September 2001 being involved in a long-planned presentation of some consequence for the organization I represented. I cannot say that my thoughts were fully focused and I am certain that neither were those of my audience.

The equipment and media available

The importance of visual aids has been mentioned and cannot be over-emphasized. They can, however, be over-complicated and over-used. The reason for their importance is that we understand and remember much more information if we are shown and told it simul-taneously, rather than if we are just told it. Abraham Lincoln and Winston Churchill spoke with enormous impact in the complete absence of such support, so any reader who can boast their class of oratory is free to ignore this advice. The rest might find visual aids as useful and helpful as I have throughout my life.

The absolute minimum a presenter should insist on is a supply of flipchart paper and pens, and some way of displaying the sheets to the audience. This is, however, far less than the desirable minimum. The next level up is a projector for 35 mm slides. The advantage with this is that the speaker can use a switch on a lead to change slides as he or she speaks, but preparing the slides is a lengthy process. Better is an overhead projector (OHP), a device on which a sheet of clear film carrying graphics and text is placed to be projected on a large screen behind the presenter's head. The options for preparing slides are between handwritten, printed or electronic.

Electronic presentations (usually using Microsoft's PowerPoint software) are prepared on a laptop and transmitted to a large electronic screen. This enables presentations of great sophistication to be given, involving video and sound as well as dissolves and so forth. The problems it presents are threefold. Not every venue has the req-uisite electronic screen; the power of the software dazzles the pre-senter and may lure him or her into spending large amounts of time to create inconsequential effects; and an inexperienced user might have problems in paging to and fro to bring up particular slides in response to questions or calls for clarification. As an occasional user I prefer to prepare my slides using PowerPoint but then to print them on to transparencies. When at the end of the presentation I am asked a question about the relationship between slides 3 and 7, it is easy to isolate and compare them. A further advantage of PowerPoint is that it allows a set of miniature slides to be printed on paper to be given to the audience for note-taking.

Planning the presentation

Taking into account the matters already considered, the plan for the presentation follows a simple template. Overall, it means telling the audience what you are going to tell them, telling them just that, then telling them what you have told them – a summary that emphasizes the need for repetition of the message. To put a little more detail on that skeleton, the main headings you can follow are these:

- introduction;
- background;
- proposal;
- justification;
- summary.

Introduction
Here you announce the topic of the presentation and summarize it ('tell them what you are going to tell them'). This part is best written last, as it is only when you have completed the planning of the presentation that you can summarize it.

Background
Cover here the reasons that the matter in hand has become an issue, and the likely consequences of doing nothing.

Proposal
Describe what you think should be done.

Justification
Explain why this course of action should be taken and no other.

Summary
Sum up: tell the audience what you have told them.

Preparing the slides

One of the worst errors in slide design is to create a script which you then read out. (I have actually witnessed this done by a senior civil servant, who also turned his back on the audience in order to read from the screen – see below.) The point of the slides is to guide you and your audience through the chain of reasoning that you plan to follow. Therefore each slide will be:

- written in headlines, not prose;
- comprised of no more than three bulleted points;
- consistent in design with its neighbours;
- written in the largest, clearest typeface available, without looking overcrowded.

Headlines, not prose
If you want to make the point that the sickness records between teams A, B and C show respectively 5 per cent, 10 per cent and 20 per

cent of days lost, do not write this out in full. Use instead the headline with which an item in the staff newsletter might introduce the story, something like 'Variable sickness record'. When delivering the pre-sentation you read out that headline, then give the detail in speech. This approach does something valuable for your presenting style, too. Instead of having to read from your script, you will know by heart the information you want to convey under each point, and will look so much more on top of your material by saying rather than reading it.

No more than three bulleted points
For some mysterious reason human beings respond to information delivered in sets of three. Listen to any politician ('more nurses, more doctors, more hospitals', 'the public is tired, fed up and rebellious'). Don't fight it but use it, and ensure that your slides follow the same pattern. That is not an inflexible rule, for there can be good reasons to ignore it now and again, but if there is no case for any particular number of points on a slide, choose to make it three.

Consistent in design
Your audience will get used to a particular style in your slides, and find it uncomfortable to have to adapt to completely different typefaces, layout, use of graphics and so on from slide to slide. This also leads to the unconscious suspicion that your argument might be as inconsistent as the slides appear to be.

You may be tempted to select a design principle that is meant to stand out from the crowd as distinctive and memorable. I would never say 'never', but for 99 per cent of the time would advocate playing safe. Once you are two minutes into the presentation and realize your approach is not working there is little you can do to save a disastrous set of slides, but all other aspects of your style can be amended as you go along.

Clear typeface, not overcrowded
Sit in the seat with the worst view in the room and simulate the conditions under which you will present. (It may be night-time when you rehearse but a bright, sunny day when you deliver: will light leaks around the curtains wash out your slides?) To give yourself the best chance all slides must be perfectly legible to all, even those with imperfect sight. As a rough rule, the three or so bullet-point headlines on your slides should be separated by at least their own depth, and

the clear space at top and bottom ought to be at least a fifth of the height, with at least a sixth of the width clear on either side.

Crib cards

Your final task before starting to rehearse is to prepare your crib cards. Most inexperienced presenters use A4 pads for their notes, writing out the script in full. This is a big mistake. A pad is awkward to handle, and there might be nowhere to put it down. Keeping your place in it is not easy, especially when there are slides to be handled too. Above all, those hand gestures that make a presentation come alive become quite alarming when amplified by cascades of paper. Finally, if you write a script the chances are you will read it, which is deadly. It kills off the spontaneity that is at the heart of good delivery.

Instead, get hold of some filing cards, about three inches by two. Each one represents a slide, and you number them accordingly. On a card you print in large letters with a broad marker the headlines of the slide. Underneath, in a different colour, you print the key points you want to make under each headline. (If this overcrowds them, switch to allocating one headline per card, but be sure to code them so that you can quickly relate them to the slide concerned.) Finally, punch holes in the top left-hand corner (or the opposite if you are left-handed) and thread through a loose treasury tag (one of those green bits of string with a metal tag at each end) – or use a piece of string. Now even if you drop them, they will still be in order when you pick them up.

Rehearsing the presentation

The more you rehearse, the more spontaneous your performance will seem to be. Apparent spontaneity makes it look as if you are on top of your subject and leads to a more professional delivery. Using the crib cards you can rehearse at any time. Sitting on a train or in a traffic jam, waiting for a call centre to answer, waiting for an agenda item that does not concern you to come to an end, as well as dozens of other odd pieces of time that crop up on any day: all present the chance to pull the crib cards out of a pocket or handbag and run through a slide or two. You do not need a projector to do this.

This is not to say that projector time is superfluous, though. Getting used to the slide changes, checking where you will put the unused and used slides, finding out where to stand so as not to block the view, walking about and making gestures as you present: all these are well worth doing.

To focus attention on the point you are currently making, lay a hex-agonal-section pen or sharp pencil on top of the slide to act as a pointer. Never use a round-section pointer as they always roll, which will amuse the audience much more than it does you.

If there is enough hanging on the result, you might wish to persuade a trusted colleague to witness a rehearsal and criticize your performance. If you choose the right person, you could learn a lot.

Before you complete rehearsals, be sure that you can turn the pro-jector on and off and focus it in the dark. Also check that it has a spare bulb and that you know what to do if the bulb fails.

Delivering the presentation
Having rehearsed, you will be confident in what you are about to deliver but understandably nervous about the next quarter of an hour. Prepare your workplace around the projector, and begin only when you have everything shipshape. If previous presenters have been considerate this will take only a second or two.

Begin with the OHP turned off. Put your first slide on the platen in the spot that you know from rehearsal will put it in the right place on the screen. Pick up your crib cards and conceal them in one hand. Smile, step forward and address the room, introducing yourself and telling the audience that you plan to give a presentation which will last for 10 minutes, followed by the chance to ask questions. Either ask for questions to be kept for the end, or allow interruptions for clarification as you are speaking. Tell the audience where they will find their hard copies of your slides.

Return to the OHP, switch it on and start. If you need to check where you are, never look at the screen, but only at the slide. Keep your pointer moving as you move on. Turn over your crib cards to make sure they are always in the right place. After plenty of rehearsal you may find that you do not need them, but keep them ready just in case you should suddenly dry up. It does happen to the most accom-plished performers; even the Royal Shakespeare Company employs prompters.

If an interruption should come, deal with it immediately. If it is to do with clarifying what you have just said, clarify and move on. If it is more substantial, it might be that you will be covering the point later in the presentation, in which case say so; if not, say that you will be happy to deal with the question at the end. Almost always an audi-ence will go along with you, for as the speaker, you have great authority. Some members of the audience might admire you for what you are doing and go so far as to shush questioners.

If you have things to say between slides, switch the projector off. (I prefer to switch the projector off when changing slides in any case, to avoid the shock and diversion caused by sudden brilliant white light.) Always remember that if there is a slide on the screen it is more powerful than anything you are saying. Switch it off if you are not directly addressing the topic of the slide.

At the end, switch off the OHP, thank the audience for their attention and say that you will take any questions. Ask anyone who interrupted if he or she would like to remind the meeting again of his/her point so that you can deal with it. Once things are truly over, thank the audience again, say where they can contact you if they so wish, pick up your materials and leave.

Dealing with questions

The vast majority of questions will be sincere expressions of puzzlement about some aspect of the matters dealt with in the presentation. Very occasionally some will have an underlying motive. The latter fall into perhaps three categories: attempts to embarrass you, attempts to use your presentation to get at someone else, or attempts to make the questioner look good. Wherever you suspect this may be going on you can play a game of your own and ask publicly if the questioner has any advice on how best to deal with the issue raised. Exposing a person with a destructive attitude by demanding that he or she behave positively can embarrass him or her deeply.

At the end of each answer, ask if you have dealt with the question to the questioner's satisfaction, and if so, move on to the next. Never speak outside your brief, but suggest that such a matter will have to be taken up with whoever is responsible. If you cannot answer, say so, and if it is appropriate to do so, undertake to get the answer for the questioner. Make a note, and make sure you do it.

Running a staff session

From time to time managers want to get staff together for a meeting. Meetings can be for discussion and decision, information sharing or creation (for example, of a new team approach to an issue). Meetings can be greatly productive, or they can be a colossal waste of time. In the latter case they are dispiriting, demotivating and frustrating to everyone attending. Managers therefore want always to run meetings that are in the former category.

The type of meeting held seated at a table is dealt with elsewhere. (Or, as one US expert advocates, held standing up – his experience that such meetings cover the same ground but are far briefer and to the point.) Here we shall deal with the kind of meeting that involves the whole team, and addresses finding agreement on either how to do something or how to do it better.

Why should the team be involved in this way? After all, isn't the manager there to manage, and isn't it his or her job to decide what is to be done and how? Yes, of course. But that principle of managerial responsibility is not affected by talking to staff. Nor is the quality of the decision likely to be worse if they are involved; indeed, it will probably be better. The clinching argument for doing it this way, though, is to do with commitment. If staff themselves have devised the procedure they are more likely to understand the need for it and hence to feel committed to making it work. Compare the two sets of possible attitudes shown in Table 9.1.

The resources needed for such a session are the team themselves, chairs, tables, flipcharts and pens, and masking tape or something else to stick paper to the walls and notepads. The room needs to be well lit and ventilated and away from interruptions. Refreshments should be handy. The suggestions below assume an ideal group size of 8 to 12; the plan can be adapted for smaller numbers, and can manage up to perhaps 20. Above that the group may need to be split or another technique employed.

The overall shape of such a session is as follows:

- focusing on the issue;
- considering the imperatives;
- generating possible methods;
- selecting a single best method;
- fixing the decision.

We shall now look at these in more detail.

Table 9.1

	Staff not involved	*Staff involved*
General attitude	Sceptical	Committed
Recognition of the need for change	Low	High
Understanding of the policy	Low	High
Commitment to the policy	Low	High

Focusing on the issue

The manager begins by setting the scene, stating the objectives and time-frame of the meeting. Immediately work begins. Staff are asked to focus on the issue individually for five minutes, noting down why it is an issue, what advantages they see from its solution and what problems they expect in the implementation of change. After five minutes they move into groups of around four, discuss their individ-ual thoughts and record their views as a group on a flipchart sheet. That might take from 10 to 15 minutes. Then the manager calls the meeting together and one member of each subgroup reports to the whole room, using as a visual aid the group's flipchart which they stick on the wall. During this the manager sits quietly as part of the audience. At the end of this activity the entire meeting will be focused on the matter in hand and the manager can move the meeting on.

Considering the imperatives

Here the manager has a choice. Either he or she can tell the group what the externally imposed imperatives are (let us say it is to speed up turnround by 25 per cent) or he/she can ask the group how much they think the matter could be improved. It is a matter of judgement which is chosen. The former case is simpler, but may create resentments from which the meeting will not recover. Equally, it may create a cohesion between group members. The manager hopes that cohesion will be directed at solving the problem, but the risk is that it will be directed to condemning the foolishness of such an aim.

If the manager chooses the second model, the group is unlikely to come up with a figure exactly matching the aim; their figure will be higher (I have known this) or, more likely, lower. Once again, the manager must judge how to handle the situation. Having got used to the idea of change, would this group be likely to accept that it should not be too difficult to improve from their proposed figure of 15 per cent to the required 25 per cent, or will they think they have been hoodwinked? (They would have generated their notional 15 per cent in the same way as before, with individual work followed by group activity. This pattern repeats itself throughout.)

If the aim is externally dictated, rather than an ambition that the team have thought up for themselves, the manager may find him or herself called upon to calm worries and deal with anger. It is vital that people are given the chance to work out their frustrations, for nothing constructive can be done until all superfluous steam has been blown off. This also gives the more constructively minded a chance to say something; rarely are they the first to speak in such a situation. The manager can build on constructive contributions, however tenuous, to steer the meeting round to thinking not how impossible the requirement is, but how it might be achieved and what resources would be needed.

Generating possible methods
Now that the meeting has agreed, however tentatively, to give some thought to the possibility of change, staff can return to thinking about ways and means. The manager will tread with care, aware that, in an extreme case such as that used for illustration, there will be many strong feelings which are not being voiced. As long as those feelings remain, and they cannot be avoided, they will impede progress.

Again staff are asked to work individually and then in groups. The timings now need to be more generous, for this is a demanding part of the session. The manager asks staff to divide a sheet of paper into three parts headed 'how the team could change to achieve the goal', 'how I could change to achieve the goal' and 'resources we would need'. This might take 15 or 20 minutes. Then groups could form (it is often a good idea to insist that group composition changes each time, which avoids the formation of cliques), discuss their individual find-ings and produce a composite view from them all. The same report-back to the whole team follows. Questions and discussion are encouraged, but the manager needs to ensure that the strong con-cealed feelings do not spill over into interpersonal tensions. After all, everyone is faced by the same problem; they ought to be able to work together to address it.

Depending on the quality of the flipcharts produced and of their accompanying commentaries, the manager may wish to create an agreed summary flipchart representing the corporate view of the team. If this is done it makes the next stage of the session easier.

Here it might be useful to mention the technique of brainstorming. This term is apparently now frowned on by those who appoint them-selves to take offence on behalf of others, as being offensive to people with epilepsy. If any offence is caused, I apologize. All I can say is that a close member of my family was epileptic, and working in the field of training and personnel, used the term freely. Brainstorming is used to think creatively without constraint, and it can often clear log-jams in thought processes. Often scenarios like the one suggested come up with a solution to 90 per cent of the problem quite readily; it is the final 10 per cent that requires brainstorming.

The idea is that you allot a short period of time (say three minutes) in which people call out all the ways of solving the problem they can think of. The session leader records the ouputs. The only rule is that there are no rules: if someone says 'deliver documents by spacerocket', down it goes on the list. The point is that someone's apparently silly suggestion can spark off an idea in someone else's mind that could actually work. In the case of the spacerocket, maybe what is really needed is a courier service that would get documents delivered in hours rather than the present days taken by the mail; or another person could be inspired to think of converting all documen-tation to e-mail. But without the spacerocket suggestion, neither of those possible solutions would have been thought of. The final stage is to delete all the obviously crazy ideas, leaving only those that might possibly work. As a quick fix technique, brainstorming can be brought into play in almost any context whenever ideas seem to be stalling.

Selecting a single best method

If all has gone to plan so far the manager will notice that the energy previously directed into hostility is now going towards trying to solve the problem. This will no doubt be welcome. The staff may also have noticed it and will be feeling warmly towards the manager for what he or she has done to help them escape from a miserable, nega-tive mindset into a more positive, problem-solving one.

The group can now define their best solution. It will probably be a hybrid formed from bits of various models put forward. Once it is agreed upon it needs to be taken apart and checked that it can really be made to work. Again the team needs to break into small groups, each possibly made up from people who work on a particular area and are therefore experts in their part of the team's operations. They think through every aspect of the new method, consider exceptions, think of things that might stop it from working and devise ways of dealing with them. Again, they report back to the group as a whole, using flipchart sheets. Those sheets are carefully collected by the manager, as they represent the new procedure that will meet the requirement placed upon the team.

Fixing the decision

As soon as possible, and no more than a day later, the manager ensures that any unanswered questions about what might be done are dealt with, liaises with other departments to make certain that the new plan will mesh with their processes, and publishes the result in a note to the team, which fixes the new system of operation in place.

Throughout the process described, the manager has played a role that some may see as minor. All the substantial work has been done by the team. Do they feel peeved at that? It's unlikely, although there might remain the odd sceptic. The facts are that, from the organiza-tion's point of view, the procedure has been designed by the best experts in that area that it employs, the people who actually run the procedure day by day; from the team's viewpoint they have at last got something they know will work, rather than something foisted on them by an ignorant outsider; and from where the manager stands the team has worked together, effectively, for the common good. And the staff can say that for once, someone has actually listened to them.

The manager needs to recognize that the whole process will have raised expectations. Not only must he or she deliver on any resources called for to execute the new plan, but there is no going back to hiding in the office and issuing edicts. Having tasted communism (with a small 'c') the team will be loth to return to traditional, hierarchical ways of determining how they work. The manager need not feel threatened by this, but may congratulate him or herself on having lib-erated a great new force, people's commitment to the life of the group, and put it to work.

Key points and tips

- Dealing with problems is one of the manager's main functions. Approaching the task methodically can make it simpler.
- How a manager uses time can determine success or failure.
- Effective chairs of meetings listen more than they speak, drawing out the contributions of everyone else.
- Presenting need not be feared; following a tried and tested template can make it straightforward.
- Involving your people in decisions affecting the team pays huge dividends: any manager can follow the simple method.

Further Reading

Belbin, R.M. *Management Teams*, Butterworth Heinemann, 1984 Further reading

Blake, R.R. and Mouton, J.S. *The Managerial Grid III – the Key to Leader-ship Excellence*, Gulf Publishing Co., 1985

Handy, C.B. *Understanding Organisations*, Penguin, 1985

Herzberg, F. *Work and the Nature of Man*, World Publishing Co., 1966 McGregor, D. *Leadership and Motivation*, MIT Press, 1966

Maslow, A.H. A theory of human motivation, *Psychological Review*, Vol. 50, 1943

Mayo, E. *The Human Problems of Industrial Civilisation*, Macmillan, 1933

Mayo, E. *The Social Problems of Industrial Civilisation*, Routledge & Kegan Paul, 1949

Index

ACAS (Advisory, Conciliation and Arbitration Service) 195
accounting systems 161
acid test 174
acknowledgement 51
advertising 112, 118, 126,
   media 118
AIDA (Attention, Interest, Desire, Action) 123
aims, personal 22 appraisal, staff 56, 191, 197
ARR (Annual Rate of Return) 183
asset stripping 72
assets, fixed and current 173 assumptions 81
authority 47

balance sheet 172 behaviour 28
Belbin, Dr Meredith 54
Berne, Erich 33
Blake and Mouton 36
boss
   your boss's 6, 21, 59 your own 20, 57
BPR (Business Process Re-engineering) 62, 69
brainstorming 202, 222
break-even analysis 180
budgeting control 182
   variance 182
   zero-based 69

cash 170
cash flow 167
   forecasting 169
change 19, 65, 192

charity sector 9, 110
communication 27, 35, 42
   HR department and 188
   visual 113
   written 44, 77, 81, 106, 113 competitors 70, 72
complexity 86
correlation linear
   90, 100
   multiple 103
costing 177
   absorption 179
   contribution 179
   marginal 180
   opportunity 178
costs, apportionment of 178
courage 13, 44
creativity 54, 111, 113
Croner's *Employment Law* 196 culture 5, 46, 187, 204

Darwinian biology 66
data 75
DCF (Discounted Cash Flow) 183 decision making 85
discipline 186
Distillers Group 68
distribution
   channels of 121
   physical 124
   statistical 90, 92

education 86
effort and achievement 51
emotional intelligence 33
   protection 195
   tribunal 18, 195, 196

example, setting 49
expectations 49
experience 85

Federal Express 7
feedback 205
finance
   and accounting 159
   sources of 166, 176
Ford 70, 150,
fraud 163, 167
frequency see distribution
fun 53

gearing 176
GEC-Marconi 65
General Electric 31
goals 78
going concern 172
Goleman, Daniel 33
GT (Group Technology) 140
Guinness 68

Harvey-Jones, Sir John 201
health 37, 55
Herzberg, Frederick 30
HR (Human Relations) 26, 32, 50, 132
   department 185, 200
      and external relationships 190
hygiene factors 31

IBM 7
implementation 204
incentive 30, 31, 51, 124
individual
   failure by 25, 29, 50
   performance 56
   potential 49
   and private life 55
   protecting 17, 43, 48, 52
   research 30, 31
   review 191, 197
   similarities and differences 28, 49, 54
information 75
   for planning process 115
integrity 17
interviewing 190, 197
IT (Information Technology) 70, 130, 156

JIT (Just in Time) 145
judgement 37, 64, 81, 84

knowledge 25, 37

law 63, 106, 155, 157
   civil 63
   employers and 194
   statute 63
leadership 48, 54, 56
learning styles 198
liquidity 169
   ratio 175
listening 41, 42, 44
loyalty 17, 21, 43, 57, 58

maintenance 156
management
   Classical School of 35
   HR School of 35
   style 56
   and fashion 35
   succession 78
   techniques 12, 15, 84
   of time 206
manager's role 77
managing people 131
manners 51
marketing 108
   and communications 112
   mix 125
Marks and Spencer 88
Maslow, Abraham 30
Mayo, Elton 31
MBO (Management by Objectives) 82
McGregor, Douglas 31, 35
meeting, chairing a 207
Mercedes 150
mergers 71

Mintzberg, Henry 32
models, mental 39
morality 17
motivation 27, 36, 38, 54, 193

National Extension College 86
new products 155
NFP (Not for Profit) sector 9, 110

objectives 49, 83, 204
Open University 86
organization
  and law 63 and
  society 63
organizational
  analysis 74
  change 69, 74, 83, 110
  environment 13, 66, 67
  remodelling 62
  setting 5, 38
orientation, task or people 36

P&L (Profit and Loss account) 171
Pareto's principle 104
payback 183
people 24
perception 38, 42
personality 37, 54
persuasion 43
PERT (Programme Evaluation and Review Technique) 84
plans
  corporate 79, 80, 82
  departmental 78
  marketing 114
politics 4, 5, 13, 62, 64
positioning 125
power 47
PowerPoint 214
PR (Public Relations) 112, 127, 188
premises
  design, layout 152
  location 151
presentation, giving a 210
probability 90, 91

problem-solving 43, 87, 201
  with staff 219
product design 125
production 129
  management principles 134
  planning 132
  and stock control 143
  batch size 137
  make or buy 154
  systems 129
  process 138
productivity 72
profit 169, 171
profitability 171
project evaluation 182
public sector 9, 110
purchasing, procurement 145

QA (Quality Assurance) 146, 148
QC (Quality Control) 94, 146
  charts 98

R&D (Research and Development) 155
ratio analysis 174, 176
records 106
recruitment 188, 190, 197
regression, statistical 90, 92
regulation 64
research 189
  market 109, 116
respect 52
responsibility 47
review 204
reward 9, 11, 51
Royal Shakespeare Company 218

safety 153, 85
sales force 123
sales promotion 126
satisficing 106
self-protection 82, 106
SMART (Specific, Measurable, Achievable, Relevant, Timed) 204
Sony 117

Index

staff
   planning 192, 197
   selection 190, 197
 statistics 84, 89, 148
stock control 142
structure 5, 62
study 38
suppliers 167
SWOT (Strengths, Weaknesses, Opportunities, Threats) 74, 81
systems, hard, soft 129, 131

TA (Transactional Analysis) 33
takeovers 71, 164, 167
targets 78
team
  building 53
  composition 54
  development 196
  goals 49
  personalities 54, 193 success with 24
Tesco 112
Theory X, Theory Y 31, 35 time management 206
trade relations 127
training 85, 165, 166, 192, 197 simulations for 198

Unilever 112

value analysis 149 variety 70, 88
  reduction 150
vendor rating 146
VW 71

work study 141

Also available from Kogan Page

Accounting for Non-Accountants: A manual for managers and students
5th edn, Graham Mott

Better Business Writing
Timothy R V Foster

Dealing with Difficult People
Roy Lilley

Dealing with the Boss from Hell: A guide to life in the trenches
Shaun Belding

Dealing with the Customer from Hell: A survival guide
Shaun Belding

Dealing with the Employee from Hell: A guide to coaching and motivation
Shaun Belding

Develop Your NLP Skills
Andrew Bradbury

Developing Your Staff
Patrick Forsyth

The Effective Leader
Rupert Eales-White

A Handbook of Management Techniques: The Best-selling guide to modern management methods
3rd edn, Michael Armstrong

Hard-core Management: What you won't learn from the business gurus
Jo Owen

How I Made It: 40 successful entrepreneurs tell all
Rachel Bridge

How People Tick: A guide to difficult people and how to handle them
Mike Leibling

How to Be an Even Better Manager: A complete A-Z of proven tech-niques and essential skills
6th edn, Michael Armstong

How to Generate Great Ideas
Barrie Hawkins

How to Manage Meetings
Alan Barker

How to Manage Organisational Change
2nd edn, D E Hussey

How to Motivate People
Patrick Forsyth

How to Negotiate Effectively
David Oliver

Improve Your Communication Skills
Alan Barker

The Inspirational Leader: How to motivate, encourage and achieve success
John Adair

The Instant Manager: Tools and ideas for practical problem solving
Revised edn, Cy Charney

Make Every Minute Count
3rd edn, Marian E Hayes

Management Stripped Bare: What they don't teach you at business school
Jo Owen

Not Bosses but Leaders: How to lead the way to success
3rd edn, John Adair